Kindest regards of
Manly P. Hall

Manly P. Hall
# All Seeing Eye
## Book Second
by
DARRELL JORDAN
Compiled and Edited

Athenaia.Co

Coeur D'Alene:
Printed and bound in
the United States, 2023

Manly P. Hall All Seeing Eye – Book Second. Compiled with graphics and edits by Darrell Jordan, Copyright © First Edition 2023. All rights reserved.

No part of this book may be reproduced in whole or in part without the written permission from the publisher, nor stored in any retrieval system or transmitted by any means, electronic, mechanical, photocopying, recording, or other, without the written consent of the publisher.

For bulk purchases, please contact the publisher.
Enquiry@Athenaia.Co

Library of Congress Cataloging-in Publication Data
Names: Hall, Manly P. | Jordan, Darrell
Title: Manly P. Hall All Seeing Eye – Book Second. / Darrell Jordan, MPS
Description: First U.S. edition. | Coeur D'Alene, Idaho: Athenaia [2023]
Identifiers: LCCN (pending) | ISBN 979-8-88556-041-2 (First Edition hardcover)
Subjects: OCC040000: BODY, MIND & SPIRIT / Hermetism & Rosicrucianism, | PHI013000: PHILOSOPHY / Metaphysics, | SOC038000: SOCIAL SCIENCE / Freemasonry & Secret Societies
LC record available at https://lccn. loc.gov

On the internet: Parallel47North.com/collections/esoteric-books

Managing Editor: Darrell Jordan
Original Author and Essay: Manly P. Hall
Executive Producer: Yuka Jordan
Book Cover Design by Darrell Jordan
Image Credits: Manly P. Hall's personal collection
Printed and bound in the United States

Publisher: Athenaia, LLC
2370 N Merritt Crk Lp, Ste 1
Coeur D'Alene, ID 83814
The United States
Enquiry@Athenaia.Co

# Manly P. Hall
# All Seeing Eye

## Book Second

by

## Darrell Jordan, MPS
### Compiled and Edited

Athenaia.Co

# CONTENTS

INTRODUCTION:     3

SEPTEMBER 1923
THE SONG OF LIFE:     6
TEN RULES OF RELIGIOUS ETIQUETTE:     7
SPIRITUAL HOBOS:     8
THE AVE MARIA:     16
QUESTION AND ANSWER DEPARTMENT:     20
BROTHERS OF THE SHINING ROBE - III:     22
PROMETHEUS THE ETERNAL SUFFERER:     25
DESCRIPTION OF LAST MONTH'S PLATE:     29
A DISCOURSE ON THE EIGHT PERFECTIONS - I:     30
IMPRACTICAL OCCULTISTS:     35
A KNIGHT OF THE HOLY GRAIL:     41
ASTROLOGICAL REWARD:     47

OCTOBER 1923
THOUGHTS:     52
DEADICATED TO OUR "OLD STUDENTS.":     53
THE CHICK AND THE SHELL:     60
THE OCCULT ACID TEST:     61
BROTHERS OF THE SHINING ROBE - IV:     63
LORD BUDDHA:     66
SPECIAL NOTICE:     72
DESCRIPTION OF LAST MONTH'S PLATE:     75
QUESTION AND ANSWER DEPARTMENT:     76
THE LORD OF THE FLAMING MOUNTAIN:     78
FADED FLOWERS:     83
A DISCOURSE ON THE EIGHT PERFECTIONS - II:     85
THE MASTER SPEAKS - II:     88
ASTROLOGICAL KEYWORDS:     89
THE NIGHT OF BRAHMA:     91

| | |
|---|---|
| OCCULT MASON - II: | 94 |

NOVEMBER 1923
| | |
|---|---|
| THE PRISON GRAVEYARD: | 98 |
| CRANKS AND CRANKISMS : | 99 |
| COURAGE VS. TIMIDITY: | 105 |
| ABSTRACTIONS: | 107 |
| BROTHERS OF THE SHINING ROBE - V: | 110 |
| THE MESSAGE OF THE GREAT INITIATES: | 114 |
| THE TEMPLE OF SIN - I: | 118 |

DECEMBER 1923
| | |
|---|---|
| THE SPIRIT OF CHRISTMAS : | 127 |
| THE SECOND COMING OF CHRIST: | 133 |
| A ONE ACT LITERARY TRAGEDY : | 136 |
| BROTHERS OF THE SHINING ROBE - VI: | 138 |
| LIVING PROBLEMS DEPARTMENT: | 142 |
| YOUR GOD AND MY GOD: | 143 |
| THE CURSE OF EGYPT'S DEAD: | 148 |
| SPECULUM ALCHYMIAE: | 150 |
| THE SYMBOLISM OF OUR NEW CROSS: | 154 |
| DESCRIPTION OF LAST MONTH'S PLATE: | 161 |
| THE DANCE OF THE VEILS: | 163 |
| THE LAW OF NON-ATTACHMENT: | 168 |
| THE WHITE ELEPHANT: | 171 |
| THE CRIME OF VACCINATION: | 176 |
| THE SONG OF THE SOUL: | 177 |
| THE KOJIKI: | 184 |
| ASTROLOGICAL KEYWORDS: | 187 |
| AUTHOR AND MANAGING EDITOR: | 189 |

# Introduction

## EDITOR'S NOTE

Manley Hall was born on 18 March 1901, in Peterborough, Canada, to William S. and Louise Palmer Hall. The Hall family moved to Sioux Falls, South Dakota, United States, in 1904. Manly Hall later settled in Los Angeles in 1919.

As a young man, he became interested in all forms of occult subjects. He subsequently joined a number of societies, among them the Theosophical Society, the Freemasons, the Societas Rosecruciana in Civitatibus Foederatis, and the American Federation of Astrologers.

In 1922, Hall wrote his first book: Initiates of the Flame and was collecting all form of esoteric/exoteric/mystical subject matter, in his own words: "late in the fall of 1922, the plan for a comprehensive work on the symbolism of western mystical societies began to take shape in my mind. It soon became apparent that research facilities for such a project were not available in Southern California... The only answer was to contact antiquarian book dealers and elicit their cooperation in the search for the items desired." In 1934, Hall founded the Philosophical Research Society, a research institute modeled on the ancient school of Pythagoras.

He was ordained a minister in 1923 to an occult/mystic congregation at the Church of the People in California. In that same year specifically in May 1923, Manly Hall began the membership/student based, not for sale magazine, all written, edited and published by Hall titled the "The All Seeing-Eye."

This Book series covers the first year of the All Seeing-Eye magazine for ease of reading. Bear in mind that Manly Hall at this time in 1923 was only 22 years old! Editing was minimal in terms of punctuation and spelling. In some cases, there are made-up words (or words that are no longer in use) in which case they were left spelled as is.

I'm sure that you will find, as did I, that Manly Hall was highly intelligent and possibly bordering on genius. Many of his stories that elucidate a particular subject were written in the first person. Whether or not this was the case, the stories demonstrate either a highly active imagination or perhaps he did, in fact, experience what he wrote in the first-person account stories or a combination thereof.

Suffice it to say, we are positive you will enjoy the many journeys Manly Hall takes you on.

SEPTEMBER 1923

## THE SONG OF LIFE

Listening for the footsteps of the Master,
Watching for the glory of his smile,
Praying for the strength that comes with knowing
As we struggle on alone each weary mile.
Seeking in the throngs that surge about us,
Waiting as the years roll slowly by,
Sighing as the burdens grow so heavy, seems would be better not to try.
Groaning as we see our brothers happy,
While our hearts grow weary with their load,
Wondering why some paths are strewn with roses
And only tears we find upon the road.
Wondering why the price of truth is sorrow,
Wondering at the bruises and the strife,
Can we really be the winners in a battle
Where only death can pay the price of life?
Why are those who live the lives of hatred
The guides that show the way to perfect love?
And why are those who live below in darkness
The ones that lead us to the light above?
And as we hear the jeers of those about us
Can we smile and bravely lay aside each fear?
And through the gloomy mask of every sorrow
Can we see the light and feel the presence near?
And with the strength that comes alone with knowing
Can we gladden other's footsteps with our song?
Can we see that every sorrow that we suffer
Is but the payment for some distant wrong?
Then sing the song of life as on we struggle
And learn from those around us every day?
Behind each Brother's form there stands a Master,
Shall we serve him or shall we turn away?

# EDITORIAL

# TEN RULES OF RELIGIOUS ETIQUETTE

1. Do not attend the meetings because you have an antipathy against the hall and do not like to associate with the class of people who sit around you. This is a proof of your ultra-refinement.

2. If you come be sure to attend irregularly and under no condition, tell anyone about the meeting or bring anyone with you. This indicates that you are exclusive and belong in the upper set.

3. Be sure that you acquire all our books but never read them. Ask the questions in class that are answered in them. This demonstrates your mental superiority beyond all doubt.

4. In securing our books and magazines, never consider the contents -always estimate their value upon the price of the paper. This is a sure sign of business shrewdness and erudition.

5. Always lock up our publications where no one else can find them or read them. This proves that you understand their esoteric value. To advertise them would be decidedly plebeian and would lessen your superiority over others.

6. Always kick about the way things are being done -the chairs, gas stoves, music, and so forth. This is very refreshing and proves your aristocracy.

7. Never put anything on the collection plate. Always give someone else that opportunity for soul growth. This shows spirituality and brotherhood.

8. Workers should never get along well together. Each one should be jealous of all the others. This shows professional temperament and helps to simplify the teacher's work, at the same time setting an illustrious example.

9. Do not spend much time studying. It isn't being done in the better circles. You should make the meeting hall a rendezvous to circulate all the latest scandals. You should also be filled with advice which you should give freely, especially on subjects about which you know nothing. This shows your occult leanings and family breeding. Every member of the student body should follow all the others and see what they do. This is deep brotherly interest.

10. If anybody should get up and do anything useful-oppose him in every way possible, crying out that he is trying to boss and run the whole show. If there is a mass movement in any direction, gather up yourself and depart, telling everyone you meet that the work is being run by a clique. This is decidedly refreshing and relieves the monotony, which might otherwise cause the work to stagnate. All of these points help to simplify matters and are of vast encouragement to all con-

cerned and, if followed religiously, will produce perfect results.

I Thank You.

## SPIRITUAL HOBOS
### A Romance in Psychologies

IT IS, alas, too true that few individuals care to be reminded of the hollows, furrows, ravines and gullies in their mental, physical and spiritual make-ups! Compliments are always in demand and a suave disposition never fails to draw around the bevies of friends and admirers who will bask in the honeyed sentiments like flies in a sugar bowl. People love to foster the fond idea that somebody else believes them to be something which they honestly know they are not.

Most of our occult students will many times declare themselves to be braced in all the weak spots, strong and courageous, ready to listen to the truth, whole truth and everything but the truth! But rarely do they demonstrate any great amount of joy when reality does strike against them or seek admittance into their consciousness. Most students tell us that they want to know their weak points, where their spiritual bunions are located and what constitutes the leading detractions of their temperaments but if we happen to intimate even for a second that they are suffering from any slight imperfection they immediately leave us-thoroughly convinced that we lack polish, grace and refinement, and are most hopelessly deficient in spiritual sentiments. While if we "gush" prettily over them, address them as "old students," "advanced souls," ad infinitum, they are then in a condition where most any living creature can separate them from their rent money, salary, and more than likely their family.

In other and shorter words, they like to be patted on the back, are willing slaves to anyone who will weave fanciful dramas around them for their own glorification-even though they really know that they possess none of the attributes in question-but if for a moment we infer that the average seeker after-the-occult is a hobo, a bum, a tramp, a nonentity, a vagabond, vandal and vampire, for some absolutely unknown reason he passes us on the street next day without recognition though he may realize that he is all of the things described, plus more known only to himself.

But let us, just for the sake of the principle involved, be truthful for once and spite the devil, admitting that at the present time the majority of seekers after things spiritual are not only looking in the wrong direction for the truth but positively ignore it when they do see it. They continue gliding through life talking themselves into believing that they are personifications of the Eternal

Seeker when in reality they are nothing but omnipotent, omnipresent, omniscient (never omni active) Incarnations of Specific Worthlessness.

These may not seem pleasant thoughts, in fact we may be called cruel, cold and unjust, but with the pure eye of logic, the brain of reason and the steady hand of the surgeon let us anatomize what we discover when we start carving modern super-spiritual cadaver and see how it sums up:

As we cast the searchlight of common sense upon the problems of modern religion and examine the fruits of philosophical endeavor, listening with rapt attention to the weird discourses which pour forth as bubbling brooks and dashing cataracts of modern Platonic reasoning, a great pessimism grips our soul and the icy fingers of doubt strangle out our tiny germ of hope as we seek to synthesize such hopelessly impossible brain-storms!

So, at last we are forced to the conclusion that most of our so-called Thinkers are neither spiritual, philosophical, intelligent nor studious but are merely brain convolution contortionists twisting their dua-mater and pia-mater into bowknots and figure-eights and then, ye gods! Inviting others to join them in their mental gymnastics. In other words, instead of being statisticians, economic reformers, teachers, and logicians, they are merely straining the cerebral vesicles and painfully spraining the mind. When we realize this, we are confronted with a great problem -what is thought? And how should its wonderful power be used to express a maximum of intelligent result?

The answer to the problem is, man must learn to think in harmony with nature and natural law. When he seeks to battle against his own intellectuality, to deny the existence of things which he daily and hourly contacts, or seeks with sheer force of will to change the direction of the universe or reverse the poles he is merely wasting power and energy on an absolutely hopeless, helpless, and non-productive series of concepts which would be comic if they were not divinely sad.

The average person does not know how to think and never will until he individually evolves the mental faculties and powers to do it with. And the first step towards this is to cease imitating the ideas of others, learn to reason out and master the problems of your own existence and being responsible to yourself instead of rushing to another fool for help-whereupon each clasps the other and both sink! The average person who believes himself to be philosophical, spiritual and ethical is merely a rambling intellectual hobo, helpless and harmless, whose every thought and action he has begged, borrowed or stolen from somebody else. Those who think other people's thoughts, lean on other people's shoulders and do not labor mentally, physically and spiritually for the things they want are tramps, imposters and human fungi as sure as there are such things in nature.

Taking the modern occult student as an example of spiritual unfoldment and moral culture, we usually find him to be merely a religious vagabond wandering from cult to creed, sleeping in intellectual box-cars, under pseudo-theological haystacks and persistently avoiding the woodpile of labor with a highly evolved efficiency that is positively uncanny. Students of the Wisdom Teachings little realize how like beggars they can become if they continue to wander from pillar to post knocking at each farmhouse door, hoping that fortune will present herself but inwardly praying that the bull-dog of adversity will not advance to the rear of their immediate environment.

There is a great Kingdom of the Unemployed and there is also that aristocratic fraternity known as Gentlemen of the Great Outdoors and, alas, it is, but too true, said institutions do many things not in accordance with the ethical statutes of our beautiful country. But let us not add infamy to insult or further scandalize their already dubious reputations by listing with them our modem spiritual students. For, 'tis sad to relate, these Gentlemen of the Open Road and non-eventuating pilgrims are never half as guilty of mental or physical vagrancy as that band of new thought and spiritual students are addicted to intellectual grafting and semi-conscientious knavery!

None of us will ever forget Tattered Tom or milord the Baron Rags and other blueblood members of the slipshod aristocracy for they are in a class unapproachable and inimical-the very acme of active indolence. As they promenade along the tar-paved boulevard resembling. animated scarecrows or bi-pedular ashcans they manifest and express in every movement of their being a nobility greater far than a scion of the House of Navarre. They are sublimely humorous, pathetically ridiculous, and always bring poetically to our minds a picture of injured innocence and over-worked ennui.

Along they go with smiles on their faces, whistling merry tunes, while clothed in a bundle of rags and tatters! Gentlemen of leisure whose motto is: "Don't work when there's anything else to do!" (the Latest psychological axiom.) You have all heard them as they gently knock at the backdoor, after making sure that the Airedale is chained, and with fringed hat in hand deliver a touching elegy with a seriousness and masterful eloquence worthy of a trained tragedian:

"Please, lady, I'm a poor man, down and out and too sick to work. I'm tryin' to get money enough to make the next city where I have a brother in business. I come from a good family, mum, -I'm not a tramp or anything like that. I'm just suffering from pecuniary embarrassment-a slight financial shortage -I wonder if it would be possible for you to give me a piece of pie or some of your husband's old clothes?"

This is a noble art-the art of begging -a cultured science which has been evolved through generations of practice, the developing of sympathetic voices, said looking eyes and cherubinic expressions that shine out with celestial radiance from beneath several days' growth of whiskers!

When poor people enter this profession and the down-and-outers promenade along the dusty road of life in someone else's clothes we call them tramps. But when they rise upward to more ethical circles of philosophical, spiritual and scientific things we then call them mystics, psychologists, philosophers, eccentric geniuses, advanced thinkers and deep students of the occult. If you will just take the average modernist in religion, however, and analyze him carefully you will find a weird and wondrous composite combination of borrowed plumage. Like Aesop of the ancient Fables, in examining said rare specimen, we find an ugly duckling with one glorious peacock plume rising from the rear. Such a sight as would give a naturalist or poultry fancier epileptic convulsions unless he knew for a certainty that the glorious tuft was not an inherent product of the bird!

Mentally, physically, never to mention spiritually, not one thing our occult student wears fits him. Surely, he represents the Ex-president of the ancient and honorable Order of Whatnots! His hat is too big and nestles grotesquely over ears that pivot and turn outward by the weight. Of course, it is no longer a dilapidated derby or gently atrophying tall silk but just a philosophical concept and shortcut to heaven he has begged off the Jones family down the street. His borrowed alchemy hangs loosely from his shoulders, gathered in by the safety-pin of someone else's ethics. His pant-legs of affirmation and denial were made for a man three times his size, consequently fit him too much, but still he is wearing them -and what makes it infinitely worse is they are not mates for he sneaked them out of Smith's backyard while Mrs. Smith was paying the iceman. His shoes, one a patent-leather the other a goulash, leave strange footprints on the sands behind, which footprints are the measure of his soul. For they are not his own either but have been begged, borrowed or stolen from some oracle along the meandering line of his pilgrimage.

Thus, he stands before you. Nothing more, nothing less than an intellectual vagabond and spiritual lounge-lizard. (Or shall we say chameleon? For as this little lizard changes his color to suit his background, so the "mystic" changes his creeds to suit his needs.) Like the ordinary tramp he hates work worse than poison, hates water like a cat, but is hoping against hope that he will get to heaven somehow if he can borrow enough old clothes to make it or can hop an empty freight going in that direction. In other words, our nondescript student of religion is eternally searching for something easy that he can secure without labor and lives ardently hopeful of finding a way to enjoy the harvest that his industrious brother creatures have stored up. Students do not mean to do this, but it seems an innate faculty of the human mind to seek to avoid exertion.

The lower in man cries out for rest while the higher spiritual powers seek to express more incessant activity. There are hobos on the physical plane of nature who claim to have been tired for fifty years and to be suffering from strange ailments which obstruct the vital energies, when the real cause of their ailment is chronic laziness. The same may be said of our spiritual seekers, for most of them are wasting away with some mystic lassitude which is nothing more nor less than a pure lack of a desire to do anything.

Sciences which seek to promote mental exertion and individual advancement become less and less popular all the time while intellectual and spiritual soothing syrups and teething rings are in ever more constant demand. Spiritual narcotics which will prevent human beings from feeling the pains of daily life are called blessings but in reality, are the greatest curses of the human race. If students could only realize that when they search for others who will answer for them the problems of their own lives with formulas and recipes which eliminate individual expression making it possible to glide en masse to the Eternal Footstool, or who will rent them pseudo-evolutionary roller skates to shorten the path-they are only being hoodwinked and deceived! And always by those who have themselves fallen slaves to their own or their brothers' absurdities.

There is no way of reaching the true position the human race is ordained to fill without individually standing upon our own feet and learning mentally, physically and spiritually to earn legitimately and honestly whatsoever quality we are seeking mastery over. There must be an equal effort expended and an honest foundation laid for everything which we want or else man is, in the sight of nature, a thief and a robber.

Those people who fondly believe that their duty ceases with the getting of things or that they can make slick transactions in religion or turn rather clever intellectual deals to their own profit have a great awakening before them, an awakening filled with sorrow and unhappiness because they have failed to realize that the Universe is governed by just, non-commercialized non-favoritism which as great abstract Intelligence governs impartially all of Its creations, rewarding each according to its works.

There is no greater crime in the world than to promise or to intimate that we can make another spiritual, intelligent or prosperous, for it is absolutely impossible to do so. And those who charge exorbitant prices for shortcuts to heaven are charging for something which they do not possess and are assessing work that only the ego of an individual alone is capable of carrying on. In other words, Mr. Jones is paying Mr. Smith for the privilege of saving his own soul. Persons who graft in such a way as this should be treated in the same manner that the Government treats oil sharks who sell shares in non-entitled wells and the like. They are mental, physical and spiritual criminals and those who patronize them are merely demonstrating a super abundance of vacuum in the cranial cavity. But the demand will always produce the supply and as long as there are people to be fooled, there will always be those pleased to do it for them.

It is perfectly legitimate to instruct man in the ways he should go (providing that the party of the first part knows what way anything should go) but to promise results is beyond the privilege of God himself. Instead of giving a spiritual tramp a meal in every case, he should be ushered into the backyard where stands the menacing wood-pile and told that if he will chop two cords, his lunch is ready. At such a moment as this the physical hobo disintegrates while his spiritual correlate dissolves into a dank cloud of iridescent dew-nose cracked, insulted and with every quill in his temperament standing on end.

We may not believe it this way, but when work is mentioned the seekers after eternal wisdom rise, one after another, and magically vanish effervescing streams of many-colored indignation-this at the bare suggestion of earning their daily bread! If he is suffering from a gouty toe or a gastronomic reaction and you tell him to watch his diet and stop eating roast goose or breaded veal cutlets he will immediately rise, a towering pillar of righteous wrath, and tell you that you are neither spiritual, ethical nor philosophical. Said student will then head for some temple of solace where he will wade through a long concentration, take an aphromatic pill or ten grains of sugar-coated sentiment and then go out to eat fried bricks and ten-penny nails a la carte until the closing of the last act when the nail he could not digest is used to hold down his coffin lid.

If you hint to the student of ancient wisdom that bathing is an inducement to health, you are ordinary, materialistic, and lack Oriental ideality. But there is not one "occultist" in a million who has studied the plumbing system of Pompeii while engaged in his ancient researches. If you tell him he has a mean disposition, you are a low-brow, a mishap, an inferior and several other things he cannot remember but which nevertheless apply to the problem on hand. However, if you will prove to him conclusively and beyond an all shadows of doubt that his spavin can be cured by some supernatural agency which requires no temperance or moderation in his own life, then indeed you are gifted of the gods. He will then peel forth the last shekel and think nothing of working at a dollar a day for fifteen years to pay you for a Latin formula or a Sanskrit delineation punctuated in Hebrew, when for a five-cent bar of Ivory soap he could be a healthy man for seventy-five years-that is, of course, if he adds to the soap the necessary exertion for applying.

There are also people, strange creatures of demented reasoning! who will condescend to study the occult if you will guarantee them illumination, unity with the Absolute, mastery and initiation, not to mention such trivial things as the seventh sense and the ability to rove on other planets or pick daisies on the Milky Way at the completion of a two-week course. If you have a dashing personality, they may even wait four weeks for their spiritual insight especially if the language you clothe the supernatural sciences in is sufficiently set with the rubies of eloquence and like the sages of old you are an orator with a silver tongue.

But when you advise said persons that mastery requires from one to three hundred and fifty million years of hard work, low pay and tough luck, he immediately tells you that you lack inspiration, that you know nothing of heaven and its mysteries, that your aura radiates bone-set tea, and that by good right you should he burned in effigy on the public square. If you warn him that his eternal salvation depends upon his own works, he is discouraged, disconcerted, and perplexed, for he knows he has never done anything worthy and can never get far on individual merit. But just whisper mysteriously in his ear a state secret all about a new way of leaning on the Lord whereby you may slip in for nothing he is thenceforth a subject of exuberant reaction, for our average student has no intention whatsoever of giving up anything he likes but will always do the thing he wants to even if it is being miserable, and some are never happy unless they are completely miserable.

To enjoy hard work at this day and age is to invite investigation from the psychopathic ward and if such a case could be found a symposium of international scientists would come into session to diagnose the extraordinary phenomenon. A person who glories in labor and in contact with the hard knocks of the world are about as rare as a total eclipse of Gloombridge or Uncle Si's three headed calf and are to be listed with the scientific marvels of the age, especially if found among spiritual students.

So they go, praying for the day when someone will build an environment for them wherein, they may be ideally happy or that a great Master will come to clean up the world, a work we ought to be doing every day or that a great Light will descend from the heavens, when we ought to be out lighting our own way. They are longing for someone else to heal them of something they have no business to have, and while they have a mean disposition and a cussedly bad temper, they long to find a way to conceal it by plastering it deep down under a thick layer of beauty mud which comes under the heading of convincing personality cosmetics.

So Tattered Tom and Frenzied Freddy address unknown, vocation unthinkable –wander from door to door asking for pie, overalls and old shoes and like the foolish virgins of old begging of the wise ones oil for their lamps instead of standing up like the men and women they claim to be, kicking out their mean dispositions, cleaning out their self-infected body and taking a good long stretch. Perhaps someday they may learn to look somebody straight in the eye and say, "There is nothing in the world equal to a life filled with works, worries, trials and troubles for it has given me the experience and strength to rise above misfortune, stand on my own feet and proclaim my inherent right to be one of the elects!"

The price of knowledge and spirituality is the proper use of the powers which man has and seventy-five squadrons of angels, three hundred battalions of gods, fifty-seven varieties of divas, two hundred and eighty-seven regiments of psychological infantry and fifteen or twenty spiritual big guns are not enough to stand forth and say "boo" to the powers of nature much less claim the responsibility of easing an individual into heaven. Sixty-five million chariots drawn by cherubim will never be able to get our big toe over if we continue to tramp around in the name of religion, vampirizing and vandalizing everyone with whom we come in contact.

Each is foreordained and predestined from before the time the universe was formed to figure his way out of and work his way out of the undesirable qualities of nature. When he sits back asleep at the switch or trusts someone else to carry him, all is lost. Never with such concepts as these will the spirit of man find rest in the lands beyond the River Styx. (He would surely drown in said river if someone didn't swim in after him.) But it seems that each leans on everything else perfectly content to let someone who can think for them, and someone who can work for them.

Instead of building the faculties, powers and qualities within themselves which entitle them to stand upon their own feet with well-fitting garments of their own making earned by the sweat of their brows, they now stand as divine incarnations of the cosmic spirit Celestial Hobo tagged out in a little bit of everything belonging to everybody else. If by any chance the people who loaned them their robes should ask them back the average mystic will stand shivering at the gates of the Great Unknown as one by one his pet concepts fly home until nothing remains but a dismal failure personifying the true inherent qualities which the student himself has evolved by his own lack of active labor.

## THE AVE MARIA

**T**HIS is the story of a spark buried deep in the heart of a dying flame, one of those tragic little legends which bring close to our soul the realization of nature's subtle working. Few realize that the shell of clay shrouds a deathless spark, and yet if the world thought they would know that this is the truth. Something hidden far within, unseen and unknown, cries eternally to be admitted and realized by its prison walls. Man must not judge his brother creature by the form alone, for behind rough exteriors of this world there is ofttimes hidden a finer, sweeter, and more beautiful spirit than we would ever dream could exist there.

Often from the shadow of a broken, discordant body there shines forth a gleam of celestial radiance. There is a strange pathos under the thoughtlessness of the world. All have felt an inner urge, a great desire to realize some hidden ideal, and man often soars heavenward upon the pinions of inspiration-only to have the ever-human crush the vision with the stony fingers of crystallization. And how often the spirit in the world of forms chafes to be free from the living corpse that holds it to the sordid things! Nature is like a string of wondrous beads; all are connected by a single thread of living gold and a tiny spark of divine life shines out between all the beads that have an end.

It is hard to realize that the tools will grow dull with age and as time slowly crushes the instrument; we wonder why the glorious dreams that fill our soul are no longer shaped to realities. We try ever to be young; even when the unseen Reaper gathers us to the Great Unknown still the divine spirit of youth within looks forward with eagerness to creation's endless adventure.

\* \* \* \* \*

It is in a little town in the old country, with its cobblestone streets, its simple folk and honest simplicity, that our story is laid. In the center of the town stood the great cathedral with tiny buildings gathered under the protection of its massive form; its grand Gothic arches rise to shadows of an endless night which hangs forever amid its lofty rafters and mysterious hallways, only but dimly lighted by the sunbeams which struggle in through the panes of many-colored glass.

A dull hush filled the building and its cold, lifeless air reminded one of the vaults of emperors and the mausoleums of kings where endless rows of marble tombs stand like phantoms in the dim uncertain light. At one end of the massive building where the altar place stood, guarded by tiny gleaming candles which sent flickering shadows on the dark stained walls, the mighty organ rises a weird mystery of tubes and pipes, a mighty sentinel guarding the holy place of God.

It is an ancient church and for many ages worshipers have knelt upon its marble floor, deep rutted by the footsteps of the pious.

Suddenly the silence was broken by footfalls which sounded hollowly in the great blank silence of the place of worship. A little figure walked slowly down through the gloomy arches to the foot of the ancient altar. It was an old man, his back bent with age, and his long white hair hanging in ringlets over his shoulders. Reaching the foot of the altar steps, he stopped and gazed lovingly up to the monster organ half concealed in the gloom of the nave. A thin streamlet of tears coursed down the old man's cheeks, and a sob echoed through the ancient hallways. And then slowly the glorious spiritual face turned away from the organ and, with his arms hanging at his sides, the old man walked away.

Day after day, he came there just for a few moments and then crept away again to his little home on the outskirts of the town. Sometimes there were others in the mighty cathedral, kneeling in prayer upon the worn flagstones. Their eyes grew misty also as they watched the old man, for they knew the sacred tragedy of his life. The white-haired figure was the organist who, since the days of his youth, had lent the voice of angels to the pipes of wood. Everyone knew the sad story of his life for in that little town there were no secrets and all lived like one great family with compassion and tenderness each to the other. The good housewives sighed when they told the story of how one day as he was playing his beloved "Ave Maria" the old man's fingers had fallen from the keys -paralyzed- and the mighty organ was silent in the midst of its melody. They knew that he had played his organ for the last time, for his dead fingers could never again move lightly across the keys.

The little story was the tragedy of the village and all hearts went out to him as day after day the lonely old man entered the ancient cathedral and gazed up at the lofty instrument which had been his friend for threescore years and ten.

Although his fingers were stilled forever, the soul of the musician was still alive. For years the mighty man-made thing with its harmony celestial had been the comrade and companion of a lonely life and up in the little balcony where the keyboard stood the organist had left his heart. In the days of sorrow when all others had deserted him, through the nights of anguish which always fill the heart of a dreamer, he had climbed the little stairway and the people outside had heard wondrous symphonies swell forth, melodies born of sadness and the shattered soul of one the world could never understand. Through pain and pleasure, through youth and manhood, and even as the snow of age gathered upon his brow, the old musician had played, loved by all and loving all but understood by none save the old organ in the great cathedral.

New fingers now played its ancient keys, another master gave it life, but still the heart of the old musician dreamed of his beloved instrument and prayed that once more he might touch its aged keys before eternity shrouded him with the endless past. So, each day he came and humbly offered his little prayer that once more his dead fingers might play the living harmonies which filled his soul.

The spirit of man never grows old, but through the ripening years of experience just learns to feel more, to be greater and closer to the divine. The life within does not age, though the frame is bent; the same glorious harmonies filled the musician's soul, but the fingers of clay no longer heeded the genius of the master's mind. But still with simple faith, he prayed for the joy of one last communion and the feeling of its possibility comforted his aching heart.

So, the years passed, the step of the musician grew tottering and broken, the very stones were worn by his footsteps and the Angel of Death hovered near him as the chill of eternal winter crept ever closer to his heart. But still he came each day to gaze upon the thing he loved, to pray, to hope and to remember.

It was late one afternoon and the setting sun was sending its last rays through the towering windows adorned with their many-colored pictures of the Master's life. The old organist had entered the church and was standing as he had so often in the past at the base of the mighty organ gazing up at the gloomy shadows which partly concealed the rows of ancient tubes. In a hushed voice, he spoke as if to a living thing: "Oh, friend of my youth! oh comforter of my old age! Inspiration in the moments of glory! silent comrade in times of sorrow! my pilgrimage is nearing its end. Will I ever play again upon your ivory keys the melodies that fill my soul but which these poor hands can bring forth no more? Still, great ideals thrill through me and the music as of angel's voices sounds ever in my ears. Ofttimes in the shades of night I hear strange songs and melodies, and had I known the fingers of the world would know many wondrous things. But, alas, it is all over-all but a dream of the deathless past! You were my life, my all, and somewhere among your ancient tubes and pipes my heart will always be, for I love you now as in the days of old. Oh, why must the soul of man remain in darkness when the clay is broken? My time here is not long, for in the shadows of the night I hear voices from a mystic land unseen; the world of spirit surrounds me, and I understand it better as the world of men grows fainter every day. Only one thing I ask before I go once more, I would play your ivory keys! Once more, to give life to your soulless being!"

Obeying an impulse which he could not understand the old organist slowly climbed the narrow stairs which led to the keyboard of the organ, and sitting down upon the ancient stool gazed lovingly at the form so darkened by age. The setting sun sent one lonely beam through the tinted panes, lighting the face of the aged man with its halo of silver locks in a glory divine. The great inspiration filled the musician's soul, the youth so far behind flooded back again as wondrous rhythms swayed his being and all the glory of the music, he loved so well thrilled through him. Instinctively he sought to raise his arms and place his fingers upon the keyboard then he realized, alas, that his youth was but a dream and with a broken sob the old man's head sank upon the organ. The ancient keys were wet with his tears as the last shades of the glorious sun shone dimly through the painted glass.

As the good folks of the city sat round their fires there suddenly broke upon their ears a sound-the voice of the mighty organ in the great cathedral pouring forth in a welling fountain of symphony and harmony! They stopped to listen-there was but one in all the world who could play such divine chords and he was paralyzed! Those who dwelt near the cathedral whispered that never before had such thunderous tones, such mellow notes, such divine sound issued from that organ. It seemed alive, and each recognized the melody that sounded forth. In the years gone by, they had heard it when the old musician was in his prime. Each knew that it was the one he loved so well, the harmony that had soothed him so many times in sorrow and inspired him in peace, the Ave Maria.

A few came out of their homes and reverently crossed the open square to the portals of the church. The very building seemed to rock and in awe and trembling they crossed themselves for a strange presence was in that cathedral, a hush, a mystic power which they could not comprehend. One by one, they gathered and knelt upon the rutted floor. Still, the harmony poured forth in welling cadences from behind the little curtain which marked the keyboard of the organ. One, a little bolder than the rest, slowly climbed the steps and gazed with reverence into the alcove where the organ stood. Then he raised his hands to his face and, with a cry, rushed down the stairs and fell in prayer at the foot of the organ. A few moments passed and then from among those gathered a good man of the town came forth, a sturdy Christian of honest principles beloved by all-the blacksmith of the town. Hat in hand, he slowly climbed the little stairs and entered the alcove from which the other had fled. He, too, gave a gasp and knelt in prayer.

On the floor in the gloom lay the body of the organist, his white face turned upward to the half shade of the descending night in which loomed the organ pipes. His beautiful spiritual face was lighted with a divine peace and his whole being seemed at rest. But this was not the miracle. Two hands were playing the organ-two wondrous, dexterous hands which flew nimbly from key to key with a power miraculous! Of body there was no sign-just the two white hands. And as the blacksmith looked, he crossed himself once more. They were the fingers of the dead musician!

The wonderous strains of the Ave Maria flooded through the cathedral in thundering symphony while the white form of the master organist lay at rest -he in union with his life's companion. The clay was shattered forever, but the soul of the musician could not go on until once more he had played the harmony he loved so well. The final notes died out. The fingers rested for a moment, caressing the keys, and then a strange stillness descended upon the cathedral. It was broken then by a sigh so faint that only a few could have heard it, and those two white hands still reaching outward toward the keys of the organ drifted slowly away into nothingness amid the gloomy shadows of the cathedral.

They say that the organ never again sounded as it did that night-never was one found who could bring such glorious harmonies from a soulless thing. They often tell of the master musician who lived and died in the little village, but the most wonderful thing of all they tell is of how he played the Ave Maria the night he died.

## QUESTION AND ANSWER DEPARTMENT

Is man a free agent or under the control of outside entities?

Ans. Nothing but God is a free agent and even He must comply with the laws of creation. So-called free-will is the power of choice and the greater the range of possibilities, the greater the power of choice. The one who can choose between three things is freer than the one who must choose between two. Only in perfect knowledge comes the greatest expression of the power of choice. Man's evolution is being assisted by outside intelligence, but he must himself make all the important decisions of his life.

What is death and what causes it?

Ans. Death is the phenomena of the separation of a life from a body. It is caused either through a shock or an accident or disease which makes the body incapable of functioning whereupon the life withdraws itself and, the center of power, having left the body because it can no longer use it the shell disintegrates.

Does the Bible contradict Reincarnation?

Ans. The Bible contradicts nothing but is a neutral work and means exactly what the reader gathers from it, as does all the works of the wise. Persecution and tyranny have been based upon the Bible, it has been used as a tool for bigotry and crystallization, and it is also the divine guide to the illuminated seeker. It does not contradict Reincarnation but seems to be based upon the idea of the law of

Rebirth being an accepted fact.

What is success?

Ans. Success is the adjustment of the individual to the plan of his work here. This plan is the result of his previous actions. Whenever he begins a new work or pays off back debts, he is walking the path of success regardless of his financial condition or his comfort. His future experiences are going to depend upon his present action, and noble, honest efforts are the basis of future success. A success is one who meets and masters every unpleasant condition and obstacle, planting flowers where thistles grew before.

What is the law?

Ans. Law is the Plan through which God, man and the Universe were differentiated, are maintained and will later be resolved into the infinite, plus individualization.

Is there anything above Law?

Ans. Those who are above the law, are above breaking it. We mean by breaking it in an attempt to oppose its dictates. NO ONE HAS EVER BROKEN A LAW; THE LAW HAS BROKEN THEM. To obey nature's laws is to make them your greatest friend; to attempt to evade them is to make them your bitter enemies. Man is walking between two lines; These parallel lines are the laws of being and as long as we keep on the road, we do not know that they exist. When we lose our true center, we strike against these walls saying we have broken a law because we suffer.

What is God's plan for man?

Ans. Harmonious adjustments with ever rarer and finer planes of consciousness. The so-called Master is one who has made adjustments to planes where the average individual has no consciousness. The degree of the Initiate's unfoldment depends upon the fineness of his adjustments.

Can consciousness be lost?

Ans. Consciousness can be lost when the vehicle connected with the plane where consciousness is becomes crystalized through age, abuse or atrophy. Consciousness upon any plane of nature depends upon a body properly functioning and attuned to the substances of that plane.

Why are we always in doubt as to what is right and wrong?

Ans. Because our scale of morals is ever changing and the thing that is right today is wrong tomorrow for, we are ever growing and demanding finer things. The highest that we know is the only thing that is ever right.

# BROTHERS OF THE SHINING ROBE - III
## CHAPTER THREE
### The Divine Presence

My trip back to England after I left the Temple of the Caves in Northern India and my Master of the Shining Robe was without event so there is little use in describing it. The long ocean trip, then the railway with its stuffy little compartments, and finally back again to the scenes of my earlier life. I was not, however, the same individual in many ways, for a great ideal had been given to me that of giving to the world the wonderful truths and inspirations that had been given to me in India.

My estates and position gave me considerable opportunity, and added to this a strange eloquence came to me after my return to England, so I sought to instruct a few of the Western world on the problems which had been unfolded to me. The way, however, was beset with difficulties. Only those who have sought to educate the human mind can realize the hopelessness of the task. Day in and day out I hammered at the wall of conventionality and popular opinion which religiously and scientifically paralyzed thought.

In many cases I met opposition and in still a more absolute thoughtlessness with no desire to change the condition. But still I kept at the task that I felt had been given to me, attempting to warn mankind of the great cataclysms, pestilences and sorrows which hung over them as the reward for their foolishness, selfishness and indolence. I gathered a few thinkers around me and also some who opposed my every move and who seemed to glory in each opportunity to tear down and destroy my selfless efforts.

One person especially appointed himself as my annihilator. Through press, pulpit and rostrum I was assailed, both personally and by this individual and through others whose instigations were based upon his maliciousness. He was a scientist of the old school, one of those narrow-minded individuals occasionally met with who, in the spirit of the Inquisition, fights tooth and nail for the perpetuation of antediluvian concepts. For many months he railed against my very being, pointing me out as a scourge to the race, for no earthly reason whatsoever except for an honest difference of opinion. Insult after insult he heaped upon me, spitting out his venom between clenched teeth, and finally challenging me to publicly meet him and prove my impossible theories.

The thought terrified me for the man in question was one of the greatest, most noted scientists that Europe had ever produced, a graduate from a dozen colleges and universities, indefatigable in his researches and unapproachable in his scientific reasoning. He had broken a dozen scientists and philosophers who had sought to question his statements. A colossal mentality and an unbreakable will with a convincing power of eloquence listed him as one of the materialistic marvels of his age. Although I realized the truth of my statements, the idea of my attempting to debate him upon his own ground seemed ridiculous for though what I said might ring true in the caves of the Himalayas, how would it sound before a group of physical scientists who did not believe anything which they could not see, weigh and measure? I was minded refusing, but something within my being whispered, "No." So, with much hesitation and many qualms I accepted his ultimatum and arrangements were settled that on a certain Friday evening I was to debate and discuss with him the continuity of human consciousness, mental evolution and the existence of the sacred schools of wisdom in the heart of the unknown East.

As the hours drew closer a peculiar sickening sensation made itself felt in the pit of my stomach and my knees wabbled in a rather undignified manner as I got into my cab and headed for the gloomy walls of a certain local club where scientists and bookworms were accustomed to gather. I felt pretty sure of what my opponent was going to say, but I had no idea whatsoever of how I was going to answer his attack in a manner convincing to materialists. So, with fear and trepidation and a mental hope that my opponent would be kind, which I greatly doubted, I entered the chili and mingled with the group of London philosophers and scientists who composed it. The professor with whom I was going to debate was introduced to me and I met my rabid disqualifier for the first time.

He was a short, portly gentleman in a nice fitting, black Prince Albert and striped trousers. His two steely gray eyes, divided by a very hooked nose, shone out from beneath brows of Darwinian proportion. He was very much bespectacled and heavily bewhiskered and his gold pince-nez insisted on sliding down his nose at the critical moment. When we were introduced, he looked me over with the air of a physician examining a specimen, answered "Humph!," and, turning on his heel, walked away, his hands clasped beneath his coat-tails. (The reader will, of course, realize that this put me entirely at my ease.) I felt like a tiny Lilliputian entirely surrounded by a mountain range of massive brows, weighty intellects and overwhelming pomposity and I also not a little feared the raging lions and tigers which intuition told me lived in the fastnesses of these mountains.

Slowly the exponents of worldly wisdom gathered and seating themselves in the massive leather arm-chairs whispered together in awful tones from the midst of clouds of tobacco smoke. Of course, I imagined that they were talking about me, probably sympathizing with my dying cause.

As I seated myself beside the professor on the small rostrum some fourscore pairs of spectacles reflected a dazzling light in my face and I seemed gazing out on a blank void edged with gleaming stars. As these exponents of learning, lost arts, and buried sciences, gazed analytically at my shrinking figure which grew smaller as the moments passed, the professor rose, and carefully arranging his notes, placed his spectacles once more, (fitting on an extra lens), cleared his throat, balanced one elbow on the reading desk and gazed benignly over the top of his glasses at the assembled group.

"Ahem! It is indeed a pleasure to address you for a few moments on this problem. There is nothing more interesting than the analysis of psychomo, blood clots on the brain in various forms of non-violent insanity and mental unbalance such as my opponent suffers from." He then began quoting eminent authorities on the problem and misquoting me profusely. As the moments passed, the professor's ire rose. He heaped infamy upon insult in endless procession, grew red around the collar band and puffed excitedly. Most of his verbose outbreaks centralized upon the first point, namely, that I was dangerously insane, completely irresponsible, and that my only possible use in the world was to die in order that scientists might have the privilege of performing a postmortem autopsy upon my cerebral vesicles purely in the interest of research. (At this point, the professor's glasses fell off, and he rearranged his notes.)

"Friends and fellow scientists, the theory of mental evolution is tommyrot, pure and simple; the outpouring of a demented imagination perpetuated only through lunatics such as the one sitting beside me now. I will defy him to prove that anything proceeds with protoplasm or follows disintegration or incineration!"

The professor then continued to explain life as being something coming from nothing through a series of scientific deductions and returning from whence it came through another series of physiological inductions. He proved (to his own satisfaction) that neither God nor spirit, life, or any energy outside of matter, was necessary in the perpetuation and procreation of specie, but that a full and complete knowledge of this indispensable fact was the basic outpouring of modern, unapproachable science. (Hearty applause at this point.)

The professor bowed and slipped one thumb under his vest flap exposing a massive gold watch-chain draped artistically across an astonishing expanse of white waistcoat. It appeared that the professor was quite a religious man for he quoted Scripture glibly and with evident gusto to discredit the doctrine of physical rebirth taught in the East and which I had been promulgating in my studies. He quoted various scientific authorities in profusion and finally wound up by presenting me with a series of questions which he demanded that I answer if I expected even a moment's recognition from the infallible sciences of which he was the omnipresent incarnation.

Handing me the slip of paper containing the questions, typewritten in mathematical precision, he sat down -a whirlwind of personality and the most perfect example of self-conceit that it has ever been my privilege to gaze upon.

I was broken. I had no oratorial harangue to come back with and I felt that my knowledge, although I knew it was true-based upon only an improbable story of apparently impossible happenings would carry no weight among this band of thoughtless thinkers and second-hand mental gymnasts.

I rose to my feet. A deep hush and a rather blank atmosphere surrounded me not half so empty, however, as my own mind which seemed incapable of any expression. What I was going to say I had no idea of, and the slip of paper in my hand seemed like a living coal, which I longed to drop.

I was the most miserable thing on the face of the earth, none excepted, and a chuckle from the professor showed that he realized this fact. (Of course, it was a very low, refined chuckle.) I had been standing some thirty seconds, which seemed like as many years, trying to gather some word or thought from the ethers which swirled in my brain, when suddenly a hand was placed upon my shoulder, and a voice whispered in my ear, "Have courage, you are not alone."

I must have started violently, although it appeared that no one noticed me. The voice was that of the Master I had left in Thibet and his hand rested upon my shoulder as it had that fatal night in the Temple of the Caves. In some mysterious way I seemed to see him there, standing behind me, his robe flowing in silver and opal, and with a great courage which seemed born of divine inspiration I opened my mouth and started to speak words that I did not understand myself but which flowed in an endless stream with a power and eloquence unquestionable.

(To be continued.)

## PROMETHEUS THE ETERNAL SUFFERER

THE seer, gazing out into the endless ages of the past, sees a phantom file of Mighty Ones passing like specters through the eons of the past, mighty powers in world creation. These silent, shadowy Unknown Ones pass down the endless corridors of time. Living, suffering, and dying, the Divine Illuminators serve a world that knows them not.

Once there was a seeker who sought to learn the meaning of life with its compound riddle, but for him the great compassion, the realization of truth and the knowledge of nature's sublime laws were still shrouded in the Great Uncertainty. So, one night he was taken far away from the haunts of men by a guide he could not see, and a strange story was unfolded to him, which made life different from it had ever been before.

This searcher, after knowledge, wandered over many mountains and through the deep blue of an endless sky, on wings of unknown power. Guided by some subtle force, he was carried to the base of a mighty mountain, which rose broken and twisted by nature's upheavals. It was a gloomy mountain whose lava-blackened rocks and lofty sides were seamed and broken as they reached up to touch the blue above. Slowly, the student was carried up the mountain through the shades of evening and as he ascended, one lonely pinnacle rose above the rest like the mighty needle of the Matterhorn.

As he neared the ragged crest, a strange sight met his vision, and he gave a gasp of astonishment. There, stretched upon the bare stones, was a human body unprotected by even a single garment from the icy blasts of snow! The form writhed and struggled in mortal agony as it feebly sought with the puny strength of man to loosen its bonds of steel which seemed cast by the gods themselves. The figure was chained to a great rock by four shackles held down by steel stakes driven deep into the stone; the arms and legs were spread, and the tortured figure was literally crucified upon the gigantic granite boulder. As the student drew near, he shuddered for the rock was red with the blood of the agonized captive and a mighty vulture -greater far than any bird known to earth, clawed and tore at the side of the chained man! The student turned aside his head; the sight was too terrible, and he could not stand it, but a power greater than his own forced his gaze back to the figure chained to the living cross of granite. As he stood there his eyes held by, he knew not what, a low moan escaped from the lips of the sufferer and two great eyes wet with tears of anguish and suffering turned toward the man who had come from earth. No word the chained being uttered, no plea for help, but the agony of his soul poured out from those great eyes of sorrow, reaching to the very depth of the seeker's soul.

"Who are you?" asked the one of earth, gazing at the massive brow bordered with locks of golden hair.

"I" gasped the Crucified One, "I am Prometheus -Friend of Man."

"Why are you chained to this rock?"

"Because," murmured the chained victim, while the vulture still gnawed at the gaping hole in his side. "Because I rebelled against Jupiter, Lord of Heaven. Not because I loved Him less, but because the woes of mankind pained me more. When the gods decreed that man must die, I stole the Sacred Fire from heaven and brought it down to earth that man might live. For this I have been chained to the rock where I must remain forever unless a champion is found on earth who can break the fetters that bind me."

The student, sick at heart and in agony unutterable, turned away and passed silently down the mountainside back again to the land of men from whence he had come.

But each day, a great sadness gnawed at his soul, even as the talons of the mighty bird clawed at the entrails of Prometheus. Through nights he prayed, through days he labored, until a great ideal was born within his soul. He would liberate the Friend of Man from that awful rock which formed his cross!

One night, after years of waiting, as he knelt in his little room, a shining form appeared to tell him of the wondrous truths which he had sought. In a ray of light, the shining figure stood and, holding out his arms, said, "Come, I will teach you how to liberate the dying Prometheus."

The candidate rose and passed with his shining companion into the darkness of a great unknown. As they went along, the guide of many-colored lights spoke, saying:

"In the days when the world was young, Great Souls suffered that man might live. A divine essence descended from heaven against the will of the gods, bringing with it the light of Truth. This Essence took up its home in the body of man, bringing with it the fire of the gods; and from this fire is born the mystic essence which feeds the mind that man may think; it has given him the flame of energy but has also brought the flame of war and the torch that burns the home. It is the birth of the passions, the lusts and the greed's; and now the Friend of Man is chained to the rock while the lower animal desires and passions of humanity feed off the life which he brought with so much suffering to illuminate man.

"Know you, oh son of man! You are the black stone. Within you is chained Prometheus the Light-Bringer, a divine intelligence, the friend of mortal things. But the perversions of man and the crystallization and degeneracy of his life have chained this World Savior and the god of life is now crucified upon the cross of matter there to remain until man shall kill the vulture which gnaws at his vitals. Our lives, while we seem to live them for ourselves alone are far more important than we think, for it is our duty to release the Savior from the darkness of His cross which our own actions have chained him to.

"For what has man done with the fire that came down from heaven? Has he burned it upon the altars of his gods? Has he returned it again to the divine from whence it came? No. He has taken the fire of the gods, given to him at such tremendous sacrifice, and has fanned it into flames of selfishness and lust, wasting it and crucifying it in useless expressions of destruction, and has utterly failed to build with it the giant of strength and power who must release Prometheus from the mountain of stone. But there is one coming, the Strong One, the Child of the Sun-Hercules, and he shall release Prometheus from his ages of torment!

"And each one of you, oh children of earth! Must become that Hercules, with the light which ye have found -the shining sun- must build of the flame brought by Prometheus the mind and the body that we may sever His bonds and pay our debt to the first Great Friend of man."

Slowly the mighty mountain rose before them in the sky and as they drew closer, they could see the lonely figure still hanging upon the slanting stone, his eyes turned in agony towards the sun that great globe of light whose rays must release him from his endless torture. Still the vulture with claw and talon tore at his liver, still the rock was spattered with his blood, and still in divine trust and a great peace that surpasseth understanding, Prometheus waited and waited for the prophecy to be fulfilled that a strong one should rise from those whom he had served -one who should release him from the cross.

The shining guide spoke. "Oh, Prometheus, Friend of Man! Have courage. Through the ages, the soul of man is awakening, and the time shall yet come when he shall know your sacrifice. Some day from the fires which you have brought him, he shall build and smelt the tools to set you free. Wait yet a little while. The world is young and the curse of the gods is terrible, but still one shall come to free you from your bonds."

The divine face of the Sufferer lighted with a glory beyond the words of human to express.

"I will wait. And I am glad in my agony, for I love man. Though it is a hundred million ages, it is not in vain. I saved man from an endless darkness and have brought upon myself a punishment that is great indeed but I am willing to bear all if man but makes himself great and glorious through my sacrifice. How little do those whom I have served realize the price that I am paying for their freedom? As the fires within man flare and burn, fed by the lowest and the worst, they little know or realize that there is One tied to the rock who feels in the anguish of his soul each perversion of the sacred flame. For not only does the fire light man's way, but by the curse of Jove, it burns as well. And the light I have brought them they have used to slay me with, but I can wait. Through ages unnumbered, since before the dawn of time I have hung upon this rock. A hundred million times has this vulture of lust and fury clawed away my life, but the curse of the gods is endless for as fast as the vulture's talons rend the flesh more grows to take its place.

"I am the Eternal Sufferer. It is I, not man, who feels the most of pain, for his abuses of my sacred fire. I brought it in a reed from heaven to kindle on the hearthstones of the world, but they have desecrated my altars; they have broken my most sacred vows. And though I saved them from oblivion, my only fear is that they may not yet escape it.

"But when one is found who purifies my fire and harnesses its flames, freeing my light from the world of sin and abuse -that one shall climb to this lofty height and free me from my agony. Until then I wait. But as you burn the fire of life away, forget not Prometheus, the Friend of Man who feels in the clawing of the vulture the abuse of that life he gave so much to bring.

## DESCRIPTION OF LAST MONTH'S PLATE

THE plate in the July issue of the All-Seeing Eye is taken, as the others have been, from the rare and unobtainable writings of Robert Fludd the medieval English alchemist and Rosicrucian who is said to have brought the teachings of C. R. C. from Germany and to have been closely connected with the early development of both Masonry and Rosicrucianism. The plate represents the hierarchies of nature and its great lesson to the student of occult philosophy lies in the analogy between elements, chemicals, planets, gods and celestial hierarchies.

The plate is divided into two grand divisions, like the horoscope of astrology. That which is below the central horizontal line represents the inferior creation while that which is above symbolizes the superior creation. As the superior creation is the cause all world there is laid out in this chart the superphysical hierarchies and the various intelligent powers behind manifestation. The upper half of the diagram is symbolical of the Masonic Lodge and the body of the enlightened Mason while the lower part symbolizes the unilluminated negation of being.

In the concentric rings are placed the names of the Powers of the universe as they are found in the various sacred arts and sciences. The sacred Hebrew names and the Sephira of the Hebrew Qabalah are found in the spaces between A and B. The superphysical hierarchies of divine beings and the leading angels and rulers of the hierarchies pass through the sphere marked by the line of B. Under C. we have the astrological worlds and under D. the natural, chemical, alchemical, mineral and animal kingdoms laid out as they are found in nature. In the outside rings beyond A. we find the primitive principles of creation with the part they play in the unfolding of a universe, an individual, or a protoplasmic cell.

This is one of the most complicated of the alchemical plates, and can never be satisfactorily explained until the individual has unfolded a very high degree of spiritual sight and insight.

The passage of man through the spiritual worlds of nature and the twelvefold constitution of his own globe and chain is the result of conscious initiation which, until it takes place, conceals from man because of his own consciousness limitation -the mysteries which are the heritage of the wise. There are really no mysteries in nature for those who have earned the right to know; neither is there anything concealed that shall not be revealed. But the only way that the unseen can be brought into conscious manifestation is when man removes the veils of limitation from his own eyes by growth and unfoldment.

Thus, these plates which we have been issuing in our magazine have a very great meaning, but like the sacred scriptures of the Illumined, are sealed forever from the ignorant by their own ignorance. No mere intellectual power is capable of unveiling the divine mysteries. Only soul qualities, the highest of the spiritual reflective powers, the co-joining of spiritual reason and mystical intuition is capable of producing true illumination.

The first step to the study of these plates is neither reading nor meditating but practical self-regeneration which will give the higher power in man an opportunity of expressing its own omnipotent knowledge. This plate contains the entire secret of spiritual rulership and analogy; but no more may be said about it than that each individual must file from his own organisms the key which shall unlock its mysteries for the wise designed these things for the use of the wise and the price of understanding the words of the Illuminated is to become illuminated yourself. This is done when the light of spirit shines forth to bring out the colors on the printed page through the regenerated lantern of the philosopher -his own sevenfold body organism.

The plate in this month's magazine is of the philosophical marriage and the philosopher's stone and is taken from the secret writings of Henry Kunrath. Its description will follow next month.

## A DISCOURSE ON THE EIGHT PERFECTIONS - I

AND the Thrice Blessed Lord Spake unto His disciple, from the heart of His lotus-throne, explaining those things which are the Great Intelligences and the basis of union with that which is Above.

By his conduct is man's salvation measured and by his works is his soul ordained. Of these Eight Intelligences, which are the Ways of Perfection, should all men learn that they may sanctify themselves in the eyes of Brahma, the One who Is.

So, the Lord of the Lotus Lips Spake, saying:

"The first Great Intelligence is the perfection of Perception, for he who perceiveth things has power equal unto his perception. And all things may be known by any who are capable of seeing them. Learn, oh son! To perfect thyself in sight that when thou lookest thou shalt see the Reality, for behind the veil of Maya is concealed all true workings. And unto those who see with eyes that God has opened all of the Plan is manifest even unto the least of the creatures, for each stick and stone tells of that which is eternal; each passing glance, each action and thought is a key to the destiny of a universe!

"Therefore, oh disciple, learn to perceive that each day new lessons shall come unto thee because thou hast found them in that which eternally is. For now, that all knowledge is about thee always but must forever remain unknown until perfect perception crowns thee with the jewels of omnipotence."

Thus, Spake the Blessed Lord of the First Intelligence, which is Perception, saying:

"Learn also that which thou seest first is not the Reality save when through perfection thou perceiveth that which is invisible. What thou first seest is Maya the great Illusion but Reality molds Illusion and he who hath a right perception perceiveth the Reality in the expressions of Its not-Being.

"Know, therefore, oh Son of Man, that mortal perception seeth nothing but the shadow while divine perception alone seeth that which Is, knowing that the Reality casteth the shadow; and he is blind who worships the reflection. Moreover, know that he who perceiveth that which is not knoweth that it shall yet be the cause of that which is, that one is threefold wise in Perception. While he who perceiveth that which is, and through his perception seeth that which is to come when the Reality gathered unto itself, the Illusion, is also wise. For now, that the great Perception is not to perceive a thing unto itself but to perceive the action of Reality upon that which is not Itself.

"Therefore, perceive three things. That which is, that which is not and that which shall be from the union of these two. For the action of one thing upon another showeth unto the wise man the power of that which is unseen and invisible save through its reactions upon illusion.

"Know, thereore, Child of Earth, that perfect Perception seeth life in death.

Not by denying death, but by piercing the veil of Maya. Perfect Perception is that which seeth good in evil. Not by denying evil but by piercing the veil of Maya or the belief in that which has no Being. Also know that perfect Perception pierceth all things save the Eye of God, which it beholdeth free of the veil of illusion.

"He who hath perfect Perception is great, for he hath seen the Reason of all things and for all things. He who hath perfect Perception seeth one reason for all things for with his perception he has perceived perfectly that diversity is born of unreality and that Unity is the Divine Reality."

These are the words which the Blessed One spoke of the First Intelligence, which is Perception, and of the way in which a man should labor if he would be free from selfish selflessness.

\* \* \* \* \*

He then opened a petal of the Lotus and said as follows:

"Behold! I would speak of the Second Perfection that which is the Intelligence of Purpose and the Perfection of Right Aim.

"By the purpose of a thing, is it measured? The best work which thou may do, be it without purpose and intelligent aim, is Maya, that is, Illusion. There must be a purpose for all works and Right Perception which is the first Intelligence must illuminate the disciple unto the path of Right Purpose. There is but one purpose wherein man may be Intelligent in Purpose and acceptable in the sight of his Lord, and that is to be worthy of Nirvana. By its reason for being is a thing measured and a man who labors without reason labors to no purpose. He who labors without ideal labors to no purpose; he who labors without sacrifice, labors to no purpose; he who labors without compassion, labors to no purpose; he who labors in selfishness, labors to no purpose. But he who labors for that which is Eternal, he labors to Perfect Purpose.

"Know, therefore, that before thou laborest for thy God, decide upon that for which thou shalt labor and by its choice shall the labor be measured insomuch as ye are chosen."

Thus, Spake the Lord of the Lotus upon the Second Great Intelligence which is Right Purpose:

"Intelligent Aim wherein man may be one with that which Is and true unto himself because he is true to all things is the basis of noble purpose. The Spark of the Flame came down for the one purpose that it might be Perfect in purpose whereas now it is imperfect in purpose. Wherefore man is to perfect Purpose by being one in his ideals with Reality.

"'There is but one Perfect Purpose and that is the Perfection of Purpose which man learns only through the vail of Maya, where he labors in imperfect purpose with that which is not so good and that which is better, thus learning the Great Perfection. Such is the Perfection of Purpose."

* * * * *

With these words, the Lord of the Ten Thousand Perfections spoke of the Third Intelligence, which is Perfect Speech, saying:

"Men speak many things. The wise men speak great truths, the foolish speak only words that they may listen to themselves. These words mean nothing save to the wise man who learns from them that the speakers of them are fools.

"Therefore, of Perfect Speech I would say: speak not too much for he who wasteth words wasteth life as words are living things. By much speaking, man becometh careless of his words, which then lose their meaning and are but sounds. Yet by much thinking man speaketh little and so becometh Perfect in Speech, whereas he sayeth much less in words but infinitely more in Truth. For Perfect Speech meaneth that all words shall be of Truth and not of Illusion. The man who speaketh with his mouth sayeth nothing, but when he speaketh with the spirit, he sayeth that which is wise.

"Therefore, it is that man should be Perfect of Speech and intelligent of words, which we know as the Third Great Intelligence."

And then Spake the Blessed Lord of the Intelligence of Perfect Speech, saying:

"Perfect speech is kind and sayeth only that which is true and serveth three the one spoken to, the one speaking, and God who hears them both.

"He who would know the bliss of union with his Lord must have control of tongue that he sayeth not that which is untrue, that which is hateful, that which injureth, or that which teareth down and is malicious, for these things are of death and not of life. And whoso controlleth not his tongue will never be one with the Immortals who speaketh only words of wisdom. He who is Perfect in Speech hurteth not another, being kind with that which is and generous with the Great Illusion. A sharp tongue hath nought with its God nor with Me, for he who hath a sharp tongue speaketh with the mouth only and use the vain words which, while often sharper than an adder's tooth, mean naught for they come from naught.

"Therefore, oh son! be Perfect in Speech that your words be kind, true, and not too plentiful; that ye speak with your mind and your heart that only which is of Truth a Reality and not with your bodies which are Unrealities."

So sayeth the Blessed Lord of the Third Perfection, which is Intelligent Speech.

\* \* \* \* \*

Then taketh He the Lotus and resumeth:

"This is the Fourth Perfection which is Intelligent Conduct, both unto thyself and unto those that surround thee. For know that a man of God who weareth the braided cord must conduct himself according to the law and must strive that his conduct be perfect insomuch as it is within his power. He who watcheth not his conduct each day soon becometh careless and faileth to conduct himself according to the Ways of Light. Therefore, I give ye these instructions that ye may live and conduct yourself in that way, which is acceptable to Brahma.

"First, conduct yourself in simplicity that there he no forward thing in you which is not good in the eyes of the Most High. Be ye not first, neither be ye last, but where ye belong according to that which you yourself knoweth.

"Second, conduct thyself with civility unto all things and with righteousness unto thy gods. Wherein ye fail to do this ye bring upon ye the calamities of which ye know."

Thus, Spake the Blessed Lord unto His disciple at the foot of the mountain of the Fourth Perfection, which is Intelligent Conduct, saying:

"By what my priests do, so am I judged and as ye conduct yourself, so men say do I, the Lord of Men, conduct myself. Therefore, be ye ever mindful that ye conduct yourself according to the ways which are of wisdom. Give not to that which is Temporal, but he is strong for that which is Eternal. Conduct yourself in peace when others are in strife, conduct yourself in meekness when others are discordant, conduct yourself in simplicity when others are vainglorious. By this shall men know that ye are seeking for that which is Eternal and not that which is of Illusion. For by your works are the gods judged insomuch as ye claim to be the mouthpiece of the gods. And realizing that ye live not of yourself but of God, live that ye may serve others through noble conduct which shall point ye out from the world of men as one trusted and beloved of the gods as their divine messenger."

In this the Blessed Lord closeth the fourth Great Perfection, which is Intelligent Conduct, and speaketh of the fifth which is Intelligent Living. For behold he liveth only who learneth at the feet of the Lord of Wisdom of that of which life is composed. So, the disciple listened while the Good Lord spoke: (To be continued.)

## IMPRACTICAL OCCULTISTS

THE greatest stumbling block that confronts students of the Wisdom Teachings seems to be the problem of proper application. A large number of so-called students are merely theorists living in a world of their own creation, separated by transcendental ideas from all of the practical problems of life. They live, move and have their being within a crystalline shell of their own making which they seem unable to break through to contact the daily problems of life.

The great cry is not for abstract ideas but for practical remedies to be applied to the world inharmonies and international diseases which we know as plagues, wars and economic disturbances!

Occultists and mystics who are not able to apply their philosophies to the great bread-and-butter necessities of life have failed entirely to grasp the real truths of Universal Knowledge. Why do we find so many students who have lost contact with their brother man? They live alone on the tops of mountains, gazing down with supercilious mien upon the tiny ants and grubs which appear mere grains of nothingness from their elevated (but not superior) position. Why does the student have the feeling that everyone is beneath him in ethics and ideals? And why, oh why! is he too good to work?

This list of questions might be continued indefinitely as one unexplainable why after another passes in endless procession-few of them complimentary to the traits and qualities exhibited by so-called students of the Wisdom Teachings.

There is no denying the fact that Mystics are unusual people but the strangest of all are the pseudo-mystics who are hanging 'twixt heaven and hell in a wonderous parachute of self-created concepts. Their eyes are upon the stars (with which they seek union) and thoughtlessly and heedlessly they push less fortunate brothers to one side, trampling on the rights of others, shirking with studious care their own responsibilities. They seem to feel, for some unknown reason, that the world should honor, adore, and bask in the presence of all who claim to be seekers of the Light and that all should hasten to cooperate in perpetuating the indolence of the average truth seeker.

The "mystic" feels and expresses in his life the idea that the world owes him a living; that it should honor, respect and support him and rush to his beck and call because his mind is filled with contemplation of the Absolute. Being engaged in such weighty and brain-wracking thoughts his inspiration should not be disturbed by the rent man, the grocer, or the cries of an atrophying stomach but that someone gathered from the worlds of the unenlightened should do these things for him and so leave the master dreamer undisturbed in his celestial nightmares.

Let us study these questions, the eternal why's, and arrange them with the analytical mind of a logical thinker, free from much spirituality and theoretical concept, and find the underlying innate reason concealed behind these eccentricies of the exponents of divine wisdom.

An old saying is that the Devil is proficient in quoting Scripture and always does it to purpose, and just so the lowest qualities in human nature eternally seek vindication beneath a mock robe of the highest and most beautiful. When we ask the question, why does not an occultist work? He excuses himself by saying he is serving the Lord, is concentrating upon world salvation, or unfolding his consciousness through hours of meditation and other strange exercises which he is forced to perform twenty-four hours a day that he may prevent an earthquake, a tidal wave, or a revolution. Another will tell you that he cannot find anything to do that is congenial with his spiritual views; another is incapacitated by a delicate constitution, et cetera. This is what they tell us but when we analyze the problem, we find that the real reason for the inertia among the "divine" is unadulterated laziness, which inherent desire to escape labor seeks to cloak itself beneath spirituality.

It is this innate quality of the lower bodies to escape the battle of the world, which is the basis of recluses, hermits, and cranks. First it is a habit, then an eccentricity, later a fanaticism, then an obsession, and finally a murderer. Man humors these lazy little principles within himself until they become giants and he is murdered by his own creations.

A large percentage of so-called students of mystic philosophy make no practical effort to be useful in world affairs or to meet the battles of life and the real reason for this is they are lazy but have found a pleasant, intellectual, highly respectable channel of human expression in which they can make themselves believe that inertia is a virtue. And whatever doctrine teaches that laziness is a desirable condition will be attended by an overflowing membership.

No one likes to work without special training. No matter how you enjoy a certain thing, if you have to do it continually, it becomes monotonous. The human soul cries for freedom from routine, and so our "mystics" assume various gymnastic poses. To quote authorities on the subject: "They aspire to soar as eagles from crag to crag." So, we see some generously proportioned disciple of things spiritual trying to balance gracefully upon one toe on a pinnacle of ethereal cloud waves or to flutter aesthetically from moonbeam to moonbeam crying in ecstasy as the gentle zyphers flush his cheeks, free as a bird!

Upon this basis of spiritual aspiration thousands of people who could make respectable grocers, clerks, window-washers, firemen and floor-walkers are now lounging around listening to delirio-scientific outbursts and waiting impatiently for their avoirdupois to become transmuted into spiritual ethers that they may slip through the window, wafted on the gentle breath of Eros!

So, we may say by way of brief condensation, that our so-called spiritual works are producing a series of lazy failures who would not do an honest day's work for the ransom of Croesus. And to top irony with calumny, they not only continue systematically to do nothing but they expect to be respected and praised for it and pointed out as glorious spiritual successes as they loll around waiting, like Wilkins Micawber, for "something to turn up."

"Occultists" with temperament are not uncommon. Some simply can't stand a breath of air! Others are overwhelmed with nausea when they contact an ordinary human being; some are shrouded in repugnance when it becomes necessary to converse with a menial person; while our scintillating lights of brotherhood edge gently away from such individuals as brick-layers, butchers and ministers. Most of our "mystics" have super nerves and a large percentage of them have that peculiar disease which turns the backbone into a wishbone, said wishbone being very wabbly and lacking sufficient strength to permit the individual leaning himself against it. This makes it necessary for him to find someone else to lean on, to tell his troubles to and blame for all his failures.

A person who is not busily engaged in something is a danger to the community, regardless of his religion. Wars, crimes, pestilences, gossip and parlor-parasites are the outgrowths and products of the germ of laziness. And never mind how "spiritual" a person may be if he is not really busy at some material, tangible and result-producing thing, he is a danger not only to himself but to others who might be infected by the bacilli he is propagating. The sooner occultists get the idea out of their system that it is degenerating to be one with the world, the sooner they will really become spiritual.

Taking it as a general entire at the present time the mystics, new thoughtists and so-called spiritual students are the most unreliable series of people alive. Their words are not worth "shucks," their powers of concentration are nil. They do not know one end of an umbrella from another, and are as lazy as all outdoors. When put to work to earn their daily bread like the rest of suffering humanity all they do is stand around and try to impress others with the necessity of realizing that an electron is smaller than a molecule or that God is all there is. This class entirely overlooks the fact that if God is all there is that it is unnecessary for one part of Him to tell the other part about it. If each will mind his own business, God will take care of the entire.

There is no class more dangerous than the soul-savers who, having just found a little light, become overly enthusiastic about it. They rouse you out of bed in the wee small hours, serenade under your windows or make you stand out in the backyard while the muffins are burning informing you that your present concepts are sure to result in a permanent Turkish bath for you after demise. It is the height of sarcasm to have some worm eaten individual, whose handclasp reminds you that your fingers have closed over a clam, whose limpid personality has neither backbone, strength, activity nor even the human attributes of cheerfulness, come up to you with tears in his eyes and try to save your soul or illuminate your consciousness in the ways of success at the same time borrow two ninety-eight until next week.

Now comes a still more important problem, oh why are all occultists "broke?" There is more pecuniary embarrassment among our modern spiritual demonstrators than in the immigrant class. Every one of them are strictly up against it and when asked why they will answer that the world has not treated them right and that their high spiritual motives make it impossible for them to join the ranks of money-grabbers and punctilious cash profiteers who make up our business systems. The "mystic" will tell you that his tender consciousness revolts against commercialism, therefore he is not well fixed because he cannot go back to that money-mad world he left behind! However, his conscience never seems to revolt against letting somebody else go out and earn it for him, and we find from proofs that when our "mystic" does get any money he is just as commercial as the person he points out as a horrible example.

Now, why, in plain English, is he broke? The answer is, he lacks concentration of purpose, system, regularity, efficiency, and worst of all, he cannot take orders. The average occultist will condescend to be the leader of almost anything but to be an office boy shocks his tender sentiments. He believes that his knowledge of rounds and periods should make him of inestimable value in a boiler factory and qualify him to be the president of a paper clip manufacturing company on general principles. The fact that he has a personal contact with God should highly recommend him in the world of affairs; when in reality, it only places the taboo mark on him, for the businessman has found that dreamy mystics do not sell china well nor peg good shoes.

One of the main reasons why occultists do not succeed in business is the fact that the world is filled with a number of people, each one of them desiring to think as he pleases, wear what he pleases, eat what he pleases and smoke stogies if he so desires. When he goes to buy a pair of shoes or have an inch sawed off of his cork leg and the salesman tries to baptize him or initiate him into the value of hops tea, he does not usually return but goes where they sell shoes instead of scintillating advice.

There is a very wide gap between heaven and earth and the businessman who lives in heaven all the time will undoubtedly lose his customers. Heaven is a very abstract space, it does not satisfy an appetite nor vulcanize tires, and the individual who tries to live there all his life will undoubtedly reach his goal prematurely as a result of starvation. And the worst part of it is that these "occultists" will never reach heaven by the routes that they have assigned themselves but day by day in every way they are going further and further astray! Their theories will not bring down the price of milk in summer nor clean the mosquitoes out of the Jersey flats. They will not inaugurate an era of brotherhood but if the modern religious mystic got hold of conditions, we would have a "smotherhood" rule instead. We have wars regularly, earthquakes per annum, pestilences, crime waves, et cetera, just as though occultists did not gather around their cold slaw like the farmers used to do down in Rumpus Ridge where they discussed the next election over the checkerboard.

And when all is taken and boiled down, in spite of much talk, there are very few occultists who have really done anything for themselves or anyone else which they couldn't have done as atheists just as well. All they have amassed is a series of intellectual concepts and theoretical speculations which have never been applied and would not work if they were. That rather hazy word "Truth" covers a multitude of sins; "the realization of God" covers a lot more; "the impersonal" is a mystic tarpaulin, while "divine love" reaches entirely across the gamut between bootleg and blackmail. But all this does not produce honest politics nor do the great international problems adjust themselves through our mystic luminaries and if it was not for the work of a few who really do know and do apply, things would be in a very sorry plight indeed.

There is but one answer to the question and that is the practical living of a life of daily service and helpfulness in the community. When the student applies to living problems which surround him the theoretical knowledge, which is useless until so applied, he will be an occultist but not before. While the occultist evades the material world, he overlooks one of nature's most fundamental laws. Let the mystic remember that he was not ordained to be ornamental, but to be useful. He should also remember that hell, not heaven, is to be the field of his activities because from last reports, heaven is quite able to take care of itself. A mystic who believes that heaven is to be his resting place and that he will be privileged to lounge forever on a bed of phoenix feathers to gargle nectar and ambrosia through sunbeam straws has a cruel awakening before him! He may as well get used to adversity right here because in accepting the Master's work he has signified his willingness to give up the comforts and peace which mark material existence and work in any way which may be given to him in the name of the great Light which he is seeking to discover.

The realization that the world's salvation depends upon the willingness of mankind to learn lessons is of great importance and students who go around fussing and stewing because of the adversity which surrounds them are not setting examples worthy of a moment's consideration. The world needs practical people; it needs better lawyers, better doctors, better ministers, government officials, and able citizens. Conscientious shopkeepers, mechanics and artisans whose work is better and more perfect will thus help to glorify the entire. All constructive works are noble and worthy and conscientious labor with the ability to master the unpleasantness of routine is necessary for advancement.

The average occultist does not realize what an important place a handshake fills in character analysis. Have you ever shaken hands with a "mystic?" Try it sometime. You will find that his hand slips out between your fingers before you can close them; his hand is clammy, mushy and semi-glutinous while the fingers never exert themselves sufficiently to close; the arm and hand droops and the mentality, power, and health is in exact accordance with the lifeless member. Their voices are sing-songy and no deeper than the front teeth; and they are prone to sighing, which is a sign, we believe, of a collapsing diaphragm. Their backs are weak, their knees wabble and they are spending their lives eating pre-digested pickles and nonprotein prunes a la zwieback in order to piece out an absolutely useless existence.

If these were outpourings of the Mystery Schools! occultism would have died ages ago. But thank goodness, these peculiar specimens are not occultists nor students of anything! They are too weak in most cases to chew their own food, mentally, spiritually, or physically and are merely collapsing organisms who are using occultism as a refined method of disintegrating.

You will find the true disciple of the Mystery School out doing things in every walk of life whether it is driving stakes, carrying girders, building homes or cleaning drain pipes, he is at work. He sings at his labors while the weak and lazy sigh at their inertia. His body is strengthened by toil, his hands are blistered with the world's work, and ever in his heart, he is the master mystic. For his hands have built the dreams of his soul into the things his brother needs! He has built homes to shelter the children of men; he has cleaned the drains that they might be well. His own work is carried on as a menial, but he is the one who has won the game. Many a god has bowed in humble servility to one far

less than he, while many a fool has stood on his hind legs to sneer at the divine!
(To be continued.)

## A KNIGHT OF THE HOLY GRAIL

THERE is no more terrible product of human individualization than that great desire for supremacy, territorial acquisition and personal vengeance which we know as the cause of war. In spite of the fact that nearly every doctrine of mankind speaks for peace and that the very faith of the world is one of love and cooperation, still the eternal combative principle of man continues to bring down upon itself that terrible pestilence that international disease which we know as war.

War is far more than what the average individual knows concerning it. Not only is it a battle of living things on this visible plane of nature, but it is also a terrible conflict of mystic beings in worlds unseen. The very elements of nature seem to conspire and strange creature's unknown unite with the endless stream of human passion, struggling, tearing and breaking. From the heights of the mountains to the depths of the sea, all nature seems to be one wild tempestuous mass of seething, twisting flame-colored forces. The armies on the field of battle are but reflections of a mighty cosmic horde, struggling, wrestling, slaying and being slain in the living ethers of the invisible worlds.

Through all of the universe a great shudder thrills as human beings lose the animal within themselves which as a giant wolf rushes across the surface of creation breathing flames of hate, playing upon the weak and foolish, tearing down the craftsmanship of the divine with murderous savagery!

If war is terrible on land, it is doubly so far out in that ever-mysterious ocean. The sea has often been called the graveyard of the world and, in truth, its ceaseless foam-capped waves seem like ghosts reaching ethereal fingers upward from the darkness of the deep. Great nations, worlds, treasures unnumbered, knowledge untold, proud ships that once sailed the seven seas, all these lies buried in the misty depths of nature's wondrous miracle where lurid shadows of strange swirling seaweeds alone mark the forests and cities of forgotten days. The lapping waves conceal in that unknown deep many a noble hope, many a great ideal; in these mighty depths, many a brave soul lies in dark oblivion; and mayhap the restless souls of those unfortunates cause its endless motion.

Here too, the spirit of war is loosened. Strange beings unseen to mortal eyes twist and writhe in the foamy depths lashing the waves to fury; great streams of fiery hate nourished by thoughts of men impregnate even the ocean's depth with powers demoniacal. The bloodshed, the lust of loosened passion and uncurbed desire thrill through the mystic currents of the sea as through the land and strange, low, moaning sighs seem to echo into a wild mystic sob which tells of the broken heart of the world.

It is not man alone who feels that awful break which stays creation's plan when the leprous pest of war is loosened, but both God and nature combine in sorrow at human ignorance and man's perversion. Plant and animal, stone and star, all feel when the red powers of Mars are loosened, all nature shudders and armies of mystic demons struggle through the clouds of smoke and gas that cover a battlefield. The salamanders battle in the flame of the firebrand and carry with lustful gleam the sparks that lay a nation hare, the twisting undines surge through the ocean clouds of spray, while from the skies the sylphs launch hurricanes of gas and wind upon that puny being called Man who feeds the worst in all the universe with his hates and his desires.

As the gods of creation wrestled in the throes of cosmic birth, so those flaming demons of darkness and armies of hate live on that mystic something, that strange effluvia of death, which rises as an unnamed stench from the battlefields of a great war! Like the drunkard gloating over the alcohol which destroys him, like the drug fiend and the morphine to which he is a slave, so the demons of death and hate live and grow strong, for a time at least, upon the thoughts and hates of man which rise in a great cloud of murky hue and float over man's greatest perversion.

All over the world this perverted energy is felt, the internal fires of the earth are loosened, and streams of lava pour down the mountainside, the curse of pestilence and crime bathes the world in blood. Each country, city and hamlet feels the presence of the Angel of Death, as the powers of hell are freed from the bonds of decency. The Spirit of the Plagues, that brooding shadow that bespeaks mortal doom, carved by human thoughts from the unformed substances of chaos, hovers as a great ghoul of evil over the world which it blasts with its flaming tongue and tears with its clawed talons. This creature is the reward of war and is given birth when man forgets he is a man and becomes a beast once more. Yes, a beast lower than a brute.

* * * * *

It was a gloomy night during the European war, probably the greatest struggle which the world has ever known, and the darkness was lighted for those who had eyes to see by millions of lurid sparks, strange snaky forms and creatures of an opium dream, the whole astral plane a seething mass of hate and glowing coals of passion. Already the low rumblings of internal flames warned that the end of human rulership had come while the beasts of desire, not the human brain, governed the actions of man.

The ocean was as silent as a tomb. Even the ceaseless moaning of the sea was so subdued as to be inaudible. Suddenly a low "swish!" and a great dark form rose out of the darkness to be silhouetted against a starless sky. A mighty ship was passing as silently as a specter through the seemingly boundless night. All lights were out and not a voice could be heard, for the vessel had entered the danger zone.

The submarine warfare which marked the European conflict was a terror hard to combat and in breathless fear and trembling each passenger waited hoping that the thing they feared would not occur and that the crash and thrill which spoke of torpedo or sunken mine would not send the gallant ship to an untimely end. The captain, his hands clutching the rail, stood on the bridge peering into the darkness, while the crew stood around with bated breaths, for the ship was carrying contraband! Any moment might be its last. Silently it ploughed on its way, the soft swish of waves and the low throbbing of engine the only audible sounds. Had the captain been able to gaze through the darkness and gloom that stretched out through the infinity of night he would have seen a dark shadow pass swiftly through the water apparently without sound nor shape. He might also have seen a thin streak of white foam pass silently over the surface of the waves towards the darkened form of the mighty vessel.

Suddenly the tense hush was broken by an explosion and a vivid flare lit up for a second, the troubled water showing the long tube-like shape of the submarine shining with silver spray as it vanished beneath the waves. In a second, all was uproar on the great liner and cries and shouts broke the stillness, for the torpedo had struck a fatal spot! An explosion followed the explosion within the ship itself, which reeled and twisted like a stricken animal. The hoarse voices of sailors, the cries of frightened passengers, the swift issue of command, the shriek of lifeboat pulleys and the unleashing of pontoons, all showed that a great excitement had taken the place of the silent dread.

A great cloud of mist suddenly swept over the ocean in dense billows shrouding the vessel and its terror-stricken passengers in a gloom intangible. The last lights vanished and nothing remained save a surging maelstrom of shadowy creatures of the fog.

Hours passed, and the rising sun scattered the clouds of darkness. But as it rose, it shone down upon a troubled sea for the waves had risen to fury, fanned by a half gale from the south, and as far as the eye could see nothing was visible but whitecapped breakers. The ship had vanished. Here and there, a broken piece of wreckage marked its resting place while an overturned lifeboat told a sad story all its own. The mighty ship was sunken forever from the sight of men and not one had survived to tell the story of it's going, for the storm swept sea had engulfed the last eager hope of those fated souls.

Hours passed, the waves stilled, and slowly the great troughs subsided until a great calm rested upon the ocean which stretched serene and blue as far as the eye could see, concealing all traces of night's tragedy. This is all that man knew. War had claimed another victim, and the hungry flames were nourished once again by the lifeblood of the innocent. But there were other things that man did not know which nevertheless tell of a wonderous plan and a wisdom divine.

Somewhere above the world where the mountain peaks of eternity touch the blue skies of a celestial land there rises a single crag higher and mightier than all the others, clouds nestling among its precipices and cliffs. While storms break in the valley below, the summit of this lofty mountain is ever bathed in sunshine. They're rising from the very peak stands a mystic castle, a temple undreamed of by mortal man, a palace of rainbow tints connected to earth by a glorious pathway of flashing jewels and mist. In the heart of this mystic temple stands a wondrous shrine guarded by the pure of the soul in the world of men. It is called the Temple of the Grail and is the home of the Lords of Compassion for from it there go forth into the world the guardians of human destiny and the saviors of the weak.

As we gaze upon the mystic castle a shining figure passes out from beneath its lofty gates, a figure robed from head to foot in garments of shining color which gleam with the shades of opal and of pearl. Down the rainbow bridge of light, the figure passes along a path which mortal feet can never tread.

Finally, at the base of the mountain where it met the waves, the mystic stranger stopped by the side of a wondrous winged boat made like a swan. Stepping into the frail craft which itself seemed but a dream and not a reality the shining figure stood and taking a thin cord of scarlet between his fingers pointed out through the blue haze which marked the unbroken skyline. The boat seemed to thrill with life and silently swift; it glided away over the surface of the water; the waves were stilled as the boat passed and like some mystic phantom, the shining figure standing in it drifted away amid the blue waters of eternity. On and on, this beautiful being passed. The mirror-like waters of peaceful blue slowly turned into surging waves of mid-ocean, the mighty mountain that touched the heavens vanished in the distance as though it had never been and the tiny figure became the only living thing in an endless expanse of water.

Suddenly, he raised his hand, and the vessel stopped. Beside him lay floating upon the water a piece of wreckage. He leaned over the side of his mystic craft and picked up the broken stick and holding it before him gazed sadly at it for several seconds, his great eyes lighted by a divine compassion. And then the shining one sank in prayer in his tiny barque 'mid that endless ocean. His prayer was turned to the mountain that touched the sky, was turned to the great temple of shining pillars, to the mystic shrine within whose holy glow the Blood of the Savior sparkled. His prayer was for the salvation of man and the redemption of the dead. As he prayed, a great glow appeared, floating over the waters. It was a cup formed of a glorious stone and in its heart surged a strange flaming liquid which seemed to pour out on to the waves below. The shining stranger rose and held out his arms to the Cup.

"Lead thou, the way!" he whispered. And as the shining Grail floated over the ocean and finally sank beneath the waves, the Brother of the Shining Robe stepped out of the boat. Instead of sinking, the waters became stilled beneath his feet and without fear or hesitation the Knight of the Holy Grail walked out over the surface of the deep, his white robe blowing slightly as the breezes fanned the water beneath him.

Reaching the trough of a mighty wave which seemed ready to break over and destroy him the shining figure reached the top of a series of mystic stairs which formed out of the water itself and seemed to reach down to endless depths. Slowly, the Shining One went down the mystic stairway and vanished beneath the water. Down, down, he passed, the light around him growing fainter and more greenish as he descended. Darker and darker it grew until finally a deep blue night enveloped him, lighted only by the glowing radiance of his own being. Strange sea creatures swam about him and as he neared the bottom of the ocean great twining arms of seaweed stretched up as though to encircle him, strange fishes, and crawling things unknown to man surrounded him but some sought to harm him not even the mighty leviathans which swam in and out among the coral arches.

Before him, brought into sight by the gleaming light of his own being, rose the hulk of a mighty vessel, in its side a gaping hole where the torpedo had struck and shivered its form. It lay caught between two mighty rocks just as it had been when floating above, save that now the deep gloom of the ocean bottom covered the scene and its passageways and corridors were filled with water and swimming things.

The mystic stood upon the deck and then slowly he passed from stateroom to stateroom, from corridor to corridor. Just a few seconds in each and then he passed on. But from the darkness of the ocean depths there arose one after another silent forms who had heard his voice and awakened from their sleep. As he climbed in and out and down into the very depths of the vessel, he gathered in the bewildered ones from the tombs of the ocean.

At last, he entered a little room where on every side lay torn and twisted machinery. They're caught among the wheels and pivots, was a lonely figure-a youth. The Master stepped up to him and spoke in his soft, sweet voice, "Brother, awaken!"

As he did so, a strange thing occurred. The tense set face of the dead man relaxed and a mystic etheric form rose out of the body.

"Who are you?" asked the youth awakened from his slumbers, "where am I? what does it mean?" and staring around in terror and amazement he held out his arms to the Shining One.

"You are in the depths of the ocean," answered the master, encircling with his arm the shoulders of the youth. "You are now in a different world from the one you have left."

"Who are you?" questioned the youth.

"I?" answered the master, "I am one who has lived in the world of men and have become, through my own labors, a citizen of two worlds. I am one of the Knights of the Holy Grail, the Invisible Helpers who labor with humanity. Come with me and I will show you your work and mine."

On and on passed the Knight of the Holy Grail. There in the darkened hold of the vessel amid the machinery torn and cracked by the explosion of boilers were those pathetic forms that had not a chance to reach the upper decks. In every case, the greeting was the same and soon a shadowy file had joined the Elder Brother as he passed on through the ocean's depths. Through the caverns of coral and forests of seaweed passed the Brother of the Shining Robe. Everywhere he found the darkness, and in every case, he brought the light. One by one, he awakened the children of men from the sleep of death and gathered them together that they once more might see the light of day.

So, the hours passed, and the minister of the gods labored far below, unseen to the eyes of men, known only to the dead who lived again through his coming. At last, the work was done and the hundreds who had been cast into the Great Eternity by that single torpedo were freed from the bonds of the unknown, freed by the Master of the Holy Grail, and shown the way to a life anew.

Slowly the shades of evening fell again over the ocean but a great peace was now upon the face of the deep for no longer the souls of men lay in darkness-the

Master had brought them Light. The little swan boat of ethers still floated upon the waves and there slowly appeared, climbing again the steps of the ocean, the gleaming figure of the Master and behind him a wraithlike train of phantom forms. Reaching the little boat, he stepped again into it and pointed in the direction from which he had come. Turning, he spoke:

"Far up in the land among the skies is the home of the Lords of Compassion, who are those of our own living and dead who have seen the Light and have labored for it. But a few short hours ago, you lay in an endless sleep of uncertainty. Now you are awakened. Over the ocean and the battlefields of this war there are thousands so laboring that man may know of the way which leads to freedom and light. I have awakened you, now go you and do likewise to those others who do not know the way but who, torn with shot and shell, are alone in an awful oblivion."

Quickly the craft moved along, passing over the surging water with the speed of the wind carrying away into the unknown the Brother of Light. Slowly, the great temple on the heights of the mountain came into view again, bathed in the glory of its endless day. The work of the Invisible Helper was done again, and the Knight of the Holy Grail returned to the mystic shrine around which gathered the Brothers of Compassion, who labor eternally for the weak.

Upon the silent battlefields, in plague-stricken lands, in pestilence, crime and disease, sorrow or death, man over turns his eyes upward to the heavens and the mountain tops from whence cometh his help. And in the moment of extremity the Knight of the Holy Grail is unfailingly there to encourage, to release and to inspire the souls of men struggling with the Great Unknown. And each day there are new ones gathered from the ranks of humanity who are ready to join that mystic band who bow before the sacred Cup in which gleams and sparkles the Life Blood of the martyred Christ.

## ASTROLOGICAL REWARD

Cancer, the fourth sign of the Zodiac, is the first of the water signs and is shown in the heavens under the symbol of a crab. Being the home of the moon, it is a fruitful sign and has been used by the ancients to symbolize the Divine Mother and the maternal instincts in nature. Briefly considered, we may analyze its general keywords as follows:

Cancer, the fourth sign of the Zodiac:
Summer, Commanding, Cold, Nocturnal, Watery, Movable, Moist, Fruitful,

Phlegmatic, Weak, Feminine, Unfortunate, Cardinal, Mute sign, Tropical, Long Ascension, Northern, The House of the Moon, The Exaltation of Jupiter, Detriment of Saturn, Fall of Mars Fall of Mars.

General Characteristics:
Cancer is not considered being a very strong sign and those under it must, under general conditions, watch their actions and lives very closely or they will not keep up to the best that they are, being apt to grow indifferent as to health and appearance. The most fruitful sign in the Zodiac.

Will power, Fair, Occasionally stubborn, Usually changeable, Being a water sign, Kind-hearted, Difficult to manage, Artistic and dreamy, Often negative, Suffer occasionally from anemia, Not usually good in speaking, Usually fairly cheerful,

Physical Appearance:
Usually fair, Often pale, Short, Round face, Slender arms and small feet, Brown hair, Usually small gray eyes, Upper part of body somewhat large, Somewhat dull in temperament and appearance, Short stature, Effeminate constitution, Phlegmatic, Heavy, Usually grows stout with age.

The Moon well posited in Cancer gives rather full symmetrical development of form while afflictions cause an overbalancing of the figure and undue development around the shoulders. Jupiter, if present in this sign, gives size and weight and a rather round appearance.

Health:
Cancer is often troubled with ill health and is subject to ailments in many parts of the body and when the moon is afflicted in Cancer, there is often considerable trouble with the liquids in the body as the blood, lymphatics, etc. The opposition of Capricorn to this sign and its malefic ray from Saturn often causes crystallization where an affliction occurs. The following are the most prevalent diseases and ailments:

Diseases of the chest and breast, Stomach trouble Coughs, Pleurisy Dropsy, Chronic indigestion, Asthma, Shortness of breath Consumption, Want of Appetite Liver trouble, Cancers Ague, Chills, Inflammation of the lungs, Injuries to the diaphragm, Ribs, Fear of insanity.

Domestic Problems: Cancer is not always fortunate in these being subject to fits of irascibility and peculiar changes in temperament and cannot always be depended upon. Is usually fond of children, however, happy in the home, and if of a highly evolved type harmonious and very likeable. Their success in this direction lies entirely with themselves.

Countries Under the Influence of Cancer:
Scotland Africa, Holland Carthage, New Zealand Algiers, Granada Tunis, Burgundy Tripoli,

Cities Under the Control of Cancer:
Constantinople Magdeburg, Venice Whittenberg, Milan St. Lucas, Genoa Cadiz, Amsterdam, St. Andrews, New York, York.

Colors:
Russet, Green, Silver.

According to Ptolemy, the two stars in the eyes of Cancer have the same influence as Mercury and also moderately like Mars. Those in the claws are like Saturn and Mercury. The nebulous mass in the breast called the Presepe has the same influence as Mars and the Moon. The two placed on either side of the nebulous mass and called the Assini, have an influence similar to that of Mars and the Sun. According to Henry Cornelius Agrippa Cancer, which rules from the 20th of June to the 20th of July, is listed in Cabbalism as follows: Of the Twelve Orders of Blessed Spirits, Cancer rules the dominations; of the Twelve Angels ruling over the Twelve Signs, it governs Muriel; of the Twelve Tribes, Manasseh; of the Twelve Prophets, Amos; of the Twelve Apostles, John; of the Twelve Plants, comfrey; of the Twelve Stones, calcedony; of the Twelve Principle Members, the breast; of the Twelve Degrees of the Damned, the revenges of wickedness.

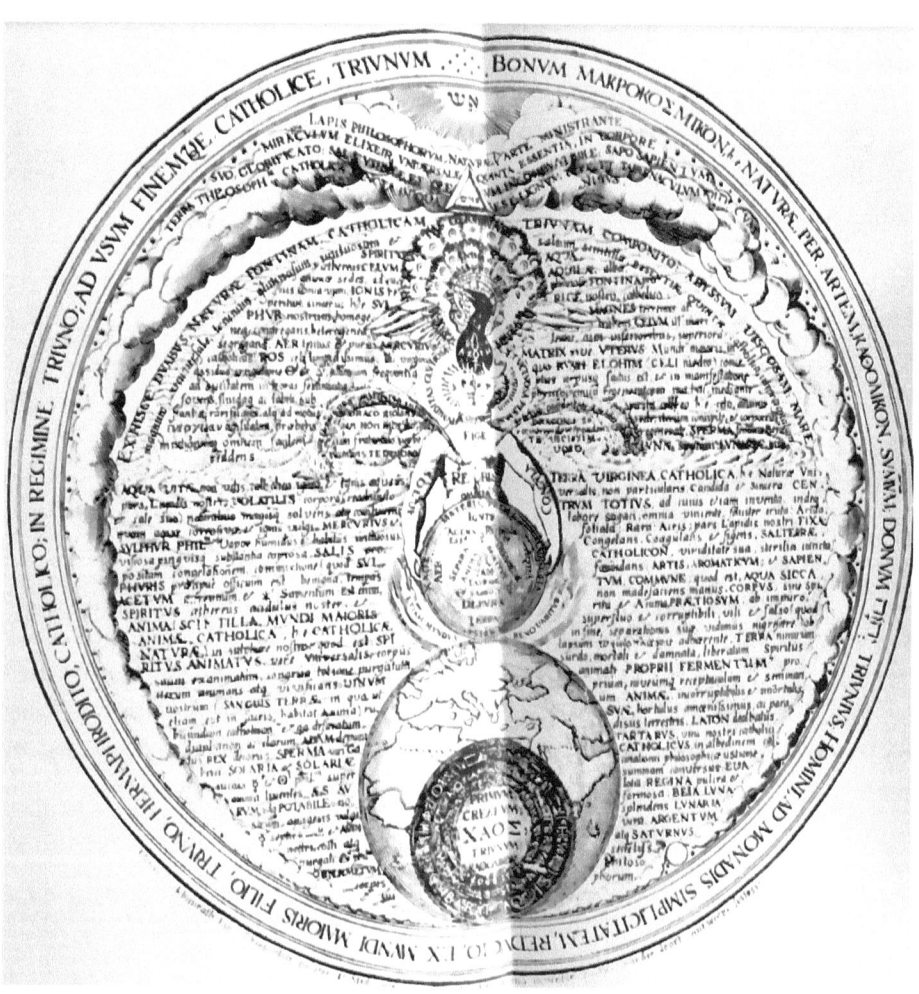

OCTOBER 1923

## THOUGHTS

There are many well-known things that no one seems to understand.

\* \* \*

Great minds and massive intellects are always surrounded by enemies of their own making for few can achieve greatness without grating.

\* \* \*

In the eyes of the ancients the acme of attainment was simplicity.

\* \* \*

Those who are absorbed by or enslaved to their labors never attain greatness.

\* \* \*

None despise egotism as do the egotists.

\* \* \*

Man's likes and dislikes stand between him and the thing he seeks.

\* \* \*

The happy person is the one who is so busy he has forgotten himself.

\* \* \*

You cannot insult an individual who is above the plane of personality.

\* \* \*

We must leave our "feelings" so far behind we cannot ever hear them when they call.

\* \* \*

If we did not want so much we would not be so dissatisfied when we do not get it.

\* \* \*

Those who build with personalities shall see their building fall. While those who build with principle build eternal.

\* \* \*

The world is filled with wonderful and talented individuals who are lost to the world and themselves because, alas, they are the first to realize their own knowledge.

\* \* \*

A word of correction from the wise is better than the applause of the foolish.

\* \* \*

No sword cuts the soul like the internal realization of failure.

## EDITORIAL
## "Ye-A-A-Ahs and Ye-A-A-Ahs!"
## DEADicated to Our "Old Students."

OCCULTISM will never grow monotonous or lack the divinely human touch while we have among us those glorious ones who emit their radiant auras of self-achievement as they promenade the by-ways of our occult groves. Wherever we turn, we find those ever-present ones, who, like rays of sunshine in our troubled lives, breeze in to tell us of their accomplishments.

Let me draw a picture for you, indeed it is a masterpiece! Poor, weary Mr. Doe, long searching 'mid the archives of the past, dropping pebble after pebble into the depthless oracles of Greece hoping against hope that some echo will waft back to him, sits surrounded by his thoughts, Hebrew lexicons, and Greek almanacs, seeking to find that which will bring him omnipotence. As he wanders midst those depthless pages which show upon their creased surfaces footprints where bookworms have trod, a voice rises and reverberates upon his dun-colored landscape. Beside him appears a strange creature, mayhap a denizen of some distant plane (Hoboken, N. J.), whose description we will try to assist you to build in that floating substance between the ears.

His name is Solomon J. Wizenheimer, and he holds the international occult talking record having kept his jaws moving continuously for ninety-two hours without saying anything. Mr. Wizenheimer is a small man about five-foot-one but what he lacks in size he makes up in conspishiation for wherever you may look from the Grand Canyon of Arizona to the Natural Bridge of Virginia, he is always the largest and most prominent object in sight. It is true that he cannot talk very clearly, having asthma and ingrowing diabetes; his glasses are about an inch and a half thick, for he is nearly blind; his upper plate falls every few moments; he dyes his eyebrows to match his toupee and his wooden leg always squeaks when he walks, but he is not so bad looking for he keeps his mange under good control. As he stands beside the struggling Mr. Doe, he is a perfect picture of the vintage of the year one.

"I see you are a student of the occult," says Mr. Wizenheimer. "So am I. I am one of the original classes of Monsieur Whoopyou will remember him, of course. He is the famous Slavonian Kabbalist. I studied with him for yeahs and yeahs and have written several books myself on physical regeneration and kindred subjects. I am the ex-grand master of the mystic Walupuk Shrine and if I do say it myself, I don't think there is another person on earth who has come so close to the realization of the mystic. I see things. As I gaze upon you, there is a peculiar greenish grey aura surrounding you. Oh yes sir, I am a seer; I go into trances! It is very wonderful when you get as far advanced as I am."

The peculiar greenish haze which was surrounding Mr. Doe was the result of that individual having become petrified with horror for fear that his studies would produce the same effect upon him as it had on Mr. Wizenheimer. The thought flashed thru his mind that if that is what occultism did for one man, he would leave it at once and join the first orthodox Fiji Island church! Swallowing his innate feelings, Mr. Doe made a graceful departing speech and hurriedly left the scenes of his late labors, leaving Mr. W. to visualize complacently the effect that his overwhelming soul growth had had upon Mr. Doe.

"My powers simply hypnotize them," murmured Mr. Wizenheimer, as he also vanished from the frame of our picture, leaving a refreshing vacuum behind him.

\* \* \*

Of course, some of our readers may feel that we have not treated this subject with justice and that we ought to have said a great deal more but we must ask them to imagine the rest upon the strength of what they have gone thru themselves while cloistered with one of these near-philosophers.

They have their place however, for utterly unknown to themselves the "old students" are the occult comedians and mirth provokers and are the basis for the laughter of the gods.

Students come up to us regularly to qualify themselves in art, philosophy, music and paternal judgment with the aid of rheumatism and white side whiskers, feeling that a snowy crest or an appearance resembling a spring freshet should deserve consideration, respect and veneration. A certain class of "mystics" just love to tell us how many cycles they have studied in this or how many decades they have immersed themselves in that, having a peculiarly distorted idea that their superiority is based upon the length of time they have expended in a certain work, failing to realize that ages of effort unwisely expended will produce nothing and that the length of time passed in study has little to do with the position of the soul in the great path, for some have done more in a few hours than some of our oldest "students" will do in a lifetime.

I must explain to you a few types of said occult mirth provokers whom we could not help but smile at if we did not realize what a tragic place they hold and what a tremendous sorrow that must come to them when they wake and realize how little they really know. The divine egotist is always with us and the trouble is the egotist seldom if ever is himself aware of his traits but blaming everyone but himself for his troubles, and claiming that others are simple because they do not agree with him, he goes on thru life never convinced of the foolishness of his own concepts. It is a tragedy in any line of life, but in spiritual things, it is doubly so. But for the good of those whom it may offend we must show you a few types commonly met with who are their own worst enemies and who in reality are never as far advanced ae the average person that they talk to. For it is the depth of the soul, the true spiritual understanding and practical works that are the basis of occult mastership and the "real old student" is the last of all who could claim that position.

It is a hard thing to say, yet it is true and must be said for the protection of others. A large number of people who claim spiritual vision and firsthand knowledge have not got it and never did have. Fifty percent of our so-called clairvoyants would be scared to death if they even saw an elemental and would run twenty miles from the first superphysical thing that confronted them, but as "old students" who should be conscious on all these planes, etc. and as nobody else is liable to be able to check them up, they tack on a few of these things for good measure to the awe of the foolish and the disgust of the initiate.

First, I want you to meet Exhibit A. Mrs. Ophelia Wobbletripe, who has tormented the community of truth seekers for about fifty years. She is a dashing dowager who has talked some of our greatest minds into a state of coma then left them perfectly satisfied that she had confounded the Elders. Madame has studied with every known swami, yogi, saint, patriarch and master since the civil war and has autographed photographs of the leading religion dispensers of the modern world (they would have given her anything they had to get rid of her). Mrs. Ophelia is a very much present student who can always be found in the front row with her mouth wide open (possibly to show her gold bridgework), going into shivering ecstasies of admiration for some exponent of things divine whom she nearly drives to distraction with an ostrich feather fan or some crinkling note papers. Mrs. Wobbletripe can quote Sanskrit by the yard, can decline Hebrew verbs, has climbed Mt. Shasta and is the proud owner of a Syriac Bible (which she uses for a paperweight.) During the first fifteen minutes of her acquaintance, you discover that she has been around the world fourteen times, has had several major operations and has relations married to the most eminent people in the country with a continuous list of husbands who pass silently to their only rest in the cemetery over the hill. She has a cousin-in-law who owns one of the largest salt licks in Arizona, has been prepared at Court without tripping on her train, and has a brother who is an eminent bootlegger. Mrs. Wobbletripe comes from a very excellent family and has a grandniece whose uncle's sister is the wife of Lord Saturday, Knight of the Bath. One of her husbands, now deceased, (and who is at rest save when she joins him on the astral plane), made millions in Chinese ques which he imported for sugar refineries and her eldest son by her ninth husband is married to the daughter of Samoa's bone fertilizer king.

All this we get in the first fifteen minutes of conversation, as I said before. She is subject to hectic delirium which she believes is a visionary condition and peculiar feelings come over her occasionally which she attributes to communication with the Masters, but is probably due to the little bubbles of uric acid poisoning which she extracts from her beefsteaks. Madame is a wonderful example of the so-called "old students" for it is safe to say that she knows absolutely nothing about anything except her own ideas which are the center and radius of her life. There is no use talking to the lady because she is completely satisfied with her own gamut of unconsciousness and knows more than any other person alive and admits it. If you are in trouble spiritually, she will have some excellent advice for you which she has never attempted to use herself but quotes it verbatim from her favorite swami. She has inflammatory rheumatism, kidney trouble, is very much overweight, won't walk, and spends half her time at Madame Gump's who is trying to eliminate seven or eight of her extra chins painlessly.

Kind reader and fellow sufferer, you may not believe that such creatures exist, but they do and can be found anywhere that students of things supernal gather. She will always be found very much in evidence and expresses herself with great confidence upon every conceivable problem.

This is an "old student." Taking the Funk & Wagnall definition of "old" we find that it says in part: "things liable to decay or having lived and existed in a certain state for a long time." This particular type has lived in a state of coma for ages and will only come out of it when nature pry's her loose. Many students have reached that enviable stage of crystallization when, having found something that to them is perfect, they sit back in complacent mental ossification and bask in the aura of their own accomplishments.

We will pass on to Type B. Section X. who is the occult antiquarian and has that wisdom which no one else can get hold of. He is the "chosen of the Masters" type. Prof. Nebuchadrezzar Nibbs has studied where no one else can go but with lofty superiority he condescends to allow others to drink occasionally at the fountain of his divine wisdom. Nebbsy is shrouded in credentials of a mystic nature, including a veterinary diploma, and being a member of several secret orders practices the pass signs every morning so as not to forget them. Neighbors watching him in the morning think he is taking calisthenics, but he is only making the secret sign of the ninth degree of the sacred order of Imperial Bunkum. He has been a private pupil of the famous Sylvester Sandstorm, one of Matilda Brainfag's inside group, has studied at the feet of Algernon Spoutly and all the other leading occult luminaries. He will tell you confidentially what they told him confidentially, misquoting leading authorities with the ease and fluency of a practiced liar. He is always surrounded by a number of gushitive individuals carrying light cargoes of mentoids who found in him the resurrection of a martyr or the reincarnation of a saint and savior within the first thirty days.

Prof. Nibbs admits that he is an old student also, and he always admits it before anyone else questions him. Everything he does is in a secret and concealed manner he even thinks in such a carefully hidden way that no other creature could possibly imagine that was what he was doing. Nebbsy admits that he is acquainted with all the leading occultists of the world and recognizes the soul growth in Exhibit A. He has had a very checkered career since he stopped working in the saloon which career, he has perpetuated in a checkered suit. He is willing to share his superior knowledge with humanity for a reasonable consideration, said compensation being as much cash as the other fellow has got.

Nebuchadrezzar Nibbs talks with the dead every night. He is out of his body half the time and out of his head the other. (We sometimes believe that he got lost on the astral plane and forgot to come back.) He is surrounded by ethereal creatures and material dupes and a bald head; a wise look and seventy-five years of stone rolling constitute his stock in trade. He knows absolutely nothing about anything but conceals this under paternal eyebrows and a saged appearance, which means absolutely nil and when asked, a quizzer always replies that information is only given out in the higher grades.

Having completed our analysis of Type B, we pass on to Type C. X 3, the Astrological Contortionist and Numerological Sprainer, Miss Delilia Wampus. No occult group is complete without her, and she is with us, even unto the end of the world. Her specialty is birth paths and evil aspects, she is perpetually suffering from acute angles and afflictions in her rising sign and can always be found seeking the hour and minute of some individual's birth and then informing them that by compound ratio or mathematical hydraulics that the Z sq. X means that their husband will run off with the chauffeur's wife or that their hours are numbered. Miss Wampus is a specialist at prognostication she has prophesied every winter that has happened during her lifetime. She knows exactly when the world will end and is waiting patiently for a certain aspect to culminate, for when it does; she is going to do great things. Miss Wam pus is an old maid, she declined three aspirants to her hand because their rising sign was not congenial with her own. Her best aspect is Saturn trine Jupiter, and she never misses an opportunity to express these good qualities and to explain that they are the base of her divine understanding. Miss Wampus also sees things occasionally and is not concentrating for prosperity, feeling quite confident that the transit of the moon will assist. She runs her life by astrology, numerology and kindred sciences and plans out her daily work according to astrological hours. She eats astrology and then, like our family cow, chews it some more; she inhales and exhales sidereal time and has her tea on the table of houses; and whenever she closes her eyes, she sees black horoscope forms. She has been pronounced demented by her relatives because she goes up to perfect strangers on the street and asks them if they have nine degrees of Taurus in the eighth house.

Leaving this specimen in its glass case, we pass on to Exhibit D. one of the most interesting and remarkable examples of "old student" formation that we have. This particular specie is known as the "mouthpiece of the gods." After having passed through thirty-five or forty years of indolent probationship he is now a self-ordained mouthpiece used by the Masters of Wisdom to sell vacuum cleaners, electric irons, magazine subscriptions and to dispense the occult wisdom generally. Yes, among our old students we find a large number who are being used by the Masters and are in constant communication with the Lords of high degree. You will always know them as they sit around discussing the haircut of their favorite patriarch. When we analyze this series of specimen, we feel certain that the only thing which the Elders could use them for would he scarecrows and danger signals and there is no doubt that many of our so-called old students in reality are warnings that if we act likewise, we may be as bad as they are. Between Indian guides, masters and departed swamis we are raising a wonderful group of old students" whose particular form of insanity leads them to believe that the Lord has singled them out as exceptionally useful instruments, when they have dispositions like the old Nick himself and bodies below the animal standard. I have seen these mouthpieces of the gods tearing hair over the back fence and declaring themselves in ardent language tinged with blue and scarlet sparks of choice profanity, then half an hour later they lead a silence meeting and wish damnation upon their opponents.

These "old students" tell you confidentially that they spent the night hobnobbing with the Lord or that the Master So-and-so told them you were to loan them two dollars and a half or that God told them that the house and lot they want will flutter down from the ethers to them. We prefer to believe that the old student is demented than that the Lords of Reason are capable of such absurdities. They are our demonstrative old students and their intelligence is just below that of a mineral.

Altogether this quartet of spiritual malformations constitutes quite a percentage of our so-called orthodox atheists. They call themselves "old students" -no one else will call them at all for fear that they may show up. They have been put out of their homes as nuisances. Most of them have ruined the next two or three generations thru their idiosyncrasies and mental acidities and now they spend their time snoozing through religion. Instead of having ripened with age, they have green spots coming out on them and are fast falling victims to the spirit of corrosion.

These are our old, advanced students. They admit it, they gloat in it, glorify in it and wallow around in it never realizing that they are the most perfect specimens of unconscious egotists that disgrace the garlands of our sciences. Will people ever get through with the idea that they know something? Self-satisfaction is the basis of decay and there are none who know as little as those who think they know a great deal. Socrates said that he was the wisest man in Athens, because he was the only man who knew he was a fool. Many an "old student" has told how much he knew and shown how much he didn't know to one he didn't have sense enough to realize was his superior.

The first thing an old student really learns to do is to keep his mouth shut and plod along. Are there any old students? Technically, no. But in this world of affairs, those who have gained the most of practical knowledge have superiority over those who have done nothing. The true old student is known by his deeper understanding of life and its problems and not by incessant pallet-calisthenics.

The jawbone of Samson's donkey is still slaying as it did of old and many a suffering mortal has gone with grey hairs to a sorrowful grave, talked to death by one of them said bone being vitalized by an "old student's" motive power.

Not one in a hundred of our so-called "old students" show any symptoms of spiritual age but the creaks that we hear when they chew indicates that the organism is dying out and that they are slowly passing into the Great Beyond as ignorant of their destiny as before, with nothing to say to their Lord except a quotation from Pythagoras or a couple of Patanjali's aphorisms! It is a very sad thing how little we strive to build for permanence and truth and how seldom we find one who is really willing to consecrate his soul to the truth and in silence and simplicity carry on his Master's work whispering his age in the wisdom of his thoughts, the depth of his understanding and the sweetness of his compassion.

## THE CHICK AND THE SHELL

MOST people are acquainted with the fact that chickens come out of eggs. This being an accepted theory, proven by repeated phenomena, no further consideration is given to the problem and we watch the wonderful processes of nature with a divine unconcern, seeing many things but thinking little about them. Now there is no greater lesson in all the world than the baby chick and the egg-shell. How wonderfully nature protects the coming in of its little creatures, how it builds around the unprotected form walls and barriers that the latent lives may gradually awaken without danger of untimely interruption! Here the embryo chick in its shell carries on, under the direction of the group spirit, the wonderful work of building a complex organism of blood, bone and feather, unseen to the eyes of a mortal creature.

But now the great lesson. The tiny chick at last completes its embryonic growth and its parent shell, the divine father and protector of its tiny life, now becomes its worst enemy. If it is unable to break through that wall, it will surely die, destroyed by its own protection. Is this not a lesson in the study of man, his growth, and his development? Are not the walls and laws and the spiritual guidance's which protect man in his early infancy the ruts and channels that he later gets into? Are not the concepts which are bred in him as necessary parts of his youth in later life of ten walls and shells which will destroy him? Are not the creeds and religions which have guarded the infancy of his unfoldment like the shells of the egg which protect him to a certain point and then strangle him? Are these not Chronus the Father of the gods, Saturn, who devoured his own children? Great light should come to the soul of man when he studies a problem of this kind.

Let us take it in another phase. Does not crystallization build around man the bodies necessary for his manifestation here? And does not crystallization also, after it reaches a certain point, inhibit the very qualities which it makes possible? Do not our thoughts build us and yet bind us by walls of our own limitations? It surely seems that they do. Our past concepts have built us and made possible our reaching human intelligence and yet, sad to say, there comes a time when our very ideals strangle us unless all of our life grows great together, unless the shell expands with the egg-which no crystallized substance can. It must break or else destroy the life growing within it.

Those who would go on to greater and more glorious fields of expression must break the shell of crystallization which holds them in, ties them down and places around them the strangle-cord of limitation. Yet in breaking this shell, we must do it with reverence, for has it not been for many years our protection, our shield, and our buckler? Our love for it, however, and our respect for the labors and growth we have passed through beneath its protection must not deter us from breaking it, for its greatest joy is in the realization that its work is done. It may rend our hearts to break the shell, but we will die if we do not and neither we nor the shell will benefit thereby.

All people who have set ideas are surrounded by shell. Sometimes these shells are large enough to allow growth to go on within them, but there are other times when the spirit is cramped within its shell. We must be willing and glad to break away from the concepts that limit us. This is one of the hardest things in the world to do, for we all love the thing we have been associated with, the things which we learned when young, the creeds, the philosophies, the ideals which helped us to grow in the years that are past. They are, in truth the fathers of the things we are and yet in order to grow; it is necessary for us to slay the parent. This point is beautifully brought out in the legend of Krishna and the Battle of Kurukshetra where the youthful prince, in compliance with the laws of Krishna, drew the arrow to the head and slew with it his own sire. Too often our spiritual channels of expression become too narrow for us but we need never be narrow ourselves, for when a creed begins to bind us then the moment has arrived when with the spear of truth and light, we must slay our own protector lest he slay us with his walls of living stones.

So, the little chick breaks the shell and comes forth or failing to break the shell dies within it and once more the father protector has slain his child with his loving embrace because the child was not strong enough to slay the parent. Like the seed in the ground, which is nourished and guarded by the green mold and yet ofttimes is murdered thereby, so the spirit of man is protected by the shell of matter which ofttimes slays its own son when the child does not rise triumphant from the protecting womb.

## THE OCCULT ACID TEST

AS precious metals are tested with acids so the spiritual doctrines and ideals of the student must be submitted to test. None should be accepted nor rejected upon advice, like or dislike, but upon the pure unemotional principles of worth should they be judged. The sacred wisdom of the ancients is now being given openly to the world but at the same time there are many false doctrines creeping in that promise much but produce nothing. The days of secretiveness and the superiority of a few are drawing to a close and all of the true occult works are being given to the world freed from the mystery of the Middle Ages. Below we list a number of questions. When investigating the merits of a doctrine, use these as the acid test. Regardless of whether you like or dislike the doctrine, stand by the decision that your conscience makes when it compares the creed with the ideal. If it be a true outpouring of the schools of knowledge, it will be:

1. A doctrine of effort and individual responsibility, striving to build and unfold each soul to perfect independence.

2. A doctrine free from the taint of commercialism, exorbitant prices and inner circles where only the financially elect can go.

3. Productive of individual thought and seeking to unfold the reason of the student, making him independent of his instructors rather than a slave to them.

4. A doctrine of evolution rather than creation, of eternal progression rather than a doctrine with an end.

5. A doctrine of cause and effect-labor for the thing desired - and not one of miracles and superhuman powers.

6. Free from the whiplash of plagues and terrors, not drawing you into it through fear of damnation.

7. Based upon principles rather than personalities, worshipping Truth and not the one who brings it.

8. Slow but sure, promising nothing but opening the doors to all.

9. Free from peace - power - and - plenty of scheming and get-rich-quick plans of all kinds.

10. A doctrine of equality with equal opportunities for all and special privileges for none.

11. Fearless in its declaration of principles and conscientious in its effort to live up to them.

12. Free from perverted sex philosophies, soul-mating, and so forth; always obeying the law of the land wherein it is.

13. Staunch in its defense of the physical body, pleading for its development and growth that it may become the living temple.

14. Based upon the doctrines of compassion, renunciation, service, and self-sacrifice; neither gloomy nor melancholy, but peaceful and true.

15. Free from much wordiness and mushiness, teaching all its truths in a simple way.

16. True to the principle that the destiny of a people rests in its own hands and that no vicarious atonement can save it.

17. Based upon the seven liberal arts and sciences and teaching, that knowl-

edge is the eternal victor over ignorance.

18. Considerate of all other creeds and doctrines, realizing and living the great truth that all religions are one.

19. Based upon the solid rock of brotherhood and cooperation and standing for the fellowship of spirit and of body.

20. Free from claims and pretenses and untouched by the spirit of egotism.

21. The last to ever say that it is great; seeking only to serve, and expecting no reward.

22. Strong in its demand for practical religion taught through right living, right thinking, right aspiring and right purification.

If the philosophy which you are interested in teaching these things in a rational way, follow it, study it and learn of it; but if it fails to live up to these thoughts, shun it as you would a leprous thing, for it will bring with it only sorrow, suffering and an untimely end. This is the acid test.

## BROTHERS OF THE SHINING ROBE - IV
### CHAPTER FOUR
### The Master Speaks
#### (Continued)

As I spoke, it seemed that I was no longer a mortal man and that instead of a human brain, my source of information was the mind of God himself. The presence of the Master behind me gave great courage and consolation so, daring all things while I knew that he was near, I told of the mysteries of life and of death.

As I looked around the room it seemed filled with white-robed forms and great streams of life and light poured into me, then seemed to radiate in waves of courage from my entire being. "How long will you search in the worlds of the dead for the living? How long will you wander in the shade instead of turning your eyes to the light? No matter how wondrous the implement, how perfect the plan-all science ends where the Divine begins. Between you and the truth of life stands a wall that nothing of material things can pierce, where even the reasoning mind cannot go, and there even the greatest scientists must stop-bowing to an Infinite All which they cannot grasp, measure or define! In hours of sickness, man cries not to science but to his God; in the great extremity, the soul leaves its reason and cries to its universal Father for courage and for strength. Upon the mystic wall of the Infinite science batters itself to pieces because it refuses to accept that which it cannot see. The greatest scientists in all the world are the ones who know that the visible is but a tiny grain floating in the endless oceans of the invisible. From the Invisible it came and to the Invisible it shall return and puny minds shall never grasp the path it goes nor understand the working of its mysterious power! Far from the eyes of man in the hidden hermitages of the Unseen are those who know its passing and are so close to the footstool of the Light that the secret things of nature to them are simple truths indeed. But if you would have the Light, you must seek where it is, realizing that neither science nor philosophy, art nor letters, nor anything of man, shall measure the boundless limits of the Divine!"

It was my voice but the Master's words and as the moments passed, he unfolded to the group gathered before me the basic principles of the ancient wisdom. He told of the sacred school of the Twelve Prophets; of the ray of the Black Light; of the Planet of Death and the sacred Lamasaries in India; of the Brothers of the Shining Robe and their labors with mankind and the powers which they have over life and death; and then of the children of men chosen to know the mysteries of God.

At last, he stopped, and my tongue grew silent too, for there seemed no more to say. And so, dazed and bewildered, I sat down with the Master still beside me. A silence followed my words, then a sigh broke from the circle of listeners. One elderly man arose.

"Your story, sir, is very remarkable. But what proof have you to offer of the things of which you tell? For years, we have been schooled in human knowledge, to the proving and trueing of things. Can you demonstrate to us anything superior to science or greater and superior to the physical world that surrounds us?"

I was about to say "No," but the Master nodded his head, and my lips uttered the word "yes." At the same time, the invisible white robed form of the Master descended from the rostrum in front of me and, unseen by the group of scientists, stepped over to an elderly man sitting in a great leather chair.

Suddenly the figure rose and raised his hand to his eyes, crying "My God! There is a face in the air in front of me. Two terrible eyes!" And with a cry, he fell forward onto the floor.

Immediately the room was in an uproar and scientists and philosophers gathered around the prostrate form of a white-haired man who lay face downward upon the Persian carpet. The professor, who had been sitting next to me and who was one of Europe's greatest physicians, elbowed his way through the crowd and knelt beside the prostrate figure. He then arose sadly and, turning to the assembled group, announced:

"Sir Richard is dead!" A gasp went around the crowd. One of England's leading astronomers and physicists had passed into the great Beyond. The Master prompted me and I spoke: "Professor, you have stated that science is unapproachable in its power. What has science to do now? Answer me a question, for I have answered yours."

"This is no time for idle argument!" exclaimed the professor.

"Yes, it is," I answered, now master of the situation. "If science is perfect and omnipotent, let it restore Sir Richard -to life."

"Fool," answered the professor, "no human power can do that."

"All right then," I answered, "there is something that science cannot do. Then explain to me, what is death? And why must all living things pass through it?"

"The organisms just stop working," announced the scientist.

"But what is the power behind the working?" I asked.

"No one knows," answered the professor.

"Yes, I do."

Again, the faces of all were turned to me and I reiterated some of the statements I had made during the evening.

"The higher consciousness and the superior bodies of man, including the spirit, the astral body and the mind, leave the physical form by passing out at the top of the skull with a twisting motion to then function on the subtler planes of nature. The consciousness has not died but has merely discarded a useless vehicle to function in a newer and finer organism."

"How can you prove that any intelligent thing has left?" demanded a voice.

"How? Why bring it back?" I answered.

I leaned over and placed my hand upon the forehead of the dead man. At the same time, the Master stooped over me, and a thrill of force passed into the organism at my feet. I took the dead man by the hand, whereupon his eyes opened and with my assistance he slowly rose to his feet and gazed around in a dazed sort of way. A gasp went around the circle of scientists.

"Did you do this?" demanded one.

"No." I answered, "I am but the mouthpiece. The great Master, I told you of who dwells in the Temple of the Caves in the heights of the Himalayas has been with me all this evening and unseen by you has performed the works to prove the truths that I have sought to give you."

Slowly, the group parted, and the wise men of Europe gathered in small clusters to discuss the problem as I passed slowly out the door and back to my apartments. I afterwards heard from one of the members of the group who talked with the professor after I left. He asked him, "Well, sir, what do you think of it?"

"Bunkum, my dear sir, bumkum pure and simple," announced the international scientist as he lighted a very black cigar and sent an attendant scurrying after a whiskey and soda. "A pure coincidence, my dear fellow, a pure coincidence, but of no scientific value whatsoever. As I said in my talk, the man is a dangerous lunatic and should be confined. There is positively nothing in the universe superior to science. I know, my dear fellow, for I have been a scientist for fifty years."

"You are certainly a marvel, professor," answered the man as he walked away.

The professor stepped over to the rostrum and picked up the crumpled piece of paper containing the questions he had written and which I had dropped after answering them. He stared for a second or two and then put on his glasses, for all the questions were answered in fine writing around the margin of the sheet.

"Most extraordinary!" exclaimed the scientist." When did he write that on there? I watched him every minute!" As he spoke, the piece of paper turned to dust and disintegrated between his fingers. The professor adjusted his extra eyeglass and gazed at his empty fingers. "Most extraordinary! That fellow is surely clever. But he will never be able to convince me that science is not the last word. Another whiskey and soda, boy, my nerves have been completely unstrung!"

(To be Continued)

## LORD BUDDHA

HE came in a packing box bound round with bands of steel and iron, dented and battered by its rough usage during a trip of many months. The packing box stood unopened for many weeks before the sacrilegious hands of uninterested servants broke it open and scattered heaps of excelsior and wrapping paper about the floor. At last, the figure stood revealed-undoubtedly one of the strangest that had ever crossed the waters from the land of the blue lotus. Lord Buddha was a wondrous, life-sized wood carving and even the servants seemed awed as they gazed upon his gilded form. Many strange stories had come with him from the silent East. It was told that the Master himself had breathed the breath of life into the ancient carving, making it sacred to all the Children of Light.

Be that as it may, the Lord Buddha was surely a thing of glory. His robes, carved with wondrous fineness out of ancient teak, were richly covered with solid gold leaf and many-colored lacquers, while his eyes were precious stones set deep into the dark wood which formed the face. Upon his forehead was a mighty diamond, one of the greatest that has ever come out of India. Even the unromantic were forced to stop for a moment and gaze in admiration at the wondrous figure of India's immortal reformer.

They took Lord Buddha from the packing case and stood him upon an ebony taboret in the Gothic library of the Chadwick home and there he remained shaded by the gloom of ancient rafters during the weeks and months that passed. Unhonored and unrevered, a breath of the mystic East amid the mold of the prostic west.

Lord Chadwick had always had a taste for antiques and his Indian appointment had given him great opportunities to indulge it. But the main reason why he secured Lord Buddha was because the Hindoos did not want him to have it. (When you know Lord Chadwick, you know that was reason enough.) We will not go into details as to how he acquired the statue, for he followed a rather-shall we say, irregular manner, not unusual among foreigners in the Orient. The Christian seldom asks the heathen for anything he wants, but just takes it. If the native protests, the Christian shoots him. So, with great expense and labor, Lord Buddha was sent to London, where he remained in silent meditation, surrounded by cobwebs and the curse of an outraged priestcraft.

A brief description of Lord Chadwick may not be out of place at this moment. He was one of those particularly affable gentlemen who is always a leading attraction among the ladies and a source of great inspiration to all who do not know him too well. While admitting his affability and his military polish it is necessary, for the proper unfolding of our story, that we unveil certain parts of his private life which are of a slightly different flavor.

Poor Lady Chadwick had been dragged through a knothole and then stepped on in the course of being duly impressed by her husband's personal omnipotence, and a strange pathetic expression appeared in her bleared eyes every time anyone congratulated her upon her choice of a husband. Not that the Earl was a tyrant or anything of that kind, just that a certain besetting sin went with the heraldry of his house. When the Earl was sober, he was a gentleman, but after a few hours at the club, he became infinitely inferior to a self-respecting animal. Every time his lordship fell victim to his indiscretion a reign of terror descended upon the household and suffering and misery formed the family lot. Not always, just when Lord Chadwick was exercising his hereditary sins. It is a strange thing how temperaments become reversed under the influence of alcoholic stimulant for Lord Chadwick sober and Lord Chadwick intoxicated were two entirely different beings-like the old story of Jekyll and Hyde.

This is not a story, however, of family skeletons but is a narrative wound around Lord Buddha who stood, through all these passing months, on his lotus throne in the silent shades of the library, his hands clasped in meditation and his flowing robe gleaming in the half light.

A certain cold December evening had given way to the bleakness of a moonless night. Lady Chadwick stood before the fire in the library, her eyes fixed on the great clock hanging on the wall those silent fingers were passing slowly round the ancient dial. A great fear oppressed her for Lord Chadwick and several of his cronies at the club had taken steps earlier in the evening which usually preceded one of milord's streaks of intemperance. This part of our story deals with the ancient fable of the worm who turned. Lady Chadwick, inspired by the flaring embers of a dying will had decided that from now on her husband would have to find within the heraldry of his house some symptom of inherited courtesy and restraint. Reared in obedience, married off in perfect obedience, beaten to further increase said obedience, milady was about to commit Europe's most terrible sin, an expression of individuality. An impermissible thing among the blueblood of the old country.

It was about half-past three when a cab pulled up at the door and two voices broke the stillness, whose tones were about as thick as the average London night.

"Five bob!" called a voice. "you heard me, five bob! not a farthing less!"

"Stooo-o mush," sounded a muffled growl. "I won't pay it!"

"Five bob! you blighty, five bob!"

Then there came the sound of a blow. The voice of the hackman broke forth. This time is pure cockney, his language consisting of one malediction after another.

"Help, help, he's strangling me!"

"Shut up!" threatened a thick voice. "take thash and thash."

At the same time, there was the sound of two heavy thuds followed by a low groan. Then unsteady steps on the pavement and a grating noise as milord tried to fit his key into the door hinge.

"Sh'wont fit-hic-sh'wont fit," he muttered. "Sh'mush be wrong key. Well, I'll fixsh it!"

The next instant there was a crash as Lord Chadwick kicked his foot through the plate glass door piece and unlatched the portal from the inside. There was the sound of steps advancing at a right oblique and as Lady Chadwick faced the library door, the form of her better half appeared in all the dignity of inebriate nobility.

Lord Chadwick was a tall, broad-shouldered man, heavily tanned by exposure to the Eastern suns, and with the muscles of an ox. He now stood swaying slightly on patent leather hinges, his tall silk hat over one eye and his evening cape dangling along the ground on the end of his cane. Putting a white gloved hand over his mouth, he hiccoughed gently behind it.

"Well, whash you lookin' at?"

Without a word, Lady Chadwick turned and, with tears in her eyes, faced the great open fireplace on the opposite side of the room.

"Whash matter?" demanded the nobleman as he reached out and hung his hat on an imaginary hook about six feet in the air. "Why donsh you speak to me?"

"John Chadwick, you are drunk again!" exclaimed his wife, turning around.

"You don't hash to tell me, I know it! Hash such a wonderful time!" and the milord swallowed hard. "But what has that got to do with it? Why donsh you come over and say good morning?"

His wife remained silent and turned again with her back to her husband.

"Well, why donsh you answer? Donsh you know I'm your husband?"

Still no sound from Lady Chadwick. A strange expression slowly came into the eyes of Lord Chadwick. He straightened up and his face grew hard.

"Come here!" he demanded. Still, his wife never moved.

"I told you to come here! When I want anyone in thish house they have got to come. If you don't come right over, I'll throw thish at your head!" And he picked up a large China vase.

Lady Chadwick remained as before and without further warning, her husband threw the China jar with all his might across the room. But he staggered as it left his hand and it missed her by several feet.

"You brute!" exclaimed his wife as the vase crashed into a great Venetian plate glass, sending fragments in all directions.

Then the thing which all his family feared happened. The spirit of ages of degeneracy and debauchery possessed him. Lord Chadwick's body slowly bent forward, and his head sank on his chest between his great arms, which swung like those of a monster ape. His lips drew back from his teeth and the white of his eyes grew red and streaked, the parlor gentleman had become the domestic beast.

With a scream, his wife shrank back as the figure slowly advanced, his steps no longer unsteady but now like the stealthy tread of an animal. Reaching a great chair, the Earl picked it up with the ease of a giant and hurled it across the room where it struck the old stone wall and was splintered to bits by the force of the blow. His wife, terrified beyond expression, crept slowly back into the corner of the room while ever closer loomed the form of her husband, now blinded with drunken rage.

At last, the corner was reached and further retreat was impossible. She had stopped beside the figure of Lord Buddha, who stood in silent contemplation, unmoved by the scene of confusion around him. As she shrank back, her shoulder touched his lacquered robe, and the chill caused her to draw aside.

Suddenly, crouching like an animal, Lord Chadwick sprang at the trembling figure of his wife and with a cry of terror, she jumped behind the statue of Lord Buddha. With an implication Chadwick rushed against the statue, throwing his arms around it to cast it aside, but though he pulled and tugged the figure of the Oriental demi-god would not move. It seemed rooted to the ground. As he tried to pass around it, it seemed that the robes spread out on each side and before the Earl realized it; he found himself twisted and hound in what seemed folds of golden lacquer. Struggling, twisting, and roaring like an angry bull, he sought to escape from the statue. His wife watched in amazement, for she saw her husband's hands and arms apparently growing to the form which he tugged and tore to escape from.

Slowly, the minutes passed. Lord Chadwick's struggles became less and less until finally exhausted and enveloped in folds of yellow lacquer he fell at the feet of the statue, his hands and arms still glued to its surface. The Earl was now thoroughly sober. The terror of his position, held prisoner by a force unknown, took all the hate out of his being.

"How am I going to get free?" he kept muttering and turned with pleading eyes to his wife. She, realizing that the fit of passion was gone, attempted to release him. But his hands seemed part of the statue and as she watched Lady Chadwick gave a scream of amazement and terror, the fingers and hands of the Earl were slowly becoming encrusted with a golden film! At the point where he grasped the statue, they had become like the teakwood beneath them. In other words, he was turning into an idol himself under the mysterious power of the sacred form of Lord Buddha.

As his wife stood there in perplexity, she heard footsteps behind her and turning she looked into the faces of three men-all of them Orientals. They must have entered through the broken doorway.

"Who are you?" she demanded, starting back. One of them bowed politely and spoke in perfect English:

"Our names will do you very little good, madam, but we have come all the way from the sacred shine in India to take Lord Buddha back to his home."

Lady Chadwick immediately replied, "Yes, yes, take the statue gladly! But how can I release my husband, for his hands and arms? Are turning into lacquer?"

The priest shook his head. "That is the curse of Lord Buddha upon those who defile his sanctity."

"Is there nothing that can be done that I may escape?" pleaded Lord Chadwick.

"There is no way but through prayers to Lord Buddha, for he is the Lord of Righteousness and if it pleases him, he may release you from his golden self. If not, you must await the end."

"I will give anything that I have to be released! My arms are growing cold and a creeping death is upon me!" cried the nobleman.

Suddenly, a strange thing happened. The mouth of the Buddha opened, and a voice seemed to breathe out from the soul of the statue: "I am Lord Buddha. Ages ago, I breathed myself into this thing of wood carved by the hands of the faithful. You stole me from my shrine, but that sin was not your greatest. Know you that those who seek protection behind the yellow robe of the Buddha shall not seek in vain. No man shall pass this gleaming robe for works of hate. I am going back again to my people who love me, honor me and revere me. But before I go, I grant you life on one condition that never again shall you abuse it. And if you do, as surely as I stand here today, you shall become a figure of wood and stone."

Slowly the hands of Lord Chadwick fell from the statue and the folds of lacquer seemed to swing and sway in the breeze that came through the open door. The statue then stepped down from its pedestal and, as the three Orientals fell on their knees before it, passed slowly out of the door, draped in its blowing robes of gold. On the ground as it passed were left strange footmarks pressed into the very surface of the floor. Without a word the three Orientals followed the carven figure and Lord Chadwick suddenly swayed with dizziness and fell across the pedestal to the floor.

\* \* \* \*

Milord suddenly sat up in his chair and gazed around him. The London Times fell from between his fingers, and he slowly drew in one foot, whose close proximity to the fireplace was undoubtedly the cause of his sudden awakening. He turned to his wife, who was sitting reading a few feet away.

"How long have I been asleep?"

"About an hour and a half, dear," she answered meekly.

"By Jove! The most peculiar dream! You know you have often asked me to stop drinking-I have half a mind to do it. By the way, I dreamed that my statue of Buddha came to life and walked off, wasn't that unusual? I must go over and look at him again. He is the most___"

Lord Chadwick had stopped and was staring at the recess in the wall where

Lord Buddha had stood. He rubbed his eyes and looked again.

"Good Lord! It's gone!"

"Really," exclaimed Lady Chadwick mildly, "are you sure you haven't mislaid it, my dear?"

"Do you know," announced his lordship, "I believe I will stop drinking!"

Suddenly, his face brightened up.

"I see it all, now," he muttered. "They told me that they would get it back. They are a strange people, those Orientals."

"If you think they are strange, they must be strange, my dear," remarked his well-regulated wife eagerly. Milord sat down again with his feet on the grating.

"I haven't lived in India for twenty years without seeing something of Oriental magic. That dream of mine was more than a dream, it was Oriental magic. They have spirited the statue away."

"I wish the spirits would wipe their shoes when they come in," murmured Lady Chadwick. "Look at those footprints all the way to the door."

The Earl gazed at them. His mind turned to the shrines of India and a strange expression came into his face. "What are those things?" asked his wife. "will you please tell me, dear?" "They are the footprints of Lord Buddha," answered the nobleman.

"What are they, John? You know I always let you do my heavy thinking for me."

"I don't understand it myself very well," answered milord as he stroked his chin reflectively. "But there goes the dinner bell and I must be at the club this evening, so you had better come, my dear."

"Yes, John."

## SPECIAL NOTICE

Six months ago, we started the publication of the All-Seeing Eye in order to find a practical manner of publishing and distributing the lectures, articles, and so forth, which our friends expressed a desire to have. During the interval, the growth of the magazine has been as rapid as could be expected considering that it has never been placed upon a newsstand or in a bookstore but as only been distributed at our own meetings and to those in personal contact with our work. As you realize, the fact that there is no price placed upon it has complicated its distribution tremendously and will continue to do so unless every one of its present well-wishers cooperate to assist in its development.

As all of our students know, the magazine was issued for six months as a tryout and no subscriptions are good for a longer time. And any of you who subscribed but have not received the entire six numbers are entitled to apply for them until the supply is exhausted.

The time has now come when a decision of importance confronts the readers. Do you wish the magazine to go on? We are perfectly willing to write and prepare it as long as those whom we publish it for are willing to cooperate with us for its maintenance, but it remains with you to say whether it shall be done or not.

An analysis of the first six months of its publication from the viewpoint of the exchequer does not show a financial success. In fact, on over half of our subscriptions, we have paid the people to take it away. About forty-four percent of our subscribers paid less than one half of the printer's cost of the magazines they received and a large number who made promises never fulfilled them.

Consequently, while the magazine is not in a bankrupt condition, it has been financed to a considerable degree by money furnished from other sources, for it has not come within nearly one-half of paying for itself. A few of our true and sincere workers have made possible its publication and presentation to you but the majority of our subscribers estimate the price of this magazine upon others which are procurable at bookstands and stores, overlooking completely two important facts:

First, only about one thousand copies are printed and the cost of setting it up is the same as though we had five hundred thousand copies printed, and the smaller the number circulated, the greater the cost of each magazine.

Secondly, all magazines on the market at the present time are either set at a price which covers cost or else pay for themselves many times over through extensive advertising. Many of the magazines which you secure at newsstands could be given to you without any cost and still be tremendous financial successes and entirely self-supporting through the hundreds of thousands of dollars' worth of advertising which they carry on their pages.

## TO OUR READER'S

These two important considerations make it impossible to estimate the cost of producing this work by comparison to those in circulation, for one copy of our little magazine costs as much as an armful of some of the popular periodicals. As a large percentage of people have been estimating upon current prices, we have absolutely lost hundreds of dollars which they have fallen under the bare printer's cost. As for the expense of writing, preparing and distributing, that has not been even thought of.

We have distributed many copies free to those who could not subscribe through financial embarrassment, probably from fifty to a hundred a month. And those who barely pay for their own subscription leave the work itself to settle the deficit.

We shall be very glad to continue publication and launch the magazine for another six months if we can depend upon your cooperation, otherwise it cannot go on. The only way that we can reduce the individual responsibility is by increasing the subscription list and if we are able to do so we may also be able to increase its size, place in its departments to handle various special problems and in many ways make it a worthier publication.

You will find with this magazine a subscription blank carrying on it three coupons or detachable slips. Each one of these carries space for the name and address of a subscriber and the mount of their subscription. If you are interested in having this magazine go on, please fill this out as generously as you can and also get two other people who will be interested and have them do likewise. Send in the three together with money order or check for the amounts and if sufficient come in to make it possible to carry the cost of publication, you will receive the next issue of the All-Seeing Eye on the 25th day of October. If there is not sufficient to meet the expense, your money will be refunded to you by that time.

If you will cooperate with us, we will be able to go on, for we are willing to do anything to make possible the continuance of the work. The greatest good that you can do us in this line is to get two people who are interested and secure their subscriptions to send with your own. In this way we can increase our list three times and reduce the expenses by nearly one half. This will enable us to put out extra work, colored supplements, etc., which we cannot do at this time because of insufficient means.

Please remember, friends, this concludes all subscriptions taken up to date as per the agreement we made when starting the magazine.

We thank you for your past cooperation and if you desire to extend that to us in the future, we will try to serve you in as efficient a manner as we can.

The fate of our little magazine now rests in your hands.

MANLY P. HALL.

# DESCRIPTION OF LAST MONTH'S PLATE

The plate in last-month's magazine which is taken from the rare and unobtainable work of Kunrath, the great alchemist, represents symbolically human regeneration and is also the key to the Philosopher's Stone. As before, the translating of it shall be left to you, because it is only in that way you can really learn its message. But we will briefly consider some of its most important symbols:

The figure rising out of the globe symbolizes spirit rising out of matter and consciousness freeing itself from the encircling and enslaving bonds of form. The two-headed figure represents the Hermetic union and the creation of Azoth the Philosopher's Stone.

In this plate we have the answer to the problem of soul-mates as only the ancient alchemist could explain it, for the male-female creature here shown symbolizes the occult constitution of man who is the male-female creation. The male figure has the sun halo or the positive ray while the female figure has the moon crown or the mother ray, representing spirit and matter, which matter being regenerated becomes the soul or bride of spirit.

This figure rises out of the globe of elements and from the heads arises a wondrous bird with the sign of Leo around its head. This blackened bird represents the unknowable secret of the phoenix or the bird of eternal life that is born out of the union of the sun and moon in the brain of man. Its tail, which is filled with eyes, represents the unfolded sense centers of human consciousness while the great circle containing all the other symbols is made to represent nature within whose protecting aura all growth is carried on.

The fire of the philosopher which rises upward and partly surrounds the central globe is the purification process in which the flame in the lower centers of the body rises upward and awakens Kundalini, the spinal spirit-fire in man, which is asleep in the egg of Brahma located in the solar plexus. This passing upward creates the figure with the two heads for these faces undoubtedly represent the pituitary body and the pineal gland which are the positive and negative poles of the spinal canal fire.

In India, the god-man Ishwari is shown as a male-female Deity and in the ancient languages, the name of God signified that He was also a male-female Divinity, for He is not only the Creator but the Creation. In a similar way man, following in the footsteps of God, is slowly arousing the latent qualities within himself and building to the day when he too shall be both creator and the creation.

The entire diagram is symbolical of the evolution of the human soul and spirit. Starting from the top downward, it is involution; working from the bottom upward it is evolution. Two streams pour from the breasts of the creature, and these represent the outpourings of fire and water or salt and Sulfur which are two of the three elements of perfection while mercury forms the third element. The band around the neck of the figure, which unites the heads, is the wedding ring of modem theology for it ties or unites as a band of spiritual gold the two extremes of human life. The upright triangle above, pointing up to the Sacred Name, is once more a symbol of human regeneration.

Taking the plate generally it refers to the cosmic scheme of things and later the individual scheme of things. The reading tells of how through the union of the universal Earth Mother and Fiery and Airy Father there is created a wondrous stone which is the answer to all the problems of life. The student recognizes that the union of the spiritual elements within himself will turn him allegorically into a two-headed creature male-female and self-reproductive through the positive pole of the brain.

Next month's magazine will contain the companion piece to this plate illustrating another of the deep, alchemical principles. Save these pictures for you will find it nearly impossible to get them again, and while you may not understand them now, as time goes on you will be grateful that you possess them.

## QUESTION AND ANSWER DEPARTMENT

What is Success?

Ans. Success is the perfect adjustment of the individual consciousness with the prenatal plan which it prepared and earned before its entrance into this life. All advancement over existing conditions is success; all stagnation or backsliding is failure.

What is the greatest of all successes?

Ans. The composite perfection which is the result of a number of small achievements, the gaining of which has been spread over numberless eternities.

Is a happy life a successful life?

Ans. A truly successful life is a happy one but experience rather than harmony is the main requisite to success in spiritual things.

Who is a failure?

Ans. A failure is one who has fallen below the standard which he himself has attained at some previous time; or one who has failed to advance that standard with every thought and action of life.

What is the greatest cause of failure at the present time?

Ans. There are many of them, but uncertainty, lack of backbone, fear of popular opinion and egotism are the greatest. Failure to live up to the purest and highest in life is the great spiritual downfall.

What is the greatest enemy of failure?

Ans. Action. For wherever this exists, growth is taking place. Though the action itself be destructive, yet through it the spirit is learning a lesson.

What is the great adjustment of man's being?

Ans. The adjustment of the self and the not-self. This is the result of the development of the mind, which becomes a neutral field-a universal solvent-in which the opposites of consciousness are capable of meeting in mutual understanding.

How may we know one who has succeeded in this adjustment?

Ans. We can know him as one who sees the divine lesson in the little things overlooked by the world in its endless rush. The one who sees the clearest is the one who sees God in the greatest number of things.

What is the reward of adjustment of life and its bodies?

Ans. Consciousness on all the planes of nature where the adjustments are made and communion with the central life within.

Who is the greatest failure at the present time?

Ans. Those who fail to recognize opportunity and conserve time by making every moment useful to all eternity-they are wasting God's most precious gifts.

What constitutes a successful speaker?

Ans. He is the one whose words, though few, still convey to the world with the greatest clearness of the ideals which fill his consciousness. He is the one who speaks the truths that others dare not think.

Who has learned to listen most successfully?

Ans. The one who has learned to hear the voice that speaks from the silence of his own soul and who knows the meaning of its quiet words.

Who is the most successful thinker?

Ans. The one whose thoughts, like God's, are in harmony with the Divine plan. Man realizes the power of God when he learns to think God's thoughts; he knows the ways of the divine when he himself has walked them.

What is adjustment?

Ans. Adjustment is the arranging or balancing of things into harmony one with the other.

## THE LORD OF THE FLAMING MOUNTAIN

UP from the shadows of swaying palms and jungle underbrush a little group of pilgrims wound their way in and out among the broken lava rocks and stubble towards a mighty mountain that rose as a looming mystery to touch the deep blue of the tropic sky. From the top of this peak, a thin trail of smoke poured eternally as though in truth this mystery of nature was the vent of Vulcan's forge. A strange group indeed it was that climbed up and up along the narrow path that led to the distant heights. They were a people we see no longer, for already eternities have shrouded them in the mantle of forgetfulness.

First came a tall and aged man, his copper skin seamed and wrinkled but his face strong and resolute. He was robed in a cape woven of bird's feathers and tilted forward upon his head was a strange, peaked cap, from the point of which hung a pendant of gold and jewels, which tossed and swayed as he walked. On his forehead was a cross, traced in white pigments, while the breeze blowing aside his cape disclosed the fact that his only other garment was a girdle of golden plates set with amethysts and rubies. In the center of the girdle was a strange face molded of solid gold, a face surrounded by a halo of flames in whose eyes sparkled rubies of a never-ending radiance. In one hand the aged man carried a carved staff painted in many colors and in the other a rattle hanging upon a tassel of human hair and composed of a gourd containing within its dried husk a tiny pebble. The long hair of the man was gray and hung in many plaits upon his shoulders while his beard, braided like an Assyrian's, hung halfway to his waist. He was the priest of the Divine Lord, Master of the Great Fire, whose temple stood alone among the lava banks and ashes of the flaming mountain.

The second member of the party was a young girl some sixteen or eighteen years of age. She, too, wore a cape of bird feathers and upon her small feet were sandals inlaid with jewels. Her head was uncovered revealing braided hair which hung in two long coils nearly to her knees and was of the shiny blackness of the lava rocks that surrounded her. She was covered with golden ornaments and chains, while her arms and ankles were encircled by bands of gold connected with links of silver and copper. But though adorned with the ransom of emperors, she seemed more a captive in bondage for her ornaments were like shackles and clanked dismally as she walked along.

Two other figures completed the group. Powerful men they were whose brown bodies glistened in the sunshine and whose forms and proportions were those of Greek athletes. They wore neither cape nor headdress, but their bodies were adorned with golden bangles and strange animals were tattooed in many colors upon their skins. The heavy girdles they wore were weighted with plates of gold and each carried in his hand a feathered staff surmounted by a globe of fiery gold.

The four figures wound in and out among the rocks and as they neared the top of the lofty mountain, thin streams of smoke rose up from the crevices at their feet; the air was filled with a moaning and rumbling; the earth shook and shivered like a thing alive; the heavy fumes of sulfureous smoke creeping up shrouded the little band in a semidarkness while the sun shone as a ball of angry red behind clouds of swirling ashes.

Evening was falling before they neared the summit and as the sun sank to rest a strange lurid glow thrilled through the atmosphere, an eerie ever-changing radiance reflected in a million different ways from the clouds of mist and vapor. Still, the little band climbed upward and upward, ever nearer to the mighty crater that loomed like a gaping pit of hell before them.

Suddenly they reached a great rock and passing around its side were confronted by a tiny hut built of stones and lava, shielded by the projecting side of the cliffs but half concealed by the seething vapors of the volcano. Reaching the door of the hut, the old priest raised his staff while the other three fell to their knees.

"Behold! This is the Temple of Anguish built on the crest of Chetoka, the Mountain of Undying Fires. This is the Place of Wailing where we sinful mortals come to ask forgiveness of our Lord and Master! For, behold! Our God speaks to us through the mountain of fire! Many days now has His voice been heard and the roaring and rumblings have whispered of His wrath. He has said to His priests: 'Bring from the people of earth a living sacrifice unto Me in the mountain of my fires!' And we have brought one even as He has said, for behold we have chosen from among our nation the loveliest and purest daughter of earth and brought her up this mountain to be the bride of the Fire King!"

He rose and entered the little hut and a fire, kindled with a broken stick, flared up, its ruddy glows revealing a massive altar above which a great flaming Face looked down-a face of gold and jewels from which poured forth streamers and rays of living light.

"Oh, Spirit of Fire! Thy children obey thy call. For it was said of thee by our father's fathers that when thou criest out for vengeance for the forgetfulness of men, behold! there must be one of the people who shall climb to the heights of thy lofty shrine and die that thy children may be saved. For thine own voice has spoken saying there shall be one acceptable in the sight of our God who shall come to make offer of their life unto our God on Chetoka the sacred mountain-and only the pure in heart are acceptable as a sacrifice unto thee. Come, oh Lord of the Sacred Mountain! and take unto thyself this one of our people who comes forth to sacrifice herself that thy wrath may not descend upon the world!"

The flaming Face gleamed and glowed in the flickering light, its eyes seeming to shine with a fire demonical. The old priest bowed, and no sound broke the stillness except a broken sob from the prisoner in her golden chains.

Slowly the old priest left the little hut and, followed by the others, climbed up and over the side of the volcano, finally standing at the very peak of a great rock that jutted over the sea of molten lava. In the center rose a mighty cone and from it flames and Sulfur came up in never-ending steam. A great rumbling and roaring rent the heavy stillness of the island night and the splashing of lava bubbles in the sea of molten rock beneath sounded like sobs on the air. All the figures were tinged red with the flames and standing alone on that pinnacle of rock in their robes of feathers and girdles of gold. They seemed like the fiery spirits of the dawn when creation was in the making instead of living creatures in a world of flesh.

The old priest raised his hands and cried outward over the lake of flames:

"We have come, oh Master! as thy law has demanded. We have brought thee thy bride. Accept our sacrifice, oh Fiery One, and destroy not our people. Send not thy flaming rivers to burn our homes with consuming fire, send not the messengers of death, the ashes and the plagues, rock not the earth with thy vengeance, oh God of Fire! But accept this, the best we have to offer thee." He knelt upon the rock and the rumblings and roarings seemed to deepen while great clouds of flame and smoke rose from the volcano's depthless center and the rocks beneath their feet shook and quivered with a life divine.

Slowly, the slender figure of the girl arose and with calm courage crossed the narrow shelf of stone. Dropping aside the robe of bird's feathers, she stood poised upon the point of rock, beneath her the surging sea of molten lava. The flames sparkled on the jewels that she wore, for these too were to be cast with her into the yawning mouth of the fire-god.

Suddenly, as she stood there, there arose from the depths of the mountain a great streaming cloud of many-colored mists. It twinkled, swayed and twisted like a thing alive and instead of passing onward and outward into the heavens it hovered and floated over the center of the crater. Slowly the streaming lights took form, the many changing vapors gathered themselves together until a Mighty Being hovered over Chetoka.

The priest raised his hands in awe and trembling and shrank backward on the rock while the two that were with him moaned and groaned in fear and agony. But the thin figure still stood alone on the point of rock, her copper skin gleaming and glowing from the flickering flames of the volcano. The great mystery shadow shape became clearer as the moments passed and the Great One hovered closely over the volcano, a creature composed of the very flames themselves, his hair a mass of flowing sparks, his fingers tapering off into points of flame, his robes of crimson fire trailing off into the mist and vapor of the volcano. Great wings of flame and fire poured from him and his eyes shone like the molten lava of the crater.

A thundering voice spoke as the Great Creature swept over the surface of his volcano towards the pinnacle of rocks:

"Behold! I am angered at thee, thou puny children of men! It is well that ye have brought your sacrifice to the top of the mountain, for ye have displeased the Spirit of the Fires. What boon ask you in exchange for the bride that ye have brought me?"

"Oh, Lord of the Flaming Mountain!" cried the priest, "for many days have the ashes poured upon our villages, for many nights has the dull glow of your anger brought terror to our hearts. We come to thee, oh Lord, asking peace and that ye shall not destroy us with the flames of thy wrath. Oh, King of the Salamanders! Son of the fiery Sparks of Fohat! accept this the purest gift of earth and freest from thy hate!"

The Lord of the volcano had reached the mighty cliff that edged his crater and reached out his arms of streaming flame to grasp in them the slender figure that stood upon the rock.

"Ye have brought your sacrifice, oh children of men, but know you not that you yourselves are the spirits of the fire? For many weeks and many years ye have wrangled and fought and hated in your villages and for that ye have brought upon yourselves the curse of the Lord of Flames. For, behold! To my mountain come the hates and griefs and wranglings of the people and from them are built the flames of my lofty peak, and were it not that ye battled in your villages my flames could not battle on this mountain peak. Ye sue for peace, but that I cannot give you while to this crater comes the flames of hate. The mumbling and the rumblings which ye hear are but shadows of your own hearts, the seething cauldrons of flames but the whisper of the flames of passion within your own soul. I am the Lord of the Flames, I am the Regent of the Red World, I am the Voice of the Eternal Fire, I love the children of men and being strong in fire, I would serve them. But they have taken my fire and desecrated it and as it seeths and boils within their own souls, so the shadows rise upon my mountain. Go back to your village and say unto them that the Lord of the Flaming Mountain has spoken, saying that only when the souls of men are at rest will my mountain slumber.

"Behold, thy sacrifice is acceptable in my sight. The heart of one that is pure can soothe the flames of creation. It is said of the gods that through all the ages, some must perish, that many may be saved! Go ye now your way and I shall return to the heart of the flaming mountain, taking with me the sacrifice that ye have made. Be not this sacrifice in vain, for it is not the first nor shall it be the last! Many a soul has perished to save the world from my wrath. Many a courageous one has entered my flames that the world should have peace. But the Lord of the Flaming Mountain is not unkind-fear not for the one that ye have given, nor fear ye for the sacrifice of your people. But come unto me with love and my flames shall warm their hearts."

Slowly the fiery figure gathered the form in its arms and floating out over the volcano passed slowly downward into its mighty center, clasping to itself the jeweled figure of the girl.

A great peace descended upon the mountain, the flames of smoke died out and the lava ceased to flow, the rumblings grew less and less until at last silence ruled supreme. The old priest rose and was turning away when a mighty voice spoke from the depths of the earth:

"I, the Lord of the Flaming Mountain, am at rest. A noble soul has sacrificed itself to bring me peace. In all the ages of the world, I have gathered unto myself many, but they are not mine. For behold, the daughter of earth is not with me in my fiery mountain but with her God and my God! And behold, she has passed through the flaming ring unscarred and in her great desire has redeemed not only you but herself as well.

"Go ye unto your people and let not this sacrifice be in vain. Remember that only when ye learn to love one another shall my mountain be at rest, for when ye wrangle and discord among yourselves ye lose my flames and turn them on the worlds of men. Then my mountain cries out for vengeance and the sword of death is loosened by the thunder and lightning of the gods. Once more art ye forgiven-go and do better. Remember who was your answer and let not the martyr die in vain.

"The Lord of the Flaming Mountain is not dead, but rests in peace under the spell of redemption. Wake him not with hate and lust for once awake. He will never sleep until another be found to pacify him, send no more brides to the top of my mountain, but live in your villages in peace as the most acceptable sacrifice unto my eyes. Fear me, for I am great, obey me, for I am kind, redeem me, for

I am salvation, and though my temple is on my mountain, rather let it be in the soul of man. While there is one that is pure, I will rest, lulled to peace by their love; but if ye live not one unto the other in friendship and in charity ye shall hear my voice again and the world shall know me and cry out in agony unto the Lord of the Flaming Mountain. But I can do nothing but use the flames which thou hast given me. Send me no flames of hate and I will not burn your homes. Live not in discord one to the other and my lava shall never flow again."

## FADED FLOWERS

OFTENTIMES in wandering through an old home among the scenes of long ago one finds pressed away in a favorite volume, possibly the Bible or the family album, a faded rose crushed between the leaves. After many years of forgetfulness, it will bring back memories of the past. Some loved one nearly forgotten in the battle of life, some dear soul we used to know, comes before the mirror of the mind. We hear a laughing voice, perhaps now hushed forever, and kind hands stretch out across the years to enfold us again in memory's embrace. How few of these faded flowers have a message to the world, yet each whisper something of the past to some responsive heart.

And how much like faded flowers are the hearts of suffering men and women wandering through life! Each faded rose was once the fairest blossom and in a distant day forgotten, its dried and falling petals shone forth with all the glory of nature and its God. As we go along the road of life, we see many wondrous blossoms filling the air with glorious fragrance and exquisite color, but when we pass that way again; we see them faded and returning again to the dust from whence they came. How like the faded flower is the life of man! The glowing ideals he came here to carry out he soon forgets his dreams of glorifying the world vanish from his memory as he struggles through the sordidness of life. In truth, he cometh forth as a flower and is cut down.

But beneath the wilted petals and beneath that broken heart of a man there still glows in embers, a light eternal. And some day the Great Magician is going to wander along that dusty road and, with the touch of his magic wand, bring back life to these faded flowers.

In the highways and byways of this world, who shall be this Great Magician? Who shall play the fairy queen and raise to life again the dead? There is within each one of us the Great Magician-the good spirit who can bring faded flowers to life and restore the broken blossoms from whose crushed petals have been formed a rosary that ends with a cross. There is this wondrous fairy godmother who can bring to life the dead rose and make it bloom again in radiant beauty, and this mystic being, the good fairy, is the sweetness and compassion of love and hope that is hidden deep in the heart of every man. Each kind word, each sweet thought, brings forth again the glow of life to the soul of some faded flower!

It is a glorious thing to have the power to make the world shine again with happiness. This is within the reach of every mystic, for into the hands of one who has earned this right, to bring back the blush of life to broken souls, a great privilege is given. No longer does he live for what the world can give him, for he has more than it can ever know. He lives to wander through the gardens of humanity where flower and blooming shrub fade each year as the snows of winter come. Gathering up the dried and withered leaves, he blesses them with the power of life and they brighten up again at his touch.

Where the mystic is, there can be no faded flowers for, he lives only to bring joy and life into the world. Hates and fears, sorrows and remorse-all these have withered the flowers of life. The roses of youth vanish from the cheek as the furrows of care appear and the eyes, once bright with laughter, soon grow dull with weeping. But the work of the master is to bring back the old-time joy and although his own heart be sad, he smiles serenely through his tears as he gathers the broken petals to mold them again into perfect flowers.

And man is walking in the footsteps of this Master. Every day, somewhere, he sees a withered rose whose petals would glow again if he would but nourish them with the waters of life. Just a kind word and the flower will become a thing of beauty in the garden of the Lord. We are to go forth in the name of the Father and gather close to our hearts these withered flowers, the broken children of men. In love and compassion, we are to serve them, in humility and simplicity to protect them, m sympathy and brotherhood to assist them that tee spirit of joy may come again into their lives as the blossoming of a flower.

Somewhere in the soul of man, no matter how cold he may seem, there is something which cries out to smile, cries out to be happy, and being happy cries some more! This is a certain soul quality explainable and known only to those who have suffered and yet through it all are drawn by bonds undefinable back to the cause of their anguish. There is something very human about the world and while it may seem a cruel place, the longer we are in it, the less we desire to leave it. It is so much like each one of us that the bonds of understanding make us love the old earth more and more.

The glory of being alive is a wonderful thing, but the still greater glory of giving life and expression to others fills the heart with a real purpose of being.

And he who turns back again into the garden of the earth to nurture and care for those withered flowers whose drooping petals bespeak the dying courage of an unawakened life, knows no other joy. It is a wondrous thing to feel that it is within our power, if we live as we should, to give these flowers new duty. From the soul of him who thus redeems the rose that was withered shall shine forth a star through the darkness, that star which is the mark of the Compassionate One.

The Sons of God labor eternally with man to build within him that sweet sadness—the sadness which is the great peace that surpasseth understanding. In simple symbol well known to our eyes, the Sons of Compassion ever seek to teach us the way that we should go, seeking to build within us the realization of the path which they have walked. They never command us to go this way or that they only show us the beauties of the path. They show us the faded flowers and then they ask if there can be anything more beautiful in all the world than a flower turned upward in adoration to the light of its God? They ask if anything is sadder than to see the blossom wither and fade away?

Then it is shown to us how we may go forth and bring to blossom the flower of spirit now budding alone in the endless deserts of materiality. So let us take their symbol of service and go out to labor in the world fields that the faded flower hidden within the heart of man, called the spirit of Christ, shall be raised from the dead to blossom forth unto perfect life.

Man is the little creator made in the image of the Great Creator containing in possibility all that God has in awakened energy.

# A DISCOURSE ON THE EIGHT PERFECTIONS - II
(Continued)

AND the Lord of Light spoke of the Fifth Perfection which is Intelligent Living, saying: "Know that the Fifth Perfection is that ye should live well to yourself and true in your dealings with others; that ye should be joyous among others, but that your living be right in the eyes of the Lord. Know that of the many things which thou hast this sheath of stone which ye call a body, is most useful to you at this time, for only through this body may ye learn that which is eternal. Realize that this body is not the Eternal I, nor God, but is rather of a demon of darkness; but you must treat it well that it may serve thee well unto the work for which God has designed it. By the Intelligence of Right Living know that he who liveth with nature in simplicity liveth with God in reality and he who would know how to live must search for life among the living and not among the dead. Man is dead, therefore search not for life there but look only unto God who is the One Life."

So saying, the Lord opened the fifth Petal:

"Of this Lotus the fifth Petal is the Perfection of Intelligent Living wherein ye shall learn that length of life is the prolonging of opportunities-when to this ye add Perception and Purpose. But the body liveth not of itself alone but of the life which is within it and which is the life of Brahma who is the Creator and Father who ever shall Be. Therefore, in all your living, live moderately and wisely; live as a brother with all other things. Thereof it is spoken in the Sacred Bharatas: Live not of the body but of the spirit. But know that living means that the bodies be preserved for the spirit and that the spirit speaks through its own reflection in the mirror of eternity."

\* \* \*

Wherein the Blessed Lord saith: "This is all that I would speak of the Fifth Perfection. So, listen unto the words of the Sixth Perfection which is Perfect Effort. Know that intelligent effort is the basis of all that expands and groweth great; effort is the measurement of reward and according to your effort, so shall it be with you in that which is Eternal. Know, oh son! -there is a reward for effort regardless of its works and know that right effort bringeth with it a sure promise of right reward. Nothing in this universe is without effort and those who do not labor shall someday be in famine for that which they have not sown. Therefore, know that in effort lies the secret of power and the Sixth Perfection is Intelligent Effort which ye gain through intelligent Perception, intelligent Speech, intelligent Purpose, intelligent Conduct and intelligent Living."

Thus, Spake the Lord of the Lotus as he pointed towards the heavens, saying of the Sixth Perfection:

"In the skies beyond the Blue Veil is the home of the saints in Sheta-loka, the home of those who have been tried and have labored for that which they are. For unto those who try is a sure reward, if ye strive with perfect effort. Ye gain not Nirvana through meditation alone; there must be works and perfect effort. Therefore, oh son, is effort greatly to be desired and when in doubt as to the labored to perform, strive with perfect effort and thy reward is sure."

\* \* \*

Thus, Spake the Mighty One of the Sixth Perfection, which is Intelligent effort, and then He saith:

"I will now speak of the Seventh Perfection, which is of the mind and is Intelligent Mindfulness. For in all thy seeking be not thoughtless lest in being such ye waste or injure. Be ye ever mindful of three things, oh son of earth! That thou mayest be perfect in Mindfulness. First, be mindful of thy conduct that it behooves thee well to watch as how thou shalt conduct thyself unto thyself. Second, be mindful of those responsibilities which are thine from the world; forget them not nor neglect them, for they are Dharma and not to be overlooked. Third, be mindful that in your eagerness ye trample not your brothers under foot but are gentle and modest in the sight of men. If it were good that ye should also be mindful of the will of God and the ways of His saints, for although ye be mindful of men ye shall not succeed if ye forget the will of God."

Thus, Spake the Blessed Lord of the Seventh Petal as He sat in the Heart of the Flower:

"Be mindful also that every labor shall increase thee in the sight of God for by this is known the Seventh Perfection -that ye have no longer the power to hurt, the power to injure nor the desire to excel but that ye are eternally mindful and considerate of the needs of others. By this shall ye reach the feet of thy Lord and Master who is ever mindful of you, and thus shall it be known that you understand the Seventh Intelligence, which is the Perfection of Mindfulness."

\* \* \*

Whereupon the Lord of Light spoke once more, saying: "There is one more Perfection whereof I would speak, namely, the Intelligence of Contemplation wherein ye become as one with God through the Contemplation of Reality. For he who can contemplate within his own soul the wonders of creation and float over oblivion on the wings of intuition and reason, he hath Perfect Contemplation which seeth life and death and yet is unmoved. Such a one shall himself live and die and yet be unmoved, whereupon may ye know that he is free from the Wheel of Birth and Death insomuch as he contemplates them as part of the Great Lesson, but is not enmeshed in them as mortal man. He that is able to stand beside the universe and contemplate upon its wonders without himself being involved therein that one has Perfect Contemplation for he seeth all things, liveth all things, contemplateth all thing and is no part of them but is one with their source."

Thus, Spake the Great Lord of the Eighth perfection, which is Intelligent Contemplation, saying:

"Behold, oh son of man! The gods are perfect in contemplation, and the universe is the fruit of their meditations. Therefore, if ye would be one with the Eternal, contemplate also upon That which Is and you will be one with the Twelve Eternal Meditators in the Fields of the Infinite. For he who seeth in all things a lesson but in nothing the personality, he is perfect in contemplation; he who seeth in all things a personality, he is perfect in ignorance. All men stand between two things, perfection in ignorance and perfection in knowledge, while the god-man sits in contemplation upon the two. They are not wise, for they are not the fruits of ignorance; they are not ignorant, for the seeds of wisdom have not been planted there. Know that Perfection of Contemplation is that which sitteth between wisdom and ignorance and meditateth upon them but is neither."

\* \* \*

"Whereupon I have finished my discourse upon the Eight Intelligences, which are the eight paths of my wisdom and the Petals of my sacred Lotus. Know ye therefore, oh Chela! that the Blessed Lord hath spoken, whereof it is written in the Sacred Books of the Trees, of that which Is and ever shall Be because it has never been, for once being it must cease to be."

## THE MASTER SPEAKS - II
(Continued)

And this was my first great experience among worldly scoffers and it was there that I learned a lesson which I never forgot. In the words of my teacher, I say: "Fear not that your words will not express your hopes and ideals for he who is carrying the Master's message is never alone. When his own words are failing, the Invisible Ones gather around and whisper in his ear. If you work and labor in truth and sincerity, never fear, for the Teacher is with you. He knows the words you need and whispers them when the moment comes.

(To be continued.)

## ASTROLOGICAL KEYWORDS

Leo as the fifth sign of the Zodiac is of special interest to students of the occult sciences for several reasons. First, being the throne of the sun, the Lion is often used as a symbol of life and power and Christ, who represents the sun-god, is often referred to as the Lion of Judah. In Masonry Leo is very symbolical, for being the chief of the cat family the Lion is said to have the same peculiarity in his ability to see in the dark consequently is used by the ancients to symbolize the Eye of God which sees into the darkness of human affairs.

The Grip of the Lion's Paw is well known, and it is symbolical of the returning of life when the sun, in his endless round, enters his throne in Leo bringing all things to life that have been dead through the long winter months.

Below we list the keywords of the sign of Leo in a simple, concise manner so that the student with slight practice will be capable of analyzing its most general characteristics. Leo is also of special interest at the present time insomuch as it forms the esoteric school of the Aquarian Age, its opposite in the Zodiac and according to geocentric astrology the Aquarian Age which is so close at hand will bring with it a powerful spiritual ray from Leo the Lion of the Tribe Judah. Leo is always symbolical of life and fire and, as in man, it governs the heart, so in the cosmos it is the home of the sun, the heart of the solar system.

Leo the fifth sign of the Zodiac:
Hot, Brutish, Dry, Barren, Fiery, Four-footed, Choleric, Broken, Eastern, Changeable, Masculine, Fortunate, Diurnal, Strong, Northern, Hoarse, Commanding, Bitter, Fixed, Violent, Estival, Long, Ascension, The day and night home of the Sun, The detriment of Saturn, Feral, Furious.

General Characteristics:
High resolve, Royal, Unbending, Ambitious, Quick-tempered, Changeable, Generous, Free, Courteous.

The Leo person takes his general characteristics from the animal in question, namely, the lion. Like that animal he chafes under confinement, rebels against over-lords and is monarch of all he surveys. If crossed or attempt is made to curb him, he is quick-tempered and noted for his roaring, ranting and cantankering. But it does not last long, and he soon quietens down. This sign is usually in important positions of trust, fond of the occult sciences, and under normal conditions makes its mark in the world of affairs.

Physical Appearances:

Usually a large body, Broad shoulders, Austere countenance, Large eyes, Dark yellow, reddish or brown hair, given to curling, Strong voice, sometimes hoarse, Full-blooded, Oval countenance, sometimes rather choppy, Later part of the sign produces weaker body with lighter hair,

Large round head, staring and goggle eyes, Middle stature but heavy arrow sides, Fierce countenance, High sanguine complexion.

Health:

While Leo is considered a healthy sign, we do find considerable sickness, especially that due to circulation and blood conditions. It governs the heart and back and its most common diseases are:

Pains in the back and ribs, Convulsions, Smallpox, Fainting, Measles, Fevers, Jaundice, Pestilences, and all hot and inflammatory diseases, Entirely barren sign, Sore eyes, The plagues, Heart trouble, Denotes accidents by fire, explosion, and combustible materials, Subject to sprains, falls, shocks, etc.

Domestic Problems:

Leo can only be said to be happy in the home when it rules the home. Monotony and drudgery do not rest well upon the Leo types and their fiery dispositions often break their homes. If they find someone, however, who is willing to allow them to do just what they want to they are usually faithful but not overly domestic, being turned more to public things.

Countries under Influence of Leo:
Italy, West of England, Bohemia, The Alps, France, Turkey, Sicily, Silesia

Cities Ruled by Leo:
Rome, Bristol, Bath, Taunton

Cremona Colors:
Yellow, Prague, Syracuse, Ravenna, Philadelphia, Damascus, Red, Brown, Green

According to Ptolemy, the stars in the head of Leo are in effect like Saturn with a ray from Mars; the three in the neck are like Saturn with some of Mercury; the bright one in the heart called Regulus agrees with Mars and Jupiter; those in the loins and the bright one in the tail are like Saturn and Venus; those in the thighs resemble Venus and, in some degree, Mercury.

According to Henry Cornelius Agrippa, of the Twelve Orders of Blessed

Spirits, Leo rules the powers; of the Twelve Angels over the Twelve Signs, Vercuil rules Leo; of the months Leo rules the 20th of July to the 20th of August; of the Twelve Tribes, Asher; of the Twelve Prophets, Hosea; of the Twelve Apostles, Peter; of the twelve plants, ladies' seal; of the twelve stones, jasper; of the twelve principal members, the heart; of the Twelve Degrees of the Damned, the jugglers of darkness.

## THE NIGHT OF BRAHMA

AT THE end of every cosmic cycle of action, there follows a period of rest, and this is the ebb and flow of energy which marks one of the fundamental expressions of the eternal plan. The periods of activity are called the Days of Brahma when the world outpouring itself from the Unknown expresses its energized and rejuvenated qualities, and with greater courage, power and speed carries on the work of universal unfoldment because of the periods of rest. At the end of each day of manifestation the Universe, the Sun of Necessity, is dissolved or swallowed up in cosmic night which was called by the ancients "Pralaya."

For every action in this world, which implies the expending of energy, there must ensure a period of inaction during which time nature rebuilds the tissues and revivifies the bodies torn down and scattered by the activities of mental, physical, or spiritual expression. There is no one who can entirely set aside the periods of rest and while for many years, lives perhaps, a powerfully constituted organism may sustain itself upon comparatively little relaxation, still at some time or other even the gods must pass into cosmic or universal sleep.

Death is merely an expression of the return of bodies to sleep. Paul says we die daily, and this is a spiritual truth, for each day we tear down the body cells and life forces which we are forced to expend in our manifestation and growth here. During the periods of cosmic sleep, the universe rebuilds its shattered vehicles and when they return to life; they start with a great impetus similar to the buoyancy we feel when we awaken from peaceful slumber. When we do not feel refreshed from sleep, it is a certainty that the vehicles have not been relaxed and that through unwise eating or physical derangement the spiritual consciousness has not completely separated itself from its vehicle of expression. The withdrawal of the life from the form constitutes death, the temporary withdrawal without rupturing the connecting links between bodies is called sleep, and this is the period of physical regeneration for night is illuminated by the moon, the generator of bodies and the ruling principle of those vitalizing forces which rebuild the depleted tissue of vehicles under the direction of the elemental intelligences.

Brahma, the incarnated intelligence of the universe, is called the Grand Man and He is supposed to be endowed with the qualities of man in a grander and more perfect degree. The sleeping and waking, the birth and death of Brahma, is correlated to the shorter periods of manifestation of man and the analogy is quite perfect. One of the greatest works that confronts the student is to accurately learn to understand the use and application of the powers of relaxation. The continued over-exertion of a body, a brain center, or an organ of consciousness will shorten the length of its life. It is true that all parts of man grow stronger with exercise, but exercise must be balanced by rest for exercise tears down the walls of resistance and saps the stores of energy used to give expression to a body or organ. Therefore, a certain part of the time, we must allow certain centers to rest and recuperate from our unbalanced use of them.

The child in school tires of arithmetic in an hour or so and then you transfer his attention to spelling or geography, bringing into play an entirely different series of sense centers. This results in the relaxation of the tired organ during which time the mind recuperates from the strain placed upon it and prepares for further active expression. The forty-three faculties of the human brain must all be given alternately exercise and rest, the result being a well-balanced consciousness and an adaptable mind. The mental breakdown is the result of the abuse of a single faculty or trying to make an organ run both night and day, year in and year out, without rest.

There are two grand phases of force. One is that expression which pours into the reservoir to supply the needs of expression; the other is that which pours out of the reservoir in active manifestation. Nothing can come out of a man that has not already gone in, for he has not yet acquired the miraculous pitcher of the gods. He can go no further than the energy stored in the reservoir; he can be no stronger than the involuted energies which he radiates. Therefore, the involution of power is absolutely necessary to the evolution of form. These two laws are intra-dependent one upon the other, for man cannot pour into his organism safely energy unless he expends a certain amount in his daily life. If he does not do this, he runs over. On the other hand, the amount within measures his capacity to draw forth. Man, involutes the expressions of this force in his material and spiritual thoughts, actions, and desires.

All life is an ebb and flow of energies. These energies pour into man from the planes of consciousness to which he has attuned himself through his own works and thoughts. They can produce no higher results than the plane of consciousness from whence they came and the quality of inflowing energy is limited by the vehicles of attraction which gather it from the cosmos.

The problem of the days and nights of Brahma is to man a divine allegory expressing as it does the requirements of his own life. Two forces govern man, solar and lunar; the solar govern the higher man, the lunar, the bodies. Each of these must alternately be given opportunity for self-expression in order that they may carry on their respective duties. So, at night, while the body is undisturbed by conscious mental or physical reaction, the reparatory, powers of nature, take charge of the organism and prepare it to support and express the life within it during the following period of action. In the daytime, the spiritual consciousness is ushered into its vehicle, where its own growth is carried on at the expense of the lower bodies. The result is a divine balance of the periods of recuperation and destruction.

Wise and careful seekers after things spiritual have learned to recognize the vital importance of giving their bodies and centers of consciousness the proper amount of exercise and relaxation. All of man's bodies have a great similarity. Our minds and emotions are subject to the same general ailments before which the physical body must bow and all through nature the law of action and repose is a governing factor. Man in his haste fails to properly consider and study the law of periodicity, consequently, he must pay the price in broken health and inefficiency. Those who would be like God in dynamic powers must develop their organism in accordance with His laws, which are the individualized needs of His composite progression.

So, through the ages, the days and nights of Brahma go on. Worlds come in and worlds go out and in shorter periods of time man passes through similar conditions which to him seem very terrible but which in reality are his greatest blessings, for God does not die when his vehicles are asleep, He is functioning in other worlds in finer and more sensitive bodies, and it is only the exhausted appendage of consciousness that is dropped and its centers allowed to rest, while in higher and finer words the consciousness is making further plans for its unfoldment and final union with the form which now it is forced to vampirize in order to exist during the days of Brahma.

## NOTE

It may be of interest to some of our readers to know that we are preparing mimeograph notes of some of our lectures, which may be secured by those desiring them on the same free-will offering basis that is used in all of our publications. The edition is limited but we will be glad to supply them while they last.

We have the following prepared for distribution at the present time:

Total Eclipse of the Sun and Effect Upon World Affairs.

This is an astrological analysis of the effect of the September eclipse upon the geographic, political, economic, and weather conditions of the world.

The Sex Problem.

These are the notes of a lecture given in Los Angeles about the effects of the modern sex teachings upon the race.

The Einstein Theory of Relativity.

A simple analysis of this intricate problem, applying it to the practical problem of human relationship.

Talks for Teachers, Parts I, II and III.

These three separate lectures deal with three phases of the work of preparing pupils for the world ministry and the labors of the coming age.

The Masters, Parts I and II.

Two lectures dealing with the Masters of Wisdom and the work of preparing oneself to be become their conscious assistants.

Books for Occult Students.

A list of nearly two hundred books and authors valuable to the student of occult teachings, which should be read and studied by all aspiring candidates on the path of self-unfoldment.

## OCCULT MASON - II
## THE TRIANGLE ON THE MASON'S RING
(Continued from May Issue in Book First)

In the first issue of our magazine, we started an article on the symbolism of the triangle, especially the flaming triangle, as it is understood in the inner Masonic lodges and mystic centers of spiritual knowledge.

The three sides of the triangle represent, of course, the three outpourings of life and energy, which are molding the threefold body of man. The triangle is composed of two substances and is shown in two ways. The upright triangle is white symbolizing the up pointing spiritual tendencies of man, the turning God-ward of the three human expressions of thought, emotion and form; while the triangle with the point downward is symbolical of the three spiritual flames descending downward from the heavens to impregnate and vitalize man. These two, with their points together, form an hour-glass which is the ancient symbol of time well known to Masons.

There are two flames in the universe, the golden flame and the black flame. The golden fire belongs to heaven and the realms of truth and light, while the black flame belongs to oblivion, the home of eternal darkness. The degenerate individual is symbolized by the black flame while the regenerated individual is typified by the golden up-pointing fire.

The Yod or Dot in the triangle represents God, who is only known or cognized through the expression of the Triangle. He is the life within or behind the glass of manifestation and the unformed, unexpressed energy manifests through the three witnesses of air, fire and water-earth. God manifests only through His creations. When He wishes to send us, a great truth needed for our development, He expresses it through the triangle of spirit, mind, and body. Spirituality is a child born of three parents: a clean body, a pure heart, and a balanced mind. This child must be nurtured and cared for as any physical baby. From this guarding and care is born the soul, which shines forth as a great aura of light and is symbolized by the glow which surrounds the Masonic triangle.

Of all the ancient and honored religious doctrines, there is none as old as the worship of the Flame. From the most ancient of times down to our modern days, the Great Unknown, the spiritual power of the universe, has been loved, protected, and revered by mankind and called the Eternal Flame. The ancients used as a symbol of this Flame the upright triangle, which precedes the G. as the sacred symbol of Masonry. In Greek, God is Deus and the first letter, D., is made in the form of an upright triangle. This upright triangle signifies the awakening of God within man as a wonderful threefold flame which divides itself through the nourishing of the three bodies. It is the thirty-third-degree symbol of the Masonic Order which, surrounded by its glowing flame, stands for the God-consciousness man.

The flaming triangle is made of three absolutely equal angles and symbolizes the divine balance in the threefold constitution. The balancing of his three bodies and their uniting to express a single central power is the basis of the thirty-third degree of Freemasonry and is the end to which all Masons aspire.

The salt, Sulfur and mercury of the ancients is a divine allegory used to conceal the secret of the philosopher's stone which is nothing more or less than the union of spirit, mind and body, the endless symbol of the human ultimate. The

When the God in man, the flaming center of the triangle, is capable of expressing itself through three perfect instruments, built by man and dedicated by the lower upon the altar of the divine, then can God find the perfect expression and the Mason himself becomes the flaming triangle surrounded by the glowing garments of his living soul.

The triangle is truly a wonderful symbol and as the Mason carries it upon the ring he wears, let him realize that its eternal plea is for the balancing of the threefold constitution united in the expression of a single divinity.

(The End)

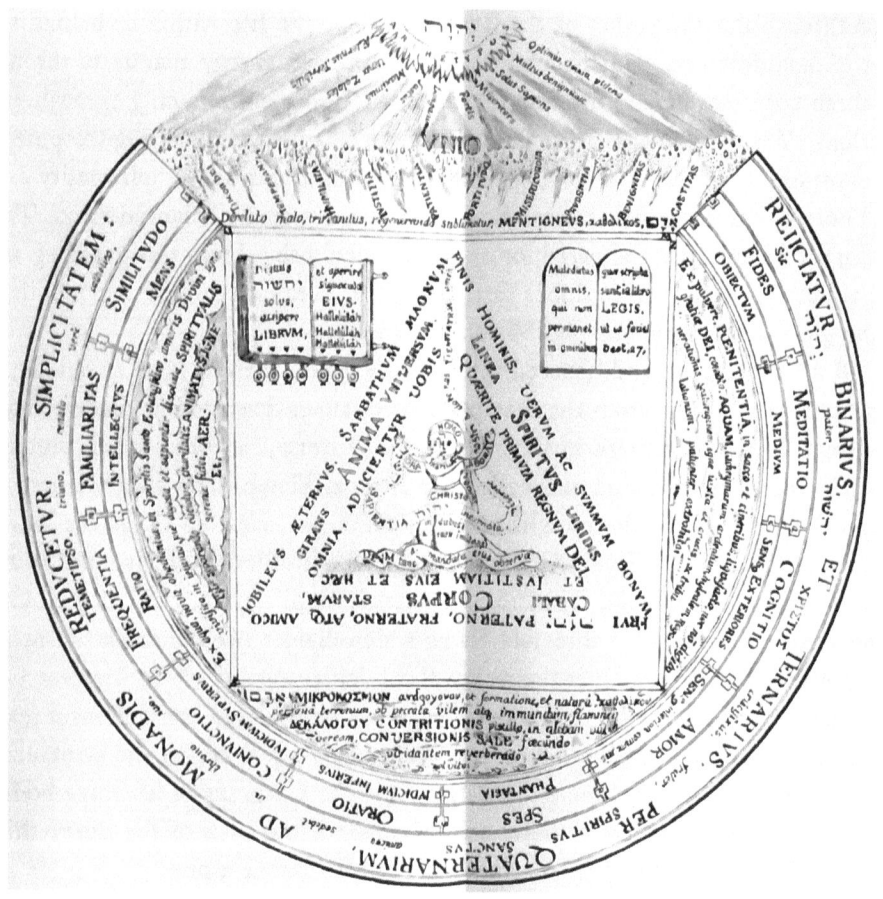

NOVEMBER 1923

## THE PRISON GRAVEYARD

Here the crest of this lonely hill
Where the tangled grasses and wild weeds creep.
In serried file neath whitewashed slabs,
The silent dead of the prison sleep.
All ill vain were their anguished prayers,
In vain were the scalding tears they shed;
They drank the cup to its hitter dregs,
And their forms were laid with the convict dead.
No tender hand to assuage the pain;
No loving kiss when the end was nigh;
No saddened voice in a last farewell;
And with dirth of these it was hard to die.
No marbled tomb nor sculptured urn
To tell what battles through life they fought,
lust a number less on the prison roll,
A soul effaced from the realms of thought.
And where was the profit, whose the gain
When these wrecks were shattered on the reef?
Ye "holier than thou" with pious mien
Do these desolate graves bring you sweet relief?
Know ye not that perchance some future day
A boyish hand from thine own may slip,
Never to nestle in thy palm again,
Whose feet to a grave like this may trip?
Were these erring lives all lived in vain,
Whose only goal was a grave of shame?
Were they destined thus by Fate's decree?
Then whose the fault, and where the blame?
Drifting about like derelicts,
With rudder broken and mainmast gone,
Flying a signal of dire distress
Fighting the tide that was driving them on.
Theirs were souls in the making yet,
With the deeper lessons of life unlearned;
The chords of their hearts were still untouched,
The passions of youth in their breasts still burned.

They gave no thought to the Universe,
They heard no hint of God's great plan
By most its thought all their hard lives taught
Was Man's Inhumanity to Man.
May these desolate graves on this lonely hill
Serve as mile posts along the way,
Revealing the needs of our fellowmen,
Guiding us on to that future day
When the Children of Earth, standing hand in hand,
Shall drink at the Fountain of Truth, and see
The Glorious Dawn so long foretold
The Brotherhood of Humanity.


EDITORIALS

## CRANKS AND CRANKISMS AS FACTORS IN INDIGESTION

THERE is that divine state of being into which it is possible for individuals to adjust themselves which humanity knows as harmony and equilibrium. This is the ultimate to which all creatures are striving, for balance is the keynote to power and success. But how seldom we find it in our world of affairs!

The human race is mostly made up of extremists and there is no doubt but that the extremes of all problems are well symbolized as the two thieves between whom the Master was crucified. The world is filled with people who live on tangents and die on angles and whenever a great truth is discovered it always gathers around it those who do it more harm than good. They are usually people who have been atheists all their lives but are converted at the eleventh hour and there are none as hopelessly bigoted in their religious viewpoints as those whose conversion is recent. They are the ones who warn you that unless you go to church regularly, you will sizzle eternally in the postmortem state and many a man has been damned heartily and eternally because he would not agree with someone else who has only been "saved" about two weeks. These problems are ever with us and now dietetics is forming a neutral point around and over which tremendous battles are being waged.

The problem before the house is: Resolved that eating is a dangerous, bar-

baric, unscientific form of nourishment and should be eliminated or, if still with us, all gastronomic influxes should be according to science.

There is no doubt in the world that dietetics molds to a great degree the consciousness of individuals, for man is in truth what he eats, but there are other considerations which must be taken up and examined in the study of this extreme problem. Each individual is building qualities and traits different from all other people and these qualities require certain elements which differ with the growth of each person. There is an undisputed fact confronting modern science, and that is, the average member of the human race is making a garbage pail, if not worse, out of his stomach by placing in, its combinations which would blow him to atoms if gathered in a chemical retort. In many cases, not only does the food we eat place us in mortal peril, but it also endangers the unfoldment of our immortal spirit. The combinations of food which the rank and file of people incorporate into their organisms in the name of a meal not only lack all constructive elements but are often of such a decidedly dangerous nature as to result in spontaneous combustion upon the slightest provocation.

Education is needed in dietetics as in all physical and super-physical sciences, but the value of the science depends upon the balance, common sense, and efficiency of the instructor. The average dietetic specialist whose life is narrowed to proteins and carbons is not in a position to make an intelligent analysis of either food qualities or the needs of his patient. The ancient philosophers were right when they said a man who knows only one thing knows nothing. There is a great deal of difference between a food expert and a crank who claims to be and they can only be differentiated when we follow, to some degree, the dictates of common sense.

There is no doubt that a large percentage of our population is suffering from stomach trouble and while much of it is the result of improper diet not a few cases are due to the frenzied notions of specialists along these lines. There are many of these mental, physical and spiritual musicians who are playing on one string and trying to produce heavenly harmony when the only sound that issues forth is a rather hashified discord in which the food specialist finally becomes so wound up in his dietetic outbursts that neither God, man nor dynamite can disentangle him.

The truly great dietetic expert knows that there is no magic formula that will bring the world health, he knows that each individual is a problem in himself, and that the food qualities which will kill one man will save another. The true scientist is a specialist in the analysis of human individuality. The true food expert realizes that the diet for each individual must be different and that no set series of personally evolved laws will ever answer the problem of indigestion.

Stomach trouble has two causes. First, ignorance; second, indolence. These two are behind practically every human infirmity. Under the general heading of indolence, are those people for whom it is too great an exertion to chew and properly masticate food or who are too lazy to exercise sufficiently to create an appetite or dispose of a dinner. The second class, the ignorant group, lists in its ranks those who do not know what nor how to eat and includes no small percentage of our so-called food experts who generally have about as many pains as their patients do.

There is no greater cause in all the world for sour stomach than a certain fraternity which is springing up among occultists and dieticians. Their slogan is: "Thou shalt not!" They are forever with us. Every time we lift a fork, gracefully balancing a luscious baked bean, a voice like the Dying Gaul whispers in our ear: "Thou shalt not or thou shalt die! Beware, brother, there is protein in that bean!" What greater cause for stomach discomfiture is there than to see these gloomy ones sitting round us at the festive board munching hour after hour and predigesting in mathematical sequence the corner of a lettuce leaf or a handful of cold slaw? Or to hear that melancholy cadence which rises as would-be Methuselahs chew graham crackers, whole bran biscuits or imported zwieback making us feel that our neighbor is gnawing on granite headstones in some outlying cemetery? There is nothing so apt to bring on indigestion as to find beside us at a pleasing meal that spirit of negation who whispers that the pickled cauliflower, we love so well will bring on fluttering of the liver or involve some nameless nerve in a compromising situation. We hate to be wound up in some mental hazard or to be bound down by the strings of the beans we eat and then have some individual, the living incarnation of failure, dyspepsia and liver trouble, tell us in a voice rising from the depths of his goulashes of the damning effect of orange ice if eaten a la shrimp.

The true food expert will never make himself obnoxious for he realizes that when he does so he loses all opportunity to be useful either to himself or his brother man. There is nothing that nauseates an individual more, irritates his gastric nerve so close to the breaking point, or sprinkles grit in his liver-pins more quickly than one of those who in the name of health bring sickness with their very presence. And many of our foremost faddists are more dangerous to general health than mushrooms, which turn the aluminum green when you cook them.

There is no class of people in the world so dangerous as fanatics and soapbox orators. As long as they will confine their faddisms to themselves all goes well for this a free country, but they do not seem to be happy unless they are inoculating the entire neighborhood with their concepts. There is no doubt that carbon, proteins, vitamins, starches, carbohydrates, etcetera, not to mention carbolic acid, strychnine, turpentine and home brew will cause trouble if taken in too large quantities. We will not dispute the fact that sour kraut and French pastry have an antipathy based upon racial characteristics; lobsters with whipped cream may also produce irritations and convulsions to the inner man. These gathered together may embarrass us, said embarrassments taking the form of rheumatism, diabetes, uric acid poisoning, toothache, dandruff, glanders, falling arches, rupe and blind staggers; but for some utterly well-known reason, the average individual gets sicker when you tell him this than when he eats the food.

Few like to be reminded of such contingencies, especially at mealtimes. The occultist must realize that the doctrine he is preaching is of tolerance and where dietetics does not receive a ready welcome, then has come the moment for the dietetic expert to gracefully retire. When he ceases to be tolerant of the desires of others makes himself obnoxious with his personally evolved ideas and runs his fads into the ground, he loses all his opportunity to be of use, takes all the joy out of life and so prejudices people against dietetics that those who do have common sense and really do know can accomplish but little.

Moderation is the keynote to all things and politeness and consideration for the feelings of others form a very important phase of philosophy. Those who lose sight of the requirements of social etiquette and who go to another man's house, pick the meals to pieces, and ruin the appetites of all members of the family, (at the same time eating the condemned vitals heartily and with relish) such a person has a small chance of being listed with the immortal benefactors of humanity. Ranters, roarers and rearers, will never gain any great amount of success; neither will those who try to force their opinions upon the world without giving the other person the privilege of declining them. Each has the right to do what he wants. If he exercises too much freedom and becomes too spontaneous in his outbursts of unleashed exuberance, he will be quietly reminded of it in civil matters by the judge, in gastric matters by his stomach, and in religious matters by a visit from the parson.

The great trouble at the present time seems to be that there are too many people taking an interest in other people's affairs and after half a dozen near-occultists have expressed their opinions on our needs, we know a great deal less than before they started. We tear our hair, perhaps the last one from our head with a cry of dismay and they put new furniture in our padded cells. After we have tried to follow a complete gamut of occult advice, our beloved ones gather round, shake their heads and whisper, "He may get over it, but he'll never be the same." Now it just so happens that we have a friend who has been suffering for many years from an acute pandemonium of the pancreas and palpitation of the pneumo-gastric nerve (which information cost him ten dollars to discover). The name of our poor, suffering fellow countryman is Ebenezer J. Wheeze. For some time, he has been trying to get the inside information on this deep inside inflammation and has applied to several scintillating exponents of dietetic science.

He has a friend who talks in his sleep, wears his hat on one ear, and only shaves occasionally who is an eminent authority on the food subject. He suggested that Ebenezer live on alfalfa and goat curds for about three months after which he was to discard the curds and take up predigested prunes and unsalted pretzels. Not feeling capable of doing the experiment himself, Uncle Ebenezer tried it on the cat who went into convulsions and has had a bleared look ever since. From that day to this, Tabby's tail swells up every time the word "dietetics" is mentioned and can only be found under the back stoop when there are any food experts around.

From him Mr. Wheeze went to another eminent authority on the subject of what to eat and how to eat it. Mr. Slump is a small man about five foot two, weighs ninety pounds, has spinal curvature and false teeth, but otherwise is a perfect picture of health. Mr. Slump analyzed it as "over-proteins" and told Ebenezer that raw cabbage and bran crackers had made him what he is today and would do the same for Ebenezer. Eb was not entirely satisfied with the example of the finished product but decided to try it and in correlation with wild onion honey and some newfangled spring water which tasted like burnt Sulphur he went into a state of agony lasting several weeks.

One day a perfect stranger came up to Ebenezer on the street and after measuring him from head to foot with a small tape measure handed him a card bearing the name of a well-known undertaking concern with a list of several beautiful plots just his size in a nearby cemetery. The same mysterious stranger also mentioned casually that silver handles were being done this year. This decided Ebenezer that the results of his labors were not harmonious with his continued manifestation on this plane of nature so he desisted from his diet and applied to another "expert."

Prof. Theodore Sneezix is now deceased, having died of convulsions a few weeks ago as the result of having eaten meat. (He found a red ant in his raw spinach.) His suggestion was a ten-day fast with a half a glass of orange juice every other day. Ebenezer tried this also but couldn't get the orange Juice the last two days, not being able to walk. Henceforward he had a dark brown taste, a rather ashen feeling and a dusty look. In other words, Ebenezer was slowly returning to Mother Matter. At the end of the fifth month, the insurance company raised his rate to the worst risk in the office and his great grand uncle who wanted his old clothes suggested that he make his will. After this experiment, it took him about eight months to build up.

Life had become just one food expert after another with Uncle Ebenezer, and he honestly tried to follow all their advice. He sharpened his fangs in caraway seed, sliced belladonna plasters and flaxseed gruel. One month he hung a piece of cuttlefish bone in the middle of the room and chewed on that, he gnawed on unbaked pie crust, chewed hickory bark, ate raw beets, decked himself out in parsley, tried a strange and mysterious concoction at the half-baked bakery, used grated raw potatoes, ate garlic and limburger and as a last resort tried chewing navy beans, split peas and unsalted lickerish bars. And day by day, in every way, he grew weaker and weaker. He tried one meal a day and then increased them to five a day; he lay down before eating and again after eating; exercised while eating by having his dinner placed on a shelf and snapping at it; tried funnels and sponges, straws and rubber tubing; chewed each mouthful ten times, then twenty times and then tried swallowing it whole, until finally he had experimented with every known method of torture conceivable to the human brain.

At the end of one full year, he had galloping jim-jams and a generally innocuous vicissitude which threatened to be fatal. Several leading doctors gathered and opened a symposium on the strength of his pocketbook, announcing as the result of a deeply heated discussion that Ebenezer was infected with creeping heaves and chronic staggers!

He had been miserable beyond expression, sick unto the breaking point, had developed crow's feet, a mean disposition, three bunions and broken up three homes. As he staggered down the street, tottering beneath the weight of gray hairs to an untimely grave, supported by a crutch and a few of his relatives, an old friend came up and slapped him on the back, nearly jarring lose his upper plate and disconnecting his spark plug, saying:

"Old man, you look down and out. Have you been watching your diet?"

Whereupon Ebenezer gave a low gurgle, draped himself upon his friend's arms and sinking upon the sidewalk stretched out his toes while the crowds gathered announcing it apoplexy. When he awoke several days later, he was staring into the face of an eminent food scientist who was feeding him barley gruel through an eye dropper! The relapse was nearly fatal.

At last, a shattered and broken wreck, he wandered alone in a heartless world, no longer able to eat a square meal because the corners scraped against some tender bit of his insides. About this time Eb found the seventh daughter of a seventh son, address unknown, age 103, who gave him the secret of longevity. She advised less worry, moderation in all things and common sense. Hope returned, for it springs eternal in the human heart!

After applying this simple recipe for a short time, Ebenezer found that it worked like a charm. He excluded things which he knew were not good for him, ate moderately of a well-balanced diet, enjoyed everything he ate and ate nearly everything he enjoyed but all in moderation and with care. He soon found the qualifications of youth returning, his fallen arches raised, and a rubber heel temperament returned. He could do a hundred yards in nothing flat, won the old man's hurdle race, did eighteen holes of golf, chopped five cords of wood before dinner and could pick up the average dietician under one arm with his following under the other. His false teeth took root, and he chewed the corner off of Webster's Unabridged.

This is the little story. Pure food and the highest of ideals plus well-balanced cooking and moderate eating bring with them health. Our hearts are very strongly with those who are fighting so bravely to prevent the murder of innocent animals for food and furs, not just because the meat makes them sick but because of a higher regard for our younger brothers in the lower kingdom. We are heart and soul with all who are seeking to help man have better bodies and better minds, and there are none who have a greater opportunity to help than those who labor with the mystery of the food which man eats. But let all be masters of their sciences rather than becoming slaves to them. Help people where they are to see things better but never become a crank or faddist, for to do otherwise will only list you with the causes of the very troubles you are seeking to remove.

## COURAGE VS. TIMIDITY

IT must be true that even the bravest occasionally have those qualms of timidity which show out so strangely from the sun-colored atmosphere of everyday life. We want to present to you a few examples of human idiosyncrasies and let you judge for yourselves the cause and cure of these conditions.

Only a few days ago we watched a perfectly contented workman, a member of the riveters' union, eating his lunch halfway out on the end of a suspended girder about two hundred and fifty feet above the ground. He was joking and talking to his pal who was sitting in the noose of a rope about the same height above the street, swinging back and forth with a ham sandwich in one hand and a boule of near beer in the other. They were the perfect picture of contentment in spite of the mere nothingness that stretched out beneath them. They showed no signs of either nervousness or worry about them. These excitements were part of the routine of life and passed practically unnoticed.

But Pat has his weak point. He must get home every night by five p.m. as he is in mortal terror of the wrath of Mrs. Murphy, his better half, who holds more horror for him than sixteen stories of rarified ether. And his companion with the sandwich is paying Dr. Soakem three-quarters of his salary because he has a strange pain inside which is frightening him to death. He worries over it day and night but thinks nothing of swinging at the end of said rope by one hand like some genial anthropoid.

In the course of our wanderings, we also come across Captain Gustave Gasp, a well-known aviator, who does all the latest fancy aeronautics. He is strapped into his machine that he may do tailspins and nose-dives and turn nineteen somersaults on a dime. Captain Gasp fully realizes that a broken wire or the slightest derangement of the mechanism of his machine would hurl him to an untimely end but still he plays with the ether bubbles in divine unconcern. But then Captain Gasp is scared to death of a certain little wart on the end of his nose and every time anyone glances at him, his face bursts into vari-colored blushes which stream out as halos of mortification from behind that tiny wart. He is so bashful that he doesn't even dare to look anyone in the face because he knows they are making fun of his nose.

In the same class, we find Reginald Gluefoot, the human fly, who plays pool with the brass ball on top of the town flagpole; also, Jimmy Shine, our well-known window washer who unhesitatingly clings to the windowsill of the nineteenth story of the Blazen Fire Insurance Company, whistling "My Country 'Tis of Thee," while thousands of people down below open their mouths in amazement just in time to have them filled with suds.

Now Reginald Gluefoot is a man of affairs. He has held on by one finger and chinned windowsills with his thumbnail a thousand times, but he will go around the very picture of misery if his necktie happens to be a little crooked. He has matrimonial difficulties and being a man of prominence rushes in terror to the newspaper offices at regular intervals praying that they will not air his domestic problems. He is more afraid of the newspaper than of twenty-nine stories of abstracted vacuum; he is frightened to death of public opinion and every time anyone even whispers his name he breaks out in a cold sweat.

With Jimmy Shine it is different. He is afraid of neither space nor time and would as soon hang on to a comet's tail as walk down Broadway. But Jimmy will not work on Friday the 13th, is scared to death of black cats, and all the money in ten kingdoms couldn't make Jimmy walk under a ladder or go against the dictates of his ruling planet.

About this time, Rebecca McFag goes over Niagara Falls in an eggshell, following this with a dive from the fifteenth story of the City Hall into a fire net. While she was receiving the applause, someone told her that she had a hole in her stocking, whereupon she fainted from stark horror.

Joseph Teasem is a man who was loosened into a brass cage with sixteen ferocious lions and glorified in the experience. This same individual however is very bashful and when he was loosened among some doting admirers of the fair sex, his terror was so great that he went into convulsions and died, his last words being, "If they had only allowed me to fight ten man-eating sharks instead of bringing me in to this social swim, I'd have been all right."

Sylvester Slide, the world's famous ski jumper, jumped two hundred and eighteen feet and landed on a track four feet wide where a single slip meant death. He does this three times a week for the consideration of ten dollars per each. But if anyone suggested that he go out without shaving, he wouldn't dare to stick his nose between the portals.

Now, friends, we will ask you once more why an individual who is willing to swing from the Ule end of a rope ladder by his toes is afraid to contradict the parson? How come's it that an individual who is perfectly willing to take a parachute jump into the Atlantic is afraid to grow whiskers when his wife says no? We repeat, why is it?

## ABSTRACTIONS

ONE of the greatest curses that confronts the student of occult philosophy is his inability to get any real information he is flooded with concepts and abstractions but not one of them is capable of solving the practical problem. There is no greater abstraction on the face of the earth than the word "Truth" which covers every doctrine and misquotation known to man. We are told that Truth is the answer to the problem, but we are not told what Truth is. Those who claim to have it, demonstrate only an abstract condition which cannot possibly he true because it does not answer any problem, solve any difficulty nor educate the human mind in any practical way.

Such words as "truth," "love," "God," "Law,""Light" and "Realization," are all of them absolutely abstract. We do not know whether the light referred to is gas, electric, or spiritual; and if spiritual, we have no idea of its dimensions, power, use, or means or perpetuation. Our so-called students of new thought pepper their entire phraseology with these abstractions which mean absolutely nothing to average heathens like us, but are used like Latin phrases by the professional people to conceal the sum of human ignorance.

So, we humbly request that these words only be used in connection with concrete, descriptive adjectives and that the process he explained along with the nouns in question.

There is no greater abstraction in the world than to say: "Believe in God." I have never met anyone who has the slightest idea of what God is and not one in a million knows the mental alchemy which must be passed through in order to hatch a belief. The average individual does not know how to believe anything. The statement "be good" is the first cousin to the above, but have two individuals ever come to a mutual understanding as to what is right and wrong? Good and bad are relative terms and have no earthly bearing upon the path of attainment.

Next door to these two is the emphasis of the "I Am" which we find so often, such statements as "I am God." These phrases and paraphrases come forth with ease and fluency but the realization of either the "I Am" or "God" is impossible for the two-by four minded person who robs these bits of language so unctuously under its tongue. It sounds good but it "don't mean nothing."

Man can only understand in a hazy way even the first principles of religion and to do so the most careful primer is necessary, one which grabs every ideal in the simplest language in order that any sort of understanding may he attained.

We know people who have "realizations," who are "living in the light" and who are "saved," and when they say these things, they say everything for they couldn't explain the process to save their neck. They have accepted some mental aphorism or tied themselves to a parrot like concept and use it as the basis of their salvation. We are sorry for them, but they do not seem to be very sorry for themselves, so we can do no more. We humbly suggest that each individual analyzes his belief and finds out whether or not he has any foundation other than a concept for his phase of religion. When he says, "I know the law" we expect an individual with a Darwinian intellect and a Spencerian brogue, a disciple of Platonic reason and it master of a priori and a posteriori reasoning to whom the mysteries of the universe are an open book and who can tell just how many granules there are in a ham sandwich, etc. Instead of this, he is some perfectly ignorant individual who doesn't even know that Spencer is sick or whether he passed out some years ago. He comes up to us in sublime and colossal ignorance and tells us that he knows the law and is saved, when he has never even been formally introduced to common sense. He tells us that he is the "victim" of a revelation and we listen expectantly for a continuation of John's divine discourse on Patmas, but nothing follows the first statement. He merely informs us that he has found the "real." Having found it, is he unable to even tell where it is?

A party came up to us a short time ago to tell us that she was "in Truth." We immediately visualized the molten sea, fed by the outpourings of living water, streaming from the souls of Zoroaster, Buddha, Krishna and Confucius. Having three or four questions we have never been able to answer, we immediately were filled with a great hope that the individual who had just arrived in Truth might be able to illuminate us on some dark corners and tear the veil from our mortal vison. We started in with an easy one, being desirous of knowing just how long the Paleozoic period lasted. We received nothing but a blank look with a hole in the center, so feeling that we may have misjudged the "ray" we presented our second difficulty, namely, why has the Chinese dragon five toes? The individual addressed took on an injured expression this time, and we politely refrained from further questioning for fear that we were offending her delicate nerves. But when this person asked us with all seriousness whether the earth revolved around the moon or bay, we began to doubt the source of their illumination and began to seek the basis of the declaration that they had discovered "Truth." We found as usual that they only thought they had, they had paid sufficient for it to buy a house and a lot. It was an aphorism dealing in a hazy way upon the relationship between Truth and Isness and so of course this put them in the "light" but their children still continue to have whooping cough every winter and they still spend half their time under the influence of aspirin.

It is a sad thing that we should have so much illumination and no light, so much knowledge and no wisdom, so much thought and no philosophy, so much logic and no reason. But we suppose it is the result of the rapid growth of minds and the tremendous influx of illumination. It must probably be that the mind is growing so rapidly that it is devouring all the brain cells. We cannot help agreeing with the ancient philosopher who said, "Oh, man! The mirror of vanity! He reflects the glory of the universe but inhales only the empty ethers."

## BROTHERS OF THE SHINING ROBE - V
(Continued)
### CHAPTER FIVE
### The Blow in the Dark

UNDER the direction of the Master, I had been carrying on my work for several years in London with ever greater success. The soul-hunger of the world, long debarred from light, had awakened in them the desire for further illumination upon the intricate problems of life. Each day I came into closer contact with the souls of men and women who were seeking in a great darkness for a light which neither theology nor science was capable of giving them. With these I worked, laboring to give to them the light which poured into me from the gray-robed figure of the Initiate.

The strange feeling that came over me when I first met that Great One never entirely vanished but the nervousness and the great chill of his presence slowly left until only an indescribable something told me when he was near. I did not often see him but sometimes upon awaking in the morning I would look for a brief moment into a face which seemed floating in the air before me and which trailed off into a nothingness as I went about the work of the day. Within my own being a great light was being born. I could feel a twisting, turning something in my own body as a mighty serpent struggling for freedom and by this, I knew that the light of the Master was slowly developing and nurturing the spark of itself within my own soul. Each day I came closer to communion with myself, closer to the realization of my own work, more and more the unseen worlds opened to me, until I seemed an inhabitant of many planes. But with it all remained that something so often lost that human touch and the mortal simplicity.

One evening as I sat alone in my study, before me a number of manuscripts which I was preparing for publication in European journals, I felt that inscrutable something which I knew to be the presence of the Teacher. Surely enough, he walked from behind my chair, around to the side of the great reading lamp and sank into an overstuffed chair beside me, his deep black eyes and slender, graceful form seeming strangely out of place among the prostic surroundings of modem London.

"Your work is going well," the Master spoke in his soft yet deep and over powering lanes. "You have met the obstacles that have confronted you honestly and truly, but your ever awakening power and the ever-broadening circle of your work is bringing you before the eyes of many people, not all of whom will accept or understand your message. There is also in the world not only the power of light but the power of opposition and as surely as the message you are giving broadens, so surely this growing light invokes the power of the shadow. Just as our sacred order has its temple in the heart of the Himalayas from which it pours forth into the world its streams of life and power, so surely there dwells in the shadows of these mountain peaks the powers of darkness. Be ever on your guard, be ever true to the light that you have, be ever prepared, for from the home of the Black Light has issued forth a rumbling. The work you have done has reached their notice and in a thousand ways they will attack you and through many innocent people whom they use as tools will seek to thwart the spreading of this sacred wisdom. Beware, my son, for they fight not with the weapons of light but with the weapons of darkness."

I turned to the Teacher: "Master," I questioned, "What is there to fear when you are near? How can the powers of darkness injure that which is ordained of the light? What power in heaven, earth, or hell should I fear?"

"Thou shouldst fear nothing, my son, for fear is a brooder of demons. Fear not, but neither be rash. The power of night is ruler of one half the circle of the hours and is equal in strength and power with the light of dawn."

The Master and I then talked for several moments about other problems, of the spreading of the work, of the labor of other Chelas in the world, and arrangements were made for the cooperation of future work.

"There is one in London now," said the Master, "whom you should know, one who passed into the Temple of Caves fifty years before you did and was the only one before you came who had entered it in three centuries. She took her initiation in the Western hemisphere but was taken by the Master out of her physical body, which remained in a state of coma for fourteen days, and carried over the top of the Himalaya mountains to Sangazi where she was privileged to receive the benediction of the Lord Maitraya. I have made the arrangements which are necessary for this meeting," The Master took from the breast of his robe a slip of paper upon which were traced a number of figures. "You know this alphabet and this writing," he said, handing it to me. "It is the secret cipher of the Adepts. This tells you where to go and you are to meet me there at eight o'clock this evening. Three of the other Masters will be there and together we will outline a program for the reconstruction of our beloved world-heavy beneath the weight of its self-created woes."

The Master rose and walking towards the wall on the opposite side of the room slowly passed through it and out of sight. I sat for several seconds wrapt in thought. The great moment of my life had come, I was to be taken into the circle of Adepts who were the Chelas of the Masters of Wisdom and was to join forces in a conscious way with the molders of human destiny. A great thrill of fear came over my being. How could I enter their august presence? And then another thought came. The sweet simplicity of my Master had always won my admiration, and I felt that the others too would be like him and was reassured.

The moments passed slowly until about seven-thirty and then dressing myself with the greatest care in order to make the best appearance possible, (with a certain element of human vanity that still remained), I called a cab and giving the driver a number, some few doors from the house where I intended to go, I sat back in the darkness of the car while we wound our way in and out through the evening traffic. Here and there a light shone out from some cafe or club, where England's upper set gathered, but soon the customary fog was upon us through which the lamps shone like haloed stars. I saw the great lions of Trafalgar go by and old Regent Circle and slowly we threaded our way out into the residential section where gray stone fronts and narrow streets spoke of the London of centuries gone by. At last, the cab stopped and the driver, in his heavy coat and over cape, opened the door and allowed me to descend under the gleam of a street lamp.

"This is 'im," the cabby remarked, nudging at empty space with his thumb. I tossed him a coin and, followed by many polite bows, headed along the street. My eyes turned to the numbers on the houses. At last, I reached the one shown on the address and looked up at a dingy old front of the early Victorian middle class which loomed down blankly upon me. The windows were small and checkered-paned, many of them broken, and the whole house seemed shaded with dissolution and death.

I looked around carefully and then slowly ascended the steps which led up to the door some dozen feet above the street. I was on about the fourth step when a peculiar sensation struck me, I felt someone behind me. It was not the presence of my Master but a cruel, cold, slimy presence that brought terror to my soul. I tried to turn. As I did so, a blow struck me directly under the heart. Staggering, and my knees bending up under me, I swayed upon the step. As I did so, I had a fleeting glimpse of the figure who stood behind me, one dimly outlined in the mist of the London fog. It was a tall heavily built form, draped in black robes, from whose hands were streaming two red flamed bolts which seemed pounding at my heart. The figure vanished. In the ethers and at the same time something welled up into my mouth, looking down, I saw the steps at my feet spattered with blood. Then everything grew black and the last thing I remember was pitching forward and downward into the fog, which seemed to rise like clouds of blackness around me. A thud, which did not seem to hurt me, and a choking, many lights dancing before my eyes, a confused sound as of voices and then utter blackness.

When my eyes opened, I found four figures gathered around me. I could not see very clearly but they seemed to be three men and one woman. One of the men I recognized as the white-robed Master. A soft musical voice spoke:

"He is coming too."

Another voice said, "Yes, but it was a very close call."

"Who struck him?" asked the musical voice again.

"It is the work of the Black School in London, I believe," answered my teacher. "Brother H. has become too prominent a figure lately to escape, but I never thought they would attack him here."

Suddenly, the four figures broke into their group, and standing in a row became silent. At the same instant another figure joined them, his body and the lower part of his face completely concealed by a black broadcloth evening cape with high turned collar. As I watched him in my lying position, I saw tiny golden flames flickering out from all parts of his body, which seemed rather small of bone and fine of texture. He spoke in a voice which sounded strangely different, as though his larynx were of gold.

"What is it?" Then he looked down at me, and leaning over, held out his hand.

"Let me help you up," he suggested, and taking my hand in his, he drew me to my feet with a strength I had not dreamed he possessed.

"Yes, it was a close shave. But come brethren, the Spiritus Sanctus is ready and there is work to be done."

Motioning me to follow him, he entered a door which suddenly appeared out of the blackness of space and into a room lighted by a glorious carved oil lamp. The doors slowly closed and be motioned each of us to a chair. Upon the table in front of us law a number of papers and documents, some of them sealed and others tied with many colored ribbons and cords. Then he in the long cape discarded his garment, and I saw a pale-faced man, slender and effeminate in form. With hair rather long and a slightly drooping mustache. He kept stroking his chin as though a beard, but there was none that any of us could see.

"Brethren," he said, taking one of the documents and breaking it open, "this is the appointed work which is to be done at this time and you four are appointed to do it." He turned to my Master.

"You, as my brother, are to take charge of this work; these three your Chelas, will labor as you direct. I am returning to Mongolia to secure further instructions from K. When I have secured these instructions, I will mail them to you with my signet. Accept nothing else."

My Master bowed his white turbaned head. "It shall be so, brother, for you speak from M. C. which is sufficient."

"Let there be doubt," answered the pale-faced stranger. And, reaching into his vest pocket, he took therefrom a small object which he concealed in the palm of his hand. He turned towards my teacher. A pale glow reflected itself from the face of the Master and he made a strange sign upon his forehead.

"It is sufficient," said my Master. "It is the seal of the Mahachohan."

The stranger resumed his cape and then, taking the letters laying upon the table, he turned them over to the Initiate of the Caves. Rising, he bowed to each in turn who stood at his departure. Only my Master remained seated.

"It is well, brethren," spoke the stranger, taking his hat in his hand. "I will be in London again in November when I shall look forward to the report of your labors. This is the year of the Great Benediction and is an important one for our work. May the grace of God rest upon you, and the power of His Holy Name protect you."

And, quickly drawing the folds of his cape around him, he vanished as though he had never been. As soon as he was gone, the Master spoke:

"He, my son, is one of the great brothers from whom we learn the will of Vaivaswati. The plans are laid the work is at hand. Now I will explain to you your appointed parts."

And, opening one of the documents, he spread out a many-colored chart upon the table, drawn in brightly colored pigments on a surface of gold beater skin. "Behold, the plan."

(To be Continued.)

## THE MESSAGE OF THE GREAT INITIATES

ALL down through the ages since the beginning of time great teachers, appointed by the spiritual hierarchies, have come to man to instruct him and reveal to him the next step in his endless path of self-unfoldment. Each of these great messengers has brought a distinct doctrine and when linked together their teachings form a golden chain of ideals which the human race must aspire to even though it may not be able to fully realize the end or the way.

For the benefit of the student of occult philosophy we list below twelve great spiritual teachers, many of them now regarded as allegorical rather than historical personages. However, the deep student realizes that mythology is the truest history of the ancient people that we have and that only in folklore and legend do we find an authentic record of the great Light-bringers and their messages to man.

1. Hermes. This great Atlantean demi-god, probably if not actually the

greatest illuminator of mortal man, taught as the key of his philosophy-analogy. The relationships existing between the inferior and the superior worlds was the basis of his doctrine and the knowledge of Ule simile was man's first revelation. Hermes is often called the first messenger of God because he is the oldest that we know and his law of analogical reasoning is the basis of every philosophy of modern times. The essence of his teaching was that God and man were made in the same mold and that all things in the lower world and the lesser sphere are made after the same pattern as the greater thing in the superior world. He taught that the realization of this was the fundamental principle of wisdom.

2. Orpheus, the Grecian demigod, taught man the law of Harmony and the great work of harmonizing the spiritual and material qualities within his own soul. The seven-stringed lyre of Orpheus represents the seven major rates of vibration known to consciousness at this time. Upon these rates of vibration, which are the basis of form, thought, growth and culture, his philosophy was based, his seven-stringed lyre representing the solar system and the seven centers in the human body and upon this he taught man to play the harmony of nature and the music of the spheres. This harmonization of the centers of consciousness was the redemption of the human soul (Eurydice).

3. Krishna, the great Indian Christ and the most beloved deity of Brahman theology, is said to have had Love as the keynote of his teaching. He taught man of the love of God for His creations, the love of the spirit within for its bodies, and the love existing always between the spiritual and the human. He taught man to live in peace with his neighbor and to recognize the fundamental duty of regard and respect for all other created things. Krishna, the Christ-child of India, is symbolical of the sun, who is in love with Radha, the East Indian symbol of nature. The marriage of the sun to nature and the love of God for His outpourings was the center ground of his divine message to man. He taught immortality and the nonexistence of death, that ignorance was the basis of oblivion and that those who love only the Light would never he in darkness.

4. Buddha, the world's most eminent reformer and regenerator of ideals, brought mankind the doctrine of Renunciation and Non-attachment as the basis of immortality. He told man to renounce the temporal for the eternal, the illusion for the reality, the lower for the higher, and the outer for the inner. He taught that attachment was the basis of sorrow and that freedom from attachment was the basis of peace. Upon his doctrines has been based the greatest religion upon the earth at the present time, a creed which has influenced the destiny of half Ule people of the earth.

5. Mohammed. The essence of the faith of Islam is the necessity for Obedi-

ence and man's perfect willingness to leave his destiny in the hands of the Immortal. Mohammed taught that the greatest glory was for him who obeyed the laws rather than for one who creates a law; that those who leave their destiny with the powers of the Divine and follow those laws in simplicity and trust, obeying them to the letter, shall never want for the treasures of the eternal.

6. Moses taught the children of Israel and the ancient world the omnipotence of Law; the justice without mercy of law, the impersonality of law and that those who would break law are themselves broken upon it. He delivered the tablets of the ten laws to the children of Israel, teaching them that law is the voice of God and that those who keep His laws are the ones He blesses and preserves.

7. Zoroaster, the great founder of the faith of the Parsees and the Fire-king of Persia, taught the doctrine of Light and said that the sun and flame were the most precious things in the universe. He taught the building of that Fire within the soul of the individual; that the fire that burnt in man is the eldest of all flames; that man is dependent upon fire and that this fire is the divine essence of God within himself. In other and simpler words, he taught the indwelling presence of the Divine.

8. Confucius, the great un-apotheosized saint of China, a god made so by the love of his people, taught that Morality was the greatest of all virtues and the most acceptable quality in the universe; that the salvation of man depended upon his relationships to his fellow creatures; that purity, chastity and fraternity were the greatest of all qualities and that religion, in essence rested upon practical works rather than theoretical dogmas.

9. Plato. Plato's doctrines were based upon the principles of Logic and he taught his disciples the orderly creation, the logical creation and the reasonable in the universe. He taught a geometrical base of all growth and instructed his followers that the universe, God, man, and nature are mathematical units capable of exact analysis.

10. Odin. This great Initiate who illuminated Scandinavia and the Teutonic countries, had as the basis of his teaching the doctrine of Courage. He taught the necessity of stamina and daring; that those who aspired to reach the footstool of light must dare all things, must battle against all opposition; and that reward comes to the victor in the battle and not to the one who remains at home.

11. Hiram Abiff, the great Masonic idol and ideal, taught in his unspoken life the doctrine of human Regeneration. Hiram, representing the spiritual essences in the human body, redeems himself and is redeemed through the path of the Masonic mysteries. Only in transmutation lays the path of immortality, and every human quality must be transmuted into a divine and eternal thing.

12. Jesus. The one teacher who is best known to the Christian world, but whose doctrines are the least understood of any of the great world teachers, is the Master Jesus. The key to his philosophy is Brotherhood and his ideal was a new faith built out of the mutual understanding and common interests of all of the others. He sought to unite all wisdom into one simple creed and also sought to show man the one simple labor which all creation is trying to achieve, each in its different way. Only those who have found harmony and are living in a state of brotherhood with other living things will ever know the message of the Master Jesus for he synthesizes all the previous world religions, for those who have the eyes to recognize that fact.

These qualities, if you will analyze them closely, you will find are absolutely dependent one upon another. There has never been a complete revelation up to date but all the revelations of the past gathered together build a monumental temple which is the expression of all known wisdom. This is the temple whose door is open to the student of the Wisdom Religion when he has learned to forsake dogma and creed, worship God in spirit and in truth rather than in clan and group. The message of the Wisdom Teachings to the modern world is, briefly, one of impartiality in which the student worships God in His many-fold expressions rather than his own crystallized concept of divinity which has so long been the basis of his faith. Only in the universal realization of the one truth, the one Light, the one path, can the student hope to make progress. The Light bearers are incidents and can receive our respect and veneration, but the Light is the thing which we should worship and not the One who brings it.

## THE TEMPLATE OF SIN - I

ON the heart of Mongolia, that unknown land of magic and sorcery, stands a strange building, pagodalike in structure and painted red and yellow. It is concealed in the wastes of a mighty range of mountains where white men seldom travel and exists as only a myth even to the natives themselves. From the corners of this grotesque building hang strange lanterns of bamboo and silk, bearing upon them Oriental designs and crude Chinese characters. A great flight of granite steps leads sheer up from the valley below, winding between the great pillars that form the gate and at last ending in a latticework door gloriously carved and lacquered in dragons and strange birds. On either side of the gate of this lonely temple stands a great dog made of wondrously colored porcelain, and on the base of each pillar where they stand is written one word. The dog upon the right carries the name Mirth and the one on the left Wrath. For many years these two animals, with their shiny porcelain bodies and heads maned like lions, their sharp gleaming teeth and great staring eyes, have stood guard at the entrance to the Temple of Sin, one of the strangest of the mysterious remnants of forgotten ages.

This temple is served and upheld by a small group of priests who stand firmly among the tottering creeds of ancient days guarding with fanatical faith this temple built by the hands of the gods to mark the place where the first man sinned on earth. The High Priest of this temple is a strange character with whom you must become better acquainted. A tall gaunt Chinaman of angular and sinister frame dressed in robes of yellow broadcloth ornately brocaded with flowers and trimmed with a crimson border, he wears upon his back a great Chinese symbol which means when translated "Immortality Forever," and upon the chest of his garment another which says "Mortality unbroken." No one knows the age of this Chinese priest but legend says it can be counted in hundreds of years and as you look at his wizened face, dried, seamed and browned, you can well believe that he really is as old as those barren mountains and withered lands that surround the temple. They say that this spot is shunned like death, for since the beginning of time, it was only meant to be visited by the sinners of the world.

The old Chinaman, with his hands crossed in his sleeves, was walking softly up and down behind the latticework of hand carved teak gilded with lilies and wondrous chrysanthemum. A faint odor of incense was born outward by the gentle breeze, filling the air with the pungent aroma of burning sandalwood, while now and then the dull boom of a temple gong told that the services of the gods were not forgotten and that the priests were gathered to pray. Suddenly, the old man held up a long finger, its nail encrusted with gold and curling some six inches beyond the fingertip; his wizened, slanty eyes opened wide and their whites, long yellowed with age, shone out like pieces of amber.

"Someone is coming over the Pass of Death," he whispered, pointing to the hills which surrounded the little vale in which the temple stood. As he spoke, the priests in the yellow robes gathered around him and looked where his finger pointed. And true enough, a thin line of dark forms could be seen in the distance, winding in and out among the hills. The aged Oriental looked long and earnestly and his old eyes seemed to gaze far beyond the mountain tops.

"He is a white man," he said after a while, "and he comes with a pack train. He is seeking rugs, rare silks and precious curios. Beware, lest he rob the temple! Close all the doors, save one and let the dogs of porcelain watch his passing." The monks bowed silently and, folding their arms in their sleeves, vanished like shadows in the temple passage way.

The old priest, upon his head a helmet of gold hung with tinkling bells and jangling ornaments, turned and entered the shrine room. Passing over the floor, soft with furs and precious rugs, he opened the doors of a tiny shrine and there before him, clasped in the claws of a teakwood dragon, stood a tiny mirror. It shone and gleamed with a depth, less light and in its burnished surface were reflected the many little flames of oil that burned in sockets on the wall. The old priest hunched his back and his cue, braided with silken cords, fell over one shoulder.

"Oh, Mirror of Quang Ke-Creator of all that is the first Being of all earth! There comes one over yonder desert whom my soul whispers are seeking to desecrate Thy shrine." He raised his thumb which bore upon it a great ring of jade and closing the doors placed upon the crack where they joined a soft wax pellet upon which he stamped the signet of the Emperor by means of the thumb ring.

"By the jade of the First Dynasty! May the Emperor of gods protect the shrine of this sacred mirror! May the five-clawed dragon twine himself around this altar that the defiler may not enter, for it is not the will of the gods that the Mirror of Sin shall be stolen!" Then, turning, he passed from the room as silently as a yellow specter and out into the courtyard of the temple.

\* \* \*

At about the same time, Hank Nicholson, buyer, and importer representing one of our largest Fifth Avenue stores, put his foot on the lowest step of the temple. Hank Nicholson was a "bad" man, but he always thought he was worse than anyone else did. He unclipped his revolver holster and with a hitch of his belt headed up the steps towards the porcelain dogs, one of which grinned while the other leered in stony salutation. Hank spoke fairly good Chinese in several dialects and soon made himself understood.

"I'm looking for rugs and curios, any good teakwood, ivory, hammered brass or idols that you may have around. Sabbee?" Hank held up a string of Chinese money and shook it under the nose of the aged Oriental.

The Chinaman, in whose eyes were a strange glint, kept perfectly poised as he gazed into the flat face in front of him and surveyed the stock of red hair that was Hank's crowning glory. He then spoke slowly:

This is no place of merchandise, of gold or silver. Or of ivory. This is the temple of a true God and has been known for ages as the Chapel of the First Sin. Here I live with a small group of priests, having no intercourse with the world of men. There is no use you're seeking here, for I have nothing to barter. To buy or to sell. I am a servant of God and not a silversmith."

"Aw, bosh and nonsense!" exclaimed Hank. "I've heard that before. How many yens for the whole damn temple and everything in it, except you? I'm lookin' for antiques and curios, but don't want anything as funny as you. Come on, Chinky, move, move aside and let's see what you got."

The Oriental bowed patiently and, stepping to one side, allowed the exponent of Brooklyn diplomacy to enter. Hank stood in the inner doorway, arms akimbo, and viewed the surroundings with an air of complacency.

"I'll get a half a million for this on Broadway!" he announced confidently. "How much Chinky?"

"I have told you, white man, I have nothing to sell."

Hank pressed with his toe against a rug before him. "That's a fine rug, Chinky, looks like a piece of genuine Thibet silk. You've got some good teakwood here too, I'll have some of my men come right in and pack it up."

The Chinaman bowed with great servility, but there was a wicked glint in his beady black eyes. "I must remind the white man of what I said before. This is a temple of God and not a curio store. God will defend His temple."

The American laughed. "A fine bunch of gods you got, Chinky! I own three of them that I use for bootjacks in Brooklyn and they haven't answered me back yet. Don't get sentimental with your religion now, because when Hank Nicholson wants somethin' he gets it, see?" and Hank pulled out his revolver and nestled it against the Chinaman's short ribs.

The Oriental looked down mildly on the gun and replied: "Three times have I enjoyed a white man's civility and alas, it has always been the same. The first white man I entertained stole my jades; the second robbed me of my temple maiden; and you, honorable sir, would take the building and all. I fear you must come to China and learn manners.

Hank stood nonplussed for a moment and then turned back to look at the room. Gazing around, his eye rested upon the shrine bearing on its closed doors the seal of wax. "What's that?" he demanded.

"In yonder shrine," answered the Chinaman, "is the Mirror of Sin made upon the eyeball of the God of Light. It is the most precious thing in all of China and rests in the claws of the sacred dragon. Those who have suffered great agony come from all parts of the world to pay homage to this mirror for as they gaze into its depths, they can see the reason for their suffering, and they know the sins for which they are accursed. So, they come to pay homage to its shrine."

"Ohhh," said Hank, "a mirror with a story like that would bring ten thousand dollars on Broadway!"

"I do not know what your wide avenue is," answered the Chinaman, "but if it is a place, the mirror shall not rest there. In my hands, I carry the temple gong. If you do not leave this holy place at once I shall ring for my priests and if so order them they will slay you where you stand and cut you into as many pieces as yon chrysanthemum has petals!"

Recognizing the flint in the old man's voice, Hank decided that discretion was the better part of valor, so he passed silently down the steps and out of the temple. But in his mind, a plan was formulating, a plan such as has; thrilled the hearts of practically every robber developed by Western civilization.

Drawing off a little distance, the American camped, and the coolies unpacked their burdens. As evening fell and shrouded the temple with its mystic lattice work, a tiny gleaming spark a few hundred feet away marked the resting place of Hank Nicholson, buyer, and his packtrain. Slowly, the monks filed out of the temple and into the little huts among the rocks where they slept and prayed. And lastly, the old priest, swinging together the temple grating, passed also like a phantom from the shrine. There was no moon that night, but the stars shone down and lighted the earth with a million fires.

As the chill blast told of the coming dawn, Hank unrolled his blanket and, in the darkness, crept across the sand among the rocks towards the gate of the Temple of Sin. The two porcelain dogs looked down in silence as he passed between them and stood before the hand carved wooden grating. An ancient Chinese lock protected the door, but this he quickly opened and passed as silently as a ghost into the inner shrine. The little oil lamp still lighted the room dimly. With an expression of diabolical greed on his face, Hank rolled-up rug after rug and his itching fingers played lovingly over the rare porcelains and carvings. At last, his eye rested on the shrine and something irresistible drew him over towards it.

"So, the old Chinaman says," muttered Hank, "that whoever looks into that mirror shall see pass before him all the sins he ever committed, that's a fine story but I'll wager it won't show up some of the little private affairs of my life."

He looked at the seal of wax for several seconds and then, taking hold of the two lower handles, drew open the door, breaking the seal. In the alcove stood the mirror, a gleaming mother-of-pearl held between the claws of the great dragon like some diamond in a Tiffany setting. A pale glow radiated from it and the American gazed into the depths of its surface in spite of himself. As he did so, he shrank back in amazement scene was unrolling itself before him! It was a lonely hill covered with clouds and seemed deep beneath the weight of approaching storms. As he watched, he saw himself. He was dressed in the yellow armor of bygone days and there swung from his shoulder a cape upon which was stamped the signet of Rome. He stood leaning upon a spear with his helmet hanging by a leathern thong from his arm. As he stood there, a rift broke in the clouds and then at his feet lay the shadow of a cross.

Suddenly Hank Nicholson gave a scream and, covering his eyes with his hands, dashed madly from the room, howling like a madman.

"No! No! God not that!" And his hurrying footsteps sounded on the steps of the temple walk while the grated door closed silently behind him. From the gloom which bordered the edge of the room, there emerged a silent figure, his hands clasped in the sleeves of his coat. The

(To be Continued)

DECEMBER 1923

## SPECIAL NOTICE TO READERS

Dear Friends: On the fourth of December next I am leaving Los Angeles for an extended trip directly around this old earth for the purpose of establishing contacts with the great religious centers of the earth, to make simpler the unification of the spiritual thought of the world by going to the very heart of each of the great world religions.

From time to time there will appear in the following issues of this magazine the results of this trip and whatever knowledge as to the spiritual, ethical, and intellectual status of the respective religions is in the world. In Kyoto are the great Buddhist universities, the greatest and most advanced of Japanese institutions. At Peking, we find the remnants of the ancient Chinese religions, while Benares has always been the home of Brahmanism. The Hermetic mysteries are outpourings of the great pyramid initiations of Egypt while Constantinople is close to the heart of the Mohammedan world. For many centuries there has existed in the soul of man a great misunderstanding of the world religions. He has come to believe that his own revelation is the one true and only spiritual doctrine. This is not so. Buddha, Mohammed, Krishna, Orpheus, Hermes, Zoroaster, Odin, Confucius, Lao Tze and many others have illuminated the world with great truths but modern Western civilization has practically ignored these great workers.

The entire trip will cover about thirty-eight thousand miles of land and sea and from it I shall gain the material to complete work on two large books of symbolism which I am now preparing and also for an occult encyclopedia which is to follow shortly. I shall be in constant touch with the headquarters of my work and the magazines and publications will appear just as though I were at home all the time.

This trip is for scientific research and investigation and not a lecture tour, though I shall probably hold meeting in the Hawaiian Islands and in London so if you have friends in those parts, it will be well for you to notify them.

Of course, during the months when I am away in order to better fit myself to express these ancient philosophies, the work will be under tremendously heavy expenses with very little revenue so I'm going to ask those of you who are interested in the maintenance of this work and who will be interested in the information which I will bring back with me to cooperate during my absence so that this slowly growing ideal shall not be crushed for want of personal supervision. The expenses of maintaining the work while I am away will probably amount to about seven hundred and fifty dollars a month. This amount divided among the total number of our students would not be felt by any but if it has to be shouldered by one or two, it is more than can be done. It would be very disastrous to go away without each one of the student bodies and those interested in our work cooperating during my absence. None of us can do it alone but if all put their shoulders to the wheel the thing is realized and if you wish to be of the great possible service during the coming month, just sit down when you can and send us a little contribution to help pay the ever-increasing bills. And if you will make it your business to sit down once a week or once a month and mail in that money which you would use to some purpose that would result in nothing permanent, you will not miss it very much and it will enable us to continue serving you more efficiently.

Please do not overlook this because during my absence the responsibility of the work divides itself among those interested and I do not want to come back and find the ship on the rocks when just a little thought on your part will keep it sailing upon the open sea.

If you will all cooperate to the best of your ability to distribute our literature and assist in whatsoever way, you feel that you can I am sure all will go well until I return from my trip.

Very truly yours
MANLY P. HALL

## EDITORIALS

## THE SPIRIT OF CHRISTMAS

THE bustle and confusion of our ever more self-centered lives is slowly killing out the beautiful spirit of Christmas. We see people fussing and stewing; we see them sinking back in their chairs at home, after a raid upon the bargain counter at the eleventh hour, with their hats over one eye and their corns singing in nine languages and three colors muttering to themselves, "Thank God, Christmas only comes once a year!" Then that other group we know so well who sends all their presents out late in order to see what the recipient sends them first and are broken-hearted if the influx is not as great as the outpouring. In other words, there are only a few people in all the world who have really preserved the true spirit of Christmas and most of these are children who have not yet been caught up in the maelstrom of our commercial ethics. The spice of Christmas is indeed losing its savor and with it's going will vanish one of man's greatest opportunities, which, like all that has gone before, he has abused and neglected.

The occultist must seek to build again in his own life the spirit of Christmas-beautiful in its simplicity, appealing in its sentiment and joyous in its ideals. Christmas whispers many things to the soul that think; it means more than merely the gift of one to another; it teaches in its mystic way the story of the divine gift which has been made by the spiritual powers of being to the worlds of men. As the child hangs up its stocking and finds it in the morning, filled with gifts and goodies, given in the name of old Santa Claus, that unknown person who is said to dwell at the North Pole, so all through life man has no greater opportunity than to give in the name of his God those things which the world needs. The spirit is Santa Claus, the Giver behind all gifts, who dwells in the North Pole of man at the upper end of the spine, and it is from here that the Ancient of Days sends out His gifts to the body, sends out His thoughts and ideals and gives His life for the glorification of the world.

Man must learn to make his gifts in the name of the spirit, not in the name of the body, for within each of us is the divine altruist seeking to be heard above the ever-crying voice of the human egotist. At Christmas the spirit of giving is said to rule the world for on that day God the Father gave His Beloved Son as His gift to the world and that Son is the spirit of life, of hope, and of truth that springs eternal in the human heart. To man has been given the work of expressing in the world of form this gift of the Father not only upon Christmas day but upon all the days of the year, for the child of God may be born in man at any time.

There is a terrible feeling that comes into the heart of a little child when the thoughtless parent or heartless playmate whispers to it that there is no Santa Claus. That is one of the heartbreaks of childhood-when that dream of the little old man with his rosy cheeks and twinkling eyes, his long white whiskers and his snug red suit, is dispelled in the mind of the child. From that time on, all the world seems false. The parents seldom realize enough of the plan of being to understand that they have destroyed a reality and not an illusion and have supplanted the reality with the false. The smiling, benevolent Santa Claus, with his ponderous comfortable figure and bag of toys, who slips down through the chimney or in some miraculous way finds his way through half inch lead pipes, is one of the sweetest concepts that man has. Santa Claus is the spirit of the Divine Humanitarian. He is always jovial, is especially fond of little children, and always brings with him dolls and toys, the playthings of the mortal man.

This jovial creature, is he not the great Olympic Jove of the Romans and the Zeus of the Greeks, is he not the spirit of the Jupiter period, expressing itself through the brain of man? The workshop of Santa Claus is the brain of man wherein the spirit conceives of the good works that it may do, the thoughts, actions and desires that it may send forth into the world to cheer the hearts of children. Directly above the eyes, at that point where the head starts to slope back to the crown, we have the home of Santa Claus, the organs of humanitarianism and ideality. It is there that this beloved Spirit of Gift, the philanthropist of human consciousness, dwells, ever hoping, ever praying for greater opportunity to give to others.

The spirit of Santa Claus, under many other names, has been in the world since time began, being brought over from the infinite not-time of eternity. In the silence of the night Santa Claus comes stealing, bringing the gifts of life and light to man. When we go to sleep at night, tired with the labors of the day, broken down by the worries and sufferings of the world, depleted by our endless battle against the substances of crystallation, the spiritual consciousness is withdrawn and we open our body for the coming in of those little workmen who, under the direction of Jehovah, the Olymphic Jove, rebuild our bodies for the day. In that way, very night, Santa Claus comes stealing, bringing us the strength, the courage, and the bodily health to carry on our endless battle. The vital forces that nourish the human body come down the sacred chimney as the manna that descended from heaven to feed the children of Israel in the wilderness. The Supreme Designer of things is ever the spirit of the benefactor, bringing light and truth and love to His children in the world.

And so, in honor of this greatest gift, the gift of life, and to prove that they realize this gift, the Christian world has set aside one day, the day which to them is the sacred of all time, the day when the Father made the supreme sacrifice and sent His only begotten Son, the spirit of love and truth, as the living bread which comes down from heaven. Man has sanctified this day and made it a time of gifts, for on this holy day, man is to renew his pact with the divine by making his gift to the children of men. Each one of us are gods in the making, each one of us carry the spark of the divine altruist within our soul, and on that day, we are to whisper this truth to the world by sending gifts to all whom we know. And these gifts must not he merely things we buy or sell but must contain the divine essence of the Eternal Humanitarian who gives the best that he is and has to his children in the world. On that day, we must give our light, which is the life of our brother men. "The gift without the giver is bare," and in order to be true to ourselves at Yuletide, we must give ourselves, our spirit, and our life with the gift that we buy. Listed below are some suggestions, some resolutions, for us to make to ourselves that we may be true to the spirit of Christmas and to the Eternal Giver who expresses Himself through the gifts of man to man.

When we realize the goodness of the universe and how Nature pours from her born of plenty her gifts to man, how Nature's eldest children, the World Saviors and Initiates, have sacrificed their lives and hopes that man may be better, when we think of the tiny children of the elements, busy night and day to make life beautiful and clean, when we think of the Masters walking the earth, living symbols of self-sacrifice and altruism, when we think of the spiritual rays of the universe pouring into us all the time our life and courage and hope, when our souls hear the music of the spheres as it thrills through our own heart and we understand better that all the universe cooperates together to serve us, to save us and give us opportunity for the fullest and greatest expression, let us realize that our duty is to be part of this great plan of salvation and send our strength, our light, our love, and our pledge that we too shall help to spread the light of life to the world of men.

At this moment let there be born in the soul of man the Christ, who is the hope of glory, that the salvation of man may come in this world of pain through that spiritual one before whom we how like the wise men out of the East, offering our three bodies for the redemption of the world. Man may offer gold and jewels, but they are not his; he may offer soft velvets and clinging silks, but they are not his; he may offer land and buildings, but the rocks belong to nature and the building is of the power of God. Man, eternally offers that which is not his, to which he is not tied by spiritual ties; he picks up handfuls of dirt and offers them to his God, to whom they belonged before. The only thing that it is his to offer is his body and the vehicles of consciousness which he has built down through the ages; he may offer his mind that through it the thoughts of God may be known to man; he may offer his heart that the love of God may be sent as a benediction to shine as a star of hope upon a world in pain; he may offer his hand with its power to mold that he may blend the elements of matter into a more conscious glorification of the eternal plan; but other than these three, he has nothing to offer. When the spirit in you is born, as on Christmas morn, you will live no longer for what the world may give you, but your joy and your life will be in giving to the world. The children of men wait, like the baby on Christmas Eve, for Santa Claus to bring his present; a world widowed in suffering waits and hopes for the coming of the light. May there be born in your Bethlehem this day that Christ in you who shall he the light of the world, the strength to steps that falter, the courage to lives that are afraid and the hope of glory to the children of creation.

Let this Christmas be different from all the others in your life insomuch as your spirit is with your gift, for a broken crust with the spirit of God is better than a string of pearls that are sent in emptiness, the heart makes the gift rich and the spirit makes it sufficient. Let us this year resolve that we shall give for the joy of giving, our reward being a happy smile in the eyes of the one who receives the token of our realization of the spirit of Christmas. The reward of the Master is to see his disciple smile for in the laughter of children sounds out a wondrous song from which pour streams of life into the heart the servant and the Master is servant of his flock. Let us this Christmas creep into the darkness of some waiting life and leave our token of good cheer, without name or symbol to show our presence, but only in the name of Santa Claus, the archetype of the Spiritual Giver, who labors all alone through the year to make the little wooden toys and dolls that bring joy to the heart of the child. And let next year be for us a year of labor that when again Yuletide comes around, we shall have a great sleigh full of toys, not perishable wood or little sawdust stuffed figures but great soul qualities built of thought and meditation which we may give to the world as truth and light just for the pure joy of giving.

Let us bury the hatchet of the past this Christmas and as one step in our realization of the brotherhood of man and the fatherhood of God send our memory and good will to those who have done ill by us, the friend who has been untrue, and the one who has broken our hearts. To such ones, let us send our token, for while the flesh has been weak enough to break our bond of friendship still, we are one in spirit. Let us give away this year that which we possess of love, truth and knowledge to a world long crying for our light, and let our first step be to make right the broken things in our own lives, the broken friendship, the broken pledge, the broken trust, let us this day forgive them all as we hope to be forgiven.

In all our giving, let it be as in the beautiful story, the gifts of Santa Claus, not a gift of men to men, not just a gift that the giver may be known. Let us slip silently in and leave our blessing and if any should ask who the giver be let us answer, there is but One, the spirit of God in man, who comes in to our soul as a babe born amidst the beasts but who someday shall lighten our way and show us the beauty of giving and sharing. Christmas is not a time for creed or clan, for family or for friend, but is a moment when all the world is banded together to keep trust with one who is the Friend of all. If they would live like Him, let each of them be this day a friend of all and like the sun, God's great gift to man, let the shining rays of our soul light the souls of the just and unjust alike, for man's is the privilege to do and God's to judge the doing.

When we sit down to our Christmas dinner, surrounded with the good things of the earth, it us not forget that we have other bodies besides this form of clay.

We feed this one many times, but how seldom do we feed the other bodies, which also grow hungry for nourishment and attention? At this Christmas dinner, may we feed the heart with its finer sentiments that great love and understanding be born there? We feed the higher bodies by the things that we do in our lives, which strengthen and harmonize with these bodies. During the year that has past, each one of us has passed through many experiences which differ with the position each holds in the world of material affairs. Part of the work of Christmas is to build into the soul body the fruitage of these experiences that the higher man may be fed with the conscious acceptance of experience, which is the only food the spirit is capable of digesting. Let us therefore take some part of this day and go away from the world and, sitting down quietly, review the last year of our lives, bringing to mind the good works we have done, the kindnesses we have shown, the mastery of over conditions which we have expressed, the harmony which we have radiated, and the services we have performed for others. Let us group all these together in our minds and spread them out before us on a spiritual table, for these things are the food of the spirit; upon this it lives and grows, by means of this it expresses ever more completely the qualities which we would that it expresses. This is the Christmas dinner of the soul where there is built into this wonderful star body of light, that robe of blue and gold, the fruitage of experience. In this way we become greater and wiser in the permanent things, feeding not only the body but nourishing also the consciousness which is the molder and regulator of bodies.

Let us also make our New Year's resolution of how we are going to conduct ourselves in the months to come; let us lay our plan to be strong where before we were weak, to grasp opportunities that before we overlooked, and to make our lives more useful every day, so that during the coming year in the workshop of Santa Claus we may prepare a greater and better harvest, more wonderful toys and beautiful gifts to shower upon the world when the spirit of Yuletide comes again.

There is nothing in all the world today sadder than man's inhumanity to man; where he should be kind, he is cruel, where he should be sweet he is heartless, and in these things he betrays the spirit of love and truth who comes to take away the sin of the world. Let him be true this year to the spirit, that the Christmas bells shall ring again with sweeter tone. How different is the sound of the hell tongue with its ringing anthem from the tongue of man, which slays its sharpness and destroys the plan with its cruelty? It is a servant of the emotions and not of the spirit.

And do not forget the Christmas tree, that sprig of evergreen which Santy brings with him. As this tree grows up through the snow and its bright green leaves never lose their color, so through mortal crystallization, through the chill of a heartless world, through the cold months of spiritual winter, the sprig of evergreen has ever been the whispering voice of immortality.

This year, let Santa Claus, the divine altruist in our own soul, bring his toys and his gifts from the North Pole and scatter them into the world. Feel him knocking at the door of your own heart and see his smiling face, inviting you to join him in the work of making people happy. He will tell you that his smile is the smile of those he has helped reflected from his own face, that he is happy and his cheeks are rosy because he is ever busy. Like the spiritual Jupiter, the humanitarian of the zodiac, he is ever seeking to make the way of life happier and more glorious. Get together with him this year and as occultists and students of spiritual things join him in making the world happy, slipping away again without ever letting anyone know who did it. Leave your blessings and be gone, give your present and leave unannounced, for the great give for the joy of giving and not in anticipation of reward; the true are rewarded enough in the realization that they are doing as the Master would have them. So, we invite you this Christmas to become a Santa Claus not a Santa Claus of make believe, but to feel in your own soul the spirit of the eternal Saint Nicholas who goes out to make the world happy.

## THE SECOND COMING OF CHRIST

FOR many years one great question has been uppermost in the minds of religious people, is this the day appointed in the Bible of the ancients for the second coming of the Christ? During the last few hundred years, many have come to teach the way of light and today many have claimed, or it has been claimed of them, that they were the second coming of our Master. Dozens of creeds have sprung up, each claiming to represent Him; dozens of those who have seen light and have given it to mankind have been pointed to as His incarnation. Many theories there are as to His coming and many wonder if they would know Him when He does come. The world is looking for a World Savior, a Great One who will bring it peace in sorrow, light in darkness, knowledge in ignorance. But, alas, few are preparing the way for such a One and His reception would indeed be a cold one if He came to the world today.

There is no doubt that the creedal theologies prohibit the coming of a World Teacher for they divide against each other and tear down their brothers' ideals and would fill His coming with wranglings and dissensions which would defile His very presence when He came. Europe is in turmoil, Asia is in revolt, America is asleep with her moneybags, and at this time there is no room for a Great One. All claim to want Him, but they would deny Him if He came, nor would they know Him if He presented Himself.

Now the questions arise: where will he come, what will He do? That is indeed a problem that needs deepest consideration. We point East, West, South and North, all need him. But all need something different; some need bread, others clothes, some need food for the intellect, and some for the soul. What will the answer be?

Theology has drawn a wonderful picture of all the people of earth bowing before a single throne, an idyllic picture but a useless one while creeds and languages, ideals and hopes are as diverse as they are today. Christians are but a wee drop in the bucket of religion and their work in the last few ages has not entitled them to very great consideration. Wherever they are suffering is with them, wherever they go, they murder, and whatever they do is with the spirit of selfishness. Their God and their lives are different things. Surely never in this way can they convince the world at large of the superiority of their doctrines.

If we are to have one Teacher to bring us light, we must first learn to live together peaceably that we may remain side by side in His presence without destroying each other, without superiority, and without hypocrisy. The world is raising its eyes unto the heavens, praying for help, but it is today still crucifying the ones who bring it help; it prays for light, then slays the bearer. In the infinite history of being man is just about four seconds old, and that is very young. He pulls hairs for his toys and fights for the front seat in everything he does.

A Teacher is needed but he must also be desired and his altar must be built among men, otherwise he can do no good. At the present time, there are many noble works in the world that are failing because they believe they are superior. But there will be a time when the one and only truth will not be taught as it is today, for East and West shall unite, North and South shall come together to teach the only and one Truth.

In looking over the messengers of God among men today, and find only egotists. They do great good and then ruin it all by claiming their superiority. Each creed is the appointed one, each messenger is the anointed one, and all the rest are less. It must bring tears to the eyes of the gods to see the foolishness of man. If ever there comes into the world a doctrine which claims to be the least and tells of the immortality of the others, such a one will flavor of divinity. But now, Smith and Brown and Jones are all anointed ones, each a little greater than the other until all three are highest. Each condescends to be kind and pity the other in order to show his Christian spirit, but all stand forth as self-ordained egotists whose usefulness is entirely destroyed by the strings of omnipotence with which they have tied up their truth.

Those who know, wait and pray, as they have waited and prayed through the millions of years that have passed, for One who is the least among men, who comes without words. And who appears not within the bonds of creed; they seek their Teacher among the hills and in the valleys, among the stones and among the stars; they wait, hoping that he shall soon come to redeem his suffering people and bring joy to broken hearts. All wait for the sending of the Anointed Son who is to lead His children from the darkness of ignorance and into the promised land. Hasten the day of His coming by living as though He were already here. He is a spirit, not a creature of this world; He is an essence, not a man; and He christens His anointed and sends them forth unto the souls of men. There shall be Christs in many lands for His spirit is legion, East, West, South and North shall feel His presence. Out of the worlds of men there come those to redeem men and upon their head is the oil of the Christ and in their hearts are His commandments, for He comes again in the hearts of His children where He has forever rested awaiting the day of resurrection. Wait not for one who comes in clouds with the chant of cherubim but rather hail one who comes enthroned in the souls of men; hail the Redeemer in the brother's heart and know that from there, he goes forth to save His people. He speaks with the voice of the martyr; He gleams out through the meditation of the monk; His sweeping sword shall prepare the way for better things, for He cometh not with peace but with a sword.

When the Christ in the heart of every one of us has stirred and whispered to the Christ in the heart of our brother, then the day of His coming shall be near and He shall Himself come into a world prepared for Him by His appointed messengers. Worlds are falling, nations are overwhelmed, peoples are torn with strife and discord, and all pray for rest, pray for the touch of the Lord Maitreya's hand to bring peace to the soul. They do not know that hand is in the hand of their brother; they do not know that voice speaks with the lips of men. If they knew, they would understand that He has come, and that the way is being prepared for a new day or righteousness and peace.

## A ONE ACT LITERARY TRAGEDY

*L*ET me relate to you a little story of one on our land who was inspired by his God to write a book in which he was to set forth some of the great mysteries of creation. In some insidious way, it was discovered that such was his fell intent. So, we open our little drama, a one act literary tragedy, in the attic where our budding author is buried in his rounds and periods. Already the manuscripts are heaped about him and strange, weird volumes, their pages embossed with symbol and design, are laying open around him. A second-hand, broken-down typewriter is pounding its very life away while the room resembles more than anything else an auction sale at Sotheby's. His mind is somewhere in the heart of the Himalayas trying to wrest from the innermost soul of his being some mighty truth to give the world, when a knock sounds upon his door.

He comes back to this mortal life with a shock and the budding idea leaves his mind forever, whereupon the world has lost a great thought-all for no other reason than that someone insists upon knocking at the door. Let us analyze the knock.

* * *

The knocker was animated by the vital principle of Mrs. Desdemona Chatterjaw who, without waiting for an invitation, walked in and sat down. "Are you Wilbermore Scribbly, young man?" asked Desdemona, adjusting her spectacles and gazing long and earnestly at the face of the author, said countenance haggard by his momentous undertaking.

"I understand you are writing a book. Now before you write it, I must tell you about some experiences I have had. You know I write books too, here's my first and greatest masterpiece, "Hoofmarks on the Sands of Time."

It is just filled with material I know you will need for your book, you know I was inspired when I wrote it. I was in the hospital recovering from the effects of an operation, oh no-no-no, I was there at that time because my husband threw a paperweight at me. It is those little things which broaden the soul, don't you know?" And Mrs. Chatterjaw looked down with benign condescension upon our poor author, who was in the last stages of passing out.

"I think you are very foolish, young man, to write a book like that. You are not sufficiently equipped for the work, your knowledge is not great enough, that is the reason why I have come to you. You know I have three masters. Here is the drawing of the spirit of an oyster that I received automatically. I know you will want this as the frontispiece of your new book, but if I were you, I wouldn't write that book at all because I have already covered the ground in mine, oh, yes, I am a teacher too, I have lived in India, yes, I have been up in the Himalayas too. If you only had the experience that I have had young man, you would be able to do great things in this world! I would have also, but you know I have such poor health. I believe I'm going to have to have another operation, but I just knew that I had to come here. I had an operation, by one of my masters. You know, I have one of the most unusual cults in the world. We have founded the New Jerusalem. If you will come there, you will be saved because all the rest of the world is going to sink. I saw it in a vision years ago!" Poor Scribbly grew weaker as the moments passed. He had not yet been able to get a word in edgewise but when Mrs. Chatterjaw stopped long enough to inhale, he broke in:

"Excuse me, madam, but at the present time, I am fully able to take care of my own affairs. I have felt inspired to write a book and, God willing, and my brother man permitting, I shall achieve the acme of my desire. In this particular part, I am dealing with silence and meditation, and I would deem it great consideration on your part if you would kindly allow me to continue this humble effort according to my own light. I am afraid that your master has misinformed you as to my crying needs for I assure you the only thing I request from humanity is that they will leave me in primeval silence and dissipate themselves to the four corners of creation."

Mrs. Chatterjaw leaned back, beaming. "Why, my dear Mr. Scribbly, you express my sentiments entirely! You know I just hate people who make themselves nuisances and I can't bear those people who talk when I am busy. I knew that we would come to a wonderful understanding! Now let me read to you from the fourth chapter of my book, thirteenth verse, it has a wonderful article on meditation in it. I know it is good, I wrote it myself!"

And Mrs. Desdemona opened her book and adjusted her spectacles. Mr. Scribbly was on the verge of that state of consciousness that editor's pass through when they drink the ink as Mrs. Chatterjaw started reading:

"Oh, enchanted ethereal vistas! how I long to be amongst thy voluptuous enchantments! Oh, isn't that beautiful, Mr. Scribbly? -my master gave that to me!" And Mrs. Chatterjaw clasped her hands and gazed at the ceiling.

"Humph!" grunted Scribbly in a tone like the Dying Gaul. "It's very nice, Mrs. Chatterjaw."

"Oh, I knew you'd love it, Mr. Scribbly! I'm going to read you some more. You know I got this one night while I was washing the dishes. I think it is one of the most beautiful things that I have ever read."

"Excuse me, please," said our fastly decomposing author, "but I am in financial embarrassment. I have paid thirty dollars a month for the use of this room and, while I love social calls, I must remind you that I cannot extract a living from them. As I must get this book finished before the rent comes Chatterjaw, I must bid yon good afternoon."

"Oh, yes, yes, yes, I mustn't detain you," answered Desdemona, sitting back in perfect ease, "but before I go, I must tell you one experience that I had on the astral plane. I was riding to the planet Venus on a green cow that had an aeroplane propeller on her front. I know you are a wonderful occultist, Mr. Scribbly, will you please give me your interpretation? Of course, I know already, but I want to find out if you agree with me."

She looked across the table and then gave a gasp. Mr. Scribbly had rolled out of his chair and lay face upward under the table, his body twitching and his eyes rolling.

"Good heavens!" exclaimed Mrs. Chatterjaw. "He's dying! Help! Help! I'll faint, I know I shall!" And gathering up her skirts and rare book, Desdemona rushed down the stairs to fall into the arms of a large Irish policeman who stood on the street corner.

As soon as he was sure that Desdemona had vanished, Scribbly got up from under the table, tiptoed carefully over to the door and locked it securely, muttering to himself, "There's no use. You gotta die to get away from 'em.'"

"Oh, where was I?" he ran his fingers through his hair-"What was I trying to write when that blizzard came in? I can't remember to save my neck!"

And here we will close our little act, leaving Scribbly to try and resurrect his thoughts from the maelstrom of thoughtlessness, with this little motto: The greatest thing you can do for your friend is to leave him alone.

# BROTHERS OF THE SHINING ROBE - VI
## (Continued)
## CHAPTER SIX
### The Plan of the Masters of Wisdom

The adept unrolled the sealed documents with care and reverence and laid out upon the table a great scroll written in strange hieroglyphic ciphers. This he read slowly to those present:

"It has been decided that drastic steps must be taken to avert the stream of perversion that at the present time is the result of a premature unveiling of occult wisdom. This knowledge has fallen into the hands of unscrupulous persons who are using the secret laws of nature to the overthrow of civilization. In order to combat this ever-increasing menace, a systematic plan is being formed to strike at the heart of each of these perverted rays. To you is given the work, with those four who are appointed under you as your Chelas, of attacking the destructive effects of cultism at the present time, both in Europe and in America. Another group has charge of the political reformation, another of the sociological reform, and still another of the economic problem. Within the next few years, a concentrated drive will be launched by the Elder Brothers through their Chelas and lay Chelas for the preparation of the birth of a new race. To this work, you are appointed. It is to unveil the false doctrines and religious viewpoints that are at the present time contaminating the ancient wisdom."

The Master laid down the scroll and looked searchingly at the three who were with him. "Yes," he answered to our unspoken questions, "we shall start at once. You brother, will remain in Europe, you sister will go to America. You," and he pointed to me, "will remain for the present with me in London while I prepare a concentrated plan of attack. Now let us briefly go over the work which is in hand.

"First, you will all know from your studies that religion is the first and last science, that all arts, sciences, trades and professions have issued from the Temple and must some time again become deified in the Temple. They are all expressions of the multi-personal power of the Logos. The development of the people rests to no small degree upon its spiritual ethics, and you know, as I know, that modern religion is rotten to the core. It preaches only death to the living and hell to the dead and has lost entirely its contact with the ancient wisdom, an empty shell floating like an astral specter with glazed eyes and unthinking brain. Our work is to revivify the dead. Each one of us must in the name of life obsess this specter and give it life with our life, strength with our strength, and truth with our truth.

"To supply the aching void in the human soul there have sprung up cults and isms one after another, based upon foolishness, served by fools, conceived by fools, but buried by wiser men. These too we must work with, for they are the outpourings of ignorance, speculation, and skepticism. In this work alone, that of awakening the dead ideals in the human soul is a labor worthy of gods. We must have a great concentration of effort and a great ordination of spirit to strengthen us in this task which we must accomplish with the diplomacy of demi-gods if we would save the plan of creation. Man must be brought back again to the ancient wisdom and reveal to the world the path of the seven lights. To this work, the Manu has appointed us, in accordance with the plan of being, and to give us these instructions the Great Brother came tonight.

"Now brethren, let us be faithful unto our work, true unto our instructions, honest unto ourselves. You in Europe must attack the black magic which is gnawing at the heart of our religious system; you in America must strike at the heart of prosperity-crazed ethics, commercialized religion and those cults and creeds that have sprung up to satisfy the lowest by the vehicle of the highest. It is a thankless work, those whom you serve will attack you, those whom you labor for will condemn, but in the infinite path of things you shall be listed with the redeemers of the ages." He turned to me: "You will continue to follow the instructions which I give you from time to time for the work that you have started in London has already been a great success and you had best continue until further information shall warn you otherwise. Next week you shall receive a certain person who will come to you concerning special instructions as to the treatment of the weighty affairs of state.

"In the meantime, a king is dying and for the purpose of saving a nation I shall hover over him, and if it be necessary I shall myself take the body that he drops. Kings are sometimes powerless, other times, have power, but I will tell you more concerning this a little later. The thread of life has not yet been broken but unless he turns from this hopeless pursuit that he is following, the Elder Brothers will destroy him.

"Now, three things I warn you of. First, the school that attacked our brother tonight has its branches all over the earth and will injure you at every turn. Our special work is to crush them, but they will not die without a struggle. Secondly, make a confidant of no one for what the world does not know it respects. Your power lies in silence. Third, eat and drink nothing that I tell you not of, for if you do, you will fail.

"Now, there is much to be done for His Majesty the king is low and I must travel halfway across Europe in order to be at his bedside. You have your instructions, here is a sealed letter for each of you which you are to open when you have left this place."

This tireless man stood, and we rose with him. He pointed to the door and one after the other we filed out; the Master bringing up the rear. He closed the door softly, and it vanished into space as we descended a rickety pair of stairs. Reaching the outer steps of the house, the Master saluted us and then dissolved into mist. I turned to the other two who were with me then gave a start, they also had vanished. I looked at the house I had just come out of and then stepped back in amazement; I was looking through the door of a highly lighted cafe. I looked on each side, but no such house as I had been in could be found for, I was standing on one of London's busiest thoroughfares. I put my hands into my pockets to find the address, but the paper was gone and in some unaccountable way, I had forgotten the number. I then realized that the house of Spiritus Sanctus was well guarded, not by soldiers and sentinels, but by the mystic power of forgotten things.

Calling a cab, I rode slowly past the brightly lighted buildings, headed for my own apartment. Suddenly I held up my hand, and the cabby stopped by a brilliantly lighted club with two crouching lions upon the steps. A figure had attracted my attention, that of a tall slender man in a high silk hat and evening cape, standing upon the steps conversing with a much shorter person. I called out to the cabby.

"Do you know who that man is?"

He looked for a second. "No sir," he answered, "but I have seen him many! l time and have driven him to the House of Lords when it was in session."

I sat back and thought. I could not be mistaken; it was that of the Great One who had come to the meeting in the little room. As I watched, he turned away, descended the steps and entered an automobile. A devilish curiosity prompted me.

"Follow that car!" I instructed the cab driver.

"Yes sir," he answered, and with a snort and a puff, the cab started off. We wound in and out through the traffic, always about a hundred feet behind the great black automobile, which spun out of the city towards the Waterloo station, and continued to curve in and out among the streets in a spiral, zigzag motion. As I sat with my eyes fixed upon it, following its every movement, a hand tapped me lightly on the shoulder. I jumped straight up about two feet and my tall silk hat went flat against the cab top. I turned nervously and there beside me on the back seat of the cab sat the gentleman in the evening cape whose car in front I had been following so earnestly.

"Did you wish to speak to me?" he asked, a smile playing around the corners of his mouth. It was the first time I had realized that the Masters of Wisdom might have a sense of humor, but I felt decidedly that the joke was on me.

"l-err-that is-I mean-"

"Yes, yes," beamed my companion, "your curiosity is quite pardonable. But do you not think a trifle unwise? A little too conspicuous, possibly for the good of all concerned?" He fingered the knob of the gold-headed cane that he carried. "Well, my good friend, I wish you a very good evening. If you are as arduous in your labors as you are persistent in your curiosity, you will do well indeed. You notice my automobile? If you have not, look closely."

I turned my eyes to the car and as I did so, it came to a stop about a hundred feet ahead. The door opened and from it stepped the gentleman with the tall silk hat who turned and waved his cane to me. I looked again at the seat beside me, but of course, it was empty. For some reason I was no longer curious and made no attempt to even note the address where he stopped.

With my squashed high hat on my ear, a very sickly feeling in the pit of my stomach and with an innate feeling that I had made a fool of myself, I told the cabby to turn around and not to stop until he reached my apartment and then sat back and closed my eyes to make sure that I didn't see anything else to awaken my curiosity.

"Two pounds, ten shillings' worth of hat," I muttered to myself forlornly, "and under it the brains of a jackass." At the same instant, a peculiar feeling came over me, as if something was drawing me upward. In a second it was over, but I felt strangely dizzy and, reaching up, took off my hat to fan my face. I looked at it in amazement-the crown had risen.

And this was my first experience of the humor of those who are supposed to be excessively stoic individuals. After thinking it over, I came to the conclusion that I was glad that it had happened because as the hat crown came up; I seemed to hear a soft laugh, and with the knowledge that I afterwards had I realized that the jester seldom smiled.

## LIVING PROBLEMS DEPARTMENT

### JUST A WORD IN PASSING

Prof. Steinmetz, one of the greatest minds of our age, who fought the battle of physical deformity and fighting against tremendous odds rose to a place of honor among his fellow men, has been released from a body which was always a living tomb to a broader and greater field of activity. With his death, another great man is found and those who would say nothing good of him, who never while he was alive, extended a hand to help him now speak of him as that great man. Why must our brothers die before we recognize their genius? Now Professor Steinmetz has gone, but his life might have been made sweeter and gladdened if a few of the words of praise that we now bestow upon him had been given him while he was alive. His battle against opposing thought was nobly fought and none know what courage might have come to his soul if someone had held out the hand of friendship to clasp his. But that hand which never extended during life now places a wreath upon his grave. Let us learn to honor our great men and women while they live instead of sainting them when they are gone.

## SPEAKING OF AUTO SUGGESTION

For those of you who are not acquainted with the fact, autosuggestion is a form of mental auto intoxication used to convince yourself that you are what you are not and have gotten over that which you know you have. The war cry is, "Day by day in every way I am getting better and better." But this form is too long for Americans while just suitable for the more voluble French, so in America the Coue string has been changed to, "Oh hell, I'm well!" We can say most anything we want to but while we live as we do, think as we do, eat and sleep in the way that we do and abuse ourselves according to fashion there is nothing upon the face of the earth that will cure us of anything.

## YOUR GOD AND MY GOD

IT was one of those little East side streets that we always find in large cities, where the rays of the sun seldom strike, where battered stone fronts and dilapidated bricks overhang streets, narrow and gloomy, and many ragged little children play on the curbstones or sail paper boats in the gutters. The bustle and confusion which marks the lower side of the life of a great city filled the air, here and there an old brick tenement rose gloomily from the surrounding shacks and the alleys were crossed and crisscrossed with clothes-lines upon which strange colored garments fluttered in the air. The day had been cloudy, and the clothes had not dried well but hung in the same dilapidated, drizzled way that the shoulders hung on those characters who slouched along the streets. The only joy seemed to be the laughter of the children, and they laughed because they were too young to cry. It was a place of sunken cheeks, hollowed eyes and furrowed brows, a land where despair dwells and where the wolf of need is ever howling at the door.

In the midst of this sordid neighborhood with its lifelessness and gloom, jammed in between a gloomy tenement and a sweatshop where a toiling humanity sold youth and life for the price of bread, stood a little one-story shack, broken in front and battered by age. Everyone knew this building, the little Buddhist church that had found its way into a land of many flags to minister to the needs of the children of India and Japan. It did not appear like the churches that we have, with rising spires and silvered belfry, but was just a little hole in the wall for it was a stranger in a strange land and the Lord of the Lotus meant little to those hungry ones who would gladly sell their souls for a crust of bread.

From across the blue Pacific and over many miles of dingy railroads there had come one from the East, bringing with him the faith of the East and the childish simplicity of the East, that indescribable something which fascinates the traveler who wanders 'mid Oriental climes. A few lonely ones in this great city had called him from the bright sunshine and green clad mountains of India, had called him to minister to their needs, so he had come out of his temple with its chanting priests, wreaths of purple incense and majesty sublime, and, as the least of the disciples of a Lowly One, came to bring the light of Asia to his people in America.

A quaint character was the little Buddhist priest. In spite of his strange gods, many of the people in that little tenement world had learned to welcome his smile and his quaint, broken English. He was just a little man, with big black eyes and kindly face, and, though the years weighed upon him, when you gazed at him you felt you were looking at a child. There was no guile in his look, no deceit in his smile, no airs about his manner, but there was something infinitely human, deeply touching, yes pathetic, in his brave. Battle against religions that opposed him.

The Buddhists loved him and came many miles around to his little church in the gloom of the tenement walls. They would go into the door in reverence but once through the portal they lived in another world for strange Oriental hangings covered the walls and the subtle odor of burning sandalwood and musk lent an Oriental atmosphere to the whole. There in a little niche of beaver board, upon which loving hands had traced the flowers of Buddha, was a little shrine in which sat their Lord and God, their minister of light, their consoler in sorrow, their hope of redemption, their voice before the Almighty, Lord Gautama, the Great Buddha. And here they came and brought their offerings, here they came to pray and sing their mantras, here they came in sorrow and in joy, young and old-far from the gods of their birth they found solace in this little temple.

One day, when the little Buddhist priest was out on the street, he saw a child playing in the gutter, playing with a little form of crockery or marble. He leaned over and there, gazing up at him from the mud, was a sad, pathetic face, carved and painted in some cheap but effective substance. The Buddhist priest gazed upon it for some minutes, then as the child ran away, leaned over and picked it from the slime. Something within his soul seemed to stir, for in that face was a haunting look that drew him irresistibly. He gazed upon it for several moments. It was just a little face broken off at the neck, that of a man with long brown hair hanging in ringlets, now grayed with the mire. Upon the head of the figure rested a wreathe of thorns and thin streams of blood were trickling down the agonized countenance which was turned with a strange pathetic look, going right into the heart of the priest. Holding the broken face in his hands, the priest of another God walked down the street and stopped at the door of a house wherein dwelt

Mrs. O'Flaherty, a kindhearted old Irishwoman who used to smile to him each morning as he went by.

Mrs. O'Flaherty often said to her better half, "Faith and begorra, that little hathen is one of the sweetest infidils I ever met. It's me mesilf that's sorry that he dinna belave in our God for I'd like to see him go to heaven."

Mrs. O'Flaherty was on the front step, waiting for the huckster, when the little Buddhist came by. Taking off his hat politely, he held out the little image and asked the broad, smiling Irishwoman who and what it was. Mrs. O'Flaherty looked for a second and then crossed herself with reverence.

"Faith, good sir, but thats the Son of the Blessed Virgin hersilf."

"Is that the One whom you call Jesus?" asked the Buddhist.

"Shure, and that it is!"

"It is a beautiful face," answered the priest, gazing in rapture at the little form. "He was a great man. Far off in my land we have heard of him and they say that he knew our Buddha and that he still wanders over the mountains hand in hand with him."

"Faith and I know nothin' of that! But I don't think he's hanging around with any hathen," answered Mrs. O'Flaherty, leaning on her broomstick and wiping her face on the edge of her gingham apron. "Sure, and if it gets much hotter, I'm going to move up on the roof again like I did last July."

"Will you tell me about your Master?" asked the Buddhist priest, still holding the little god in his hand. "I would know of him, for my soul tells me he, too, was a mighty Buddha."

"Shure! Sit down right here on the step and I'll tell yer about him till the dago comes with me potatoes, then Mikey's comin' home from the dump-yard and I'll have to be gettin' him some dinner."

Motherly old Mrs. O'Flaherty cast anchor, plunked herself down on the upper step, while the little Buddhist sat on the step below still gazing at the little broken image. Then Mrs. O'Flaherty in her homely way, gave her story of the Master's life.

The potatoes never came and for two hours they talked there. A great light came into the eyes of the Buddhist priest and something touched Mrs. O'Flaherty also for the childlike peace and simplicity of the Hindoo stirred her very soul. At last Mrs. O'Flaherty had to go and the little Buddhist, clasping the broken face to his heart, crept quietly down the street, shaded by the falling night, to his little hole in the tenement wall where his people came to pray.

\* \* \*

One night in December, as I was passing by the little Buddhist church, I stopped for a moment in amazement. A door was hanging by one hinge and its panels had been broken in with an axe. The windows were shattered, and the broken sashes were banging dismally in the evening air. There was a thin flurry of snow that day. The sidewalks were slippery, and the hurrying passersby did not stop to look in at the windows. All seemed dark inside, and I wondered what had happened to the little Buddhist church.

As I stood undecided whether to go on or to push aside the broken door and enter, a sound broke the silence. It was a broken sob, just one heart-breaking wail so low as scarcely to be heard but which seemed to strike the very heartstrings. Quickly pushing aside the broken door, I entered the little church. Everything inside was in disorder, the draping's placed with so much love was torn away, the little beaver board altar with the lotus blossoms traced upon it had been kicked to pieces, the little brine was overturned and on the floor in front of it lay the shattered body of Lord Buddha, his gilded form crashed in by the blow of an axe. One little taper alone was burning and cast its shadow over the scene of dissolution. On the floor, at the foot of the broken shrine and the shattered bits of the gilded statue, lay the Buddhist priest. From a wound upon his forehead, blood dropped upon the broken statue.

"What is the matter?" I cried, "how did this happen?" And kneeling down, I raised the limp body of the priest. He looked at me for a moment and then the tears broke out afresh. In the Western world, men do not cry, but in the Eastern world, it is different. I knew that it was not pain that brought the tears, but an ache in the soul.

"Tell me what has happened?" I asked in sympathy. And in broken bits I got the story; a story that is often told in the Western world though mayhaps not in just the same words.

"Oh, how hard I have tried to carry into your beautiful land the light of our God! He is a god of love and light, if you could only learn of my god, you would not slay your brothers, had you the love of my god this wrecked shrine would not lie here today. I came from far off India, a stranger in a strange land, to bring the blessing of my priest who sent me out to minister unto my people here, here in this land where people think only of themselves. This was my little shrine where I used to come at night and here, I have ever found love and light in the gaze of my Buddha. In the stillness I could hear his soft voice whispering courage to me in my labors. I have never injured anyone, nor have I ever sought to lead your people from their gods, I have just come to keep my own. Far across the sea they told me that this was a free land where people could believe in whom they would and pray unto whatsoever God they would, I came and for five years I have labored among my people here. I have tried to serve them with love and patience.

Last night when all was still, I came and knelt before my Buddha-before your God and my God, and as I sat here dreaming of the days when my Lord walked on earth and of the time when His blessing should he upon me, a harsh voice suddenly broke my meditation. 'Open the door!' it said. I rose and opened the door and several white men stood there. One said to me, 'Get out of the way, you dirty heathen!' Another said, 'We will have no more devil worshippers in our district!' A third said, 'To hell with those who worship wood and stone!' Then they came into my beautiful temple and broke the furniture, tore down the draping's -and one of them took a great axe and aimed a blow at my poor Buddha-my Buddha whom I brought with me from the caves of Gunga far up in the snow! My Buddha was made when the great Lord himself walked the earth and for over two thousand years has inspired and guided my people, I could not stand it! I rushed between my Buddha and the blow, then all grew black. How long I have been here I do not know, but it must have been many hours. When I came to this is what I saw. Is this what your God has taught you? Is this the one to whom you pray that he should kill the faith of other men? But, it is nearly done with me, I cannot battle with your world. Already I can see my home, I can see in these wrecked walls the snowcapped peaks of my mountains. For many years I have served my God in spirit and in truth and now I am going to him, I am going into Nirvana, into the home of Buddha. But before I go-say unto the world that I will go to my Buddha and I will pray to Him for those who broke his shrine, I will pray unto my God for his love and his compassion."

The heart-broken little priest raised himself for a moment and his hands closed over the broken statue of his Buddha. He turned the body around and there in the back was a hollow such as is often found in Eastern gods wherein they put their treasured trinkets or their books of mantrams. The blow of the ax had fallen deeply and had cut the body of the god in two and as he held it there fell from the broken opening two pieces of crockery. Picking them up and joining them together, I found that they formed the face of Jesus.

"How come they are here?" I asked.

The Buddhist answered softly, "Many months ago I found that little face in the street where children were playing with it in the gutter. Its sad look made me sad, and I brought it home and put it in the heart of my Buddha that the heart of my God might make your God glad."

He looked down at the pieces.

"Look," he whispered, "the blow that broke my Buddha's heart, broke your God's face is it not so, my friend? Is not your God glad with my God? Is he not sad with my God?" The Buddhist picked up the broken bits of plaster. "Look, they have shattered his face. In striking at my God they have broken their own, and I loved his face. It was so sad. But it can be no sadder than his heart this day. I can see a face beside me." The little Buddhist held up his hands. "Oh, Master with the Wreath of Thorns, I see you. You have come to me, God of another people. I loved you, but those who slew me have slain you. Look, I see the mountain in the sky, Om mani, padma hum! Lord Buddha, I come."

The form grew limp, and the tragedy was ended. A broken god and two little bits of plaster lay on the floor.

## THE CURSE OF EGYPT'S DEAD

LET us roll back the scroll of time to the day when rows of massive tombs, columns of sphinxes, and mighty temples lifted their crested domes in the Valley of the Kings, when a civilization now lost and gone ruled the world with the feather of Atlantean law. Man, little realizes the power of these dead peoples, nor does he accept their occult art, but every little while he is faced with indisputable evidence of the reality of the unknown.

Let us enter one of these tombs. A great Pharaoh is being laid to rest, surrounded by the scepters of his state, his body embalmed and preserved with spices and rich oils, and wrapped in the winding sheets of linen. With the golden mask of his state, he lies within the many mummy cases, carved and painted with glorious colors by the artists and artisans of a lost world. There also are the mourners, howling and wailing and beating their breasts; there are the councilors with their robes and serpent staffs; there too is the priest of Isis, with the mighty scepter of his state, the great hierophant of the Egyptian mysteries, who wield the power of life and death. The torch's light from the scene, sending flickering glows among the shadows to reflect strange lights from the golden ornaments.

On a couch carved in the shape of a lion lies the body of Egypt's dead. Beneath it are many vessels and jars containing the separately embalmed vital organs of the Pharoah. With him is buried the ritual of the dead, the papyrus of the doom and the wondrous rites by which the deceased may pass over the mountains of eternity, cross the river of death, bow before the throne of Osiris, God of the underworld, and finally pass on to glory in the Elysian fields. The walls of the tomb are carved with the faces of the gods and the judges of Egypt's dead gaze down in majestic splendor. The eye of Horus gaze unblinkingly upon the scene and Khepara Scarabus spreads its mighty wings as a symbol of the resurrection.

For a second, silence descended upon the scene and the priest spoke of the death ritual of the king. Then raising his staff and pounding it upon the floor, the priest muttered these words:

"Oh, Spirits of the Shadowland! Sons of Set! Children of Typhoon, Intestine-born! guard thou this tomb. Hear these my words which I speak of Osiris and of Isis. May the Ka of this dead pass on to resurrection but guard thou this body. The curse of the gods be upon he who shall touch it, he who shall break the sacred resting place! The curse of death be upon him who shall disturb its peace or defile its sanctity! Woe unto him who has not reverenced in the presence of the dead, who touches one stone, one jewel, who breathes upon the face of the dead, let him rot as the dead rots. Let him rot from the inside outward, let him become a living corpse for his audacity. It is said in the law that the dead shall rest in peace, and that this may be fulfilled I set the four sons of the demons upon this tomb to guard it through all eternity. One I place upon the north corner, one I place upon the south corner, one I place upon the east corner, one I place upon the west corner; then above and below, around and about, I encompass it with the curse of the gods and woe unto him who shall enter this living ring which I have placed! For upon him shall descend the curse of Ammon Ra, the curse of Osiris the protector of the dead, the curse of Isis the Mother of heaven, the curse of Nepthus the Mother of hell, the curse of Typhoon the Crocodile, the curse of Set the god of the dead, the curse of the seventy-two thousand Gatemen be upon him -may his bones wither, and his eyes fall out, that he shall die of the agony of decay. May the hand that touches this tomb wither, the eye that gazes upon it become blind, the heart that dares to enter become cold and the mind that dares conceive it become a blank. This is the curse of the Ring of Death, for it is said disturb, not the shade!"

The priest brought down his staff upon the floor. And so, it was done the laying of the curse of Egypt's dead, a curse which will not be forgotten, nor shall it pass unknown. Slowly, one by one, the figures filed away, and the light of the torches vanished in the distant corridors. The mummy lay upon its couch of lions, while at the corners sat four dim, misty figures, their hands upon their knees and their eyes turned upon the heart of the dead. They were the Silent Watchers, set to guard the body of the righteous dead. In the air floated strange creatures, twining strain after strain of fine thread around the body of the Pharoah, the soft beating of their wings unheard by mortal man.

There in the days of Egypt's glory that tomb was sealed, that graved was sanctified, that spot was hallowed. The rust of ages and the passing tide has laid low the arches of the ancients, the avenues of sphinxes are covered with dust, the papyrus columns are broken and overturned, and here and there a mound of broken rocks alone marks the resting place of Egypt's dead; but through all those ages time has had no power and the dead of Egypt still lie in state upon their couches of lions, still surrounded by their jewels and ornaments, still surrounded by the demons.

Man dares anything. And who shall say whether it is right or wrong that he should dare? That is the problem of his soul. But let him who dares be prepared to face the folly of his daring nor feel offended if the price of his folly is heavy. Today into the Empire of the Nile pours the scientists of many lands, seeking to establish the records of the past by robbing the graves of Egypt's dead. If they can succeed, let them proceed. It is their will and their life. But let them go prepared to face the curse for in all these ages the demons have not moved but like faithful watchdogs still kneel at the corners of their emperor's tomb and he who lays his finger upon Egypt's dead shall feel their curse. Through all ages the grave-robber has borne upon himself the curse of death and the fact that science needs the knowledge does not make the scientist other than a grave-robber.

So, as he enters in, the demon moves; as he touches, the demon strikes for the guardians of Egypt's dead know no rulership but the grave invocation that placed them there. It may be coincidence, but one after another, the defilers of tombs pass away as the curse narrates; one by one the grave-robbers sink to rest in the tombs they themselves have defiled. Whether they be right or wrong their own souls must judge, but this we do know, that the curse strikes and the silent specter's power is as great today as when the glory of Egypt was the envy of the world.

## SPECULUM ALCHYMIAE
### The True Glass of Alchemy
### BY ROGER BACON

salute or greet unto thee, most dearly beloved, the Class of Alchemy, which in my heart I have figured or printed, and out of the books of wise men have drawn, in the which is contained fully all that they have gathered to the perfection of Alchemy-I do give it unto your person, and in the which all things which are required to this Art be here gathered together, and those which be in diverse places dispersed: I shall thus answer unto your produce and wisdom, all things be created of the four Elements, and they be the Roots and matters of all things, and the diversity of things consisteth in three, that is to say, Color, Taste and Smell. There is not to me but three, viz. Diversities of Elements, divers Propertions, divers Decoctions, and divers Mixtions. Wherefore if ye will one Metalline Body transform into another, ye must know the Nature of one contrary and of another in every diversity, and when you know this, then you may by Addition and Subtraction, put to more of one Element, and the less of another, and seeth them together well or evil, and also to mix them together well or evil unto your own will and desire. And that may a Man do well in Metals if he might know without error how to separate the Elements, that is to say, to reduce them to their first Matter and Root, which Root is Brimstone and Quicksilver and Sulfur and Mercury, and then that is the Root or Matter nearest or nearer; but because the separation of Elements in Metals is difficult and hard, the Matters did seek how to get the Roots nearest without any labor, from Brimstone and quicksilver, and of these they made their separation of Elements, which they used, and said that only the Elements did cleave in Metals, and that strange Elements of other things, as the blood, eggs and hair, do not enter but by Vertue or by commixtion of them, with the aforesaid Elements, drawn of the Spirits and Bodies Metalline; but because we cannot resolve or separate as Nature doth, for Nature separateth without apposition of any strange thing in the space of a thousand years, and we cannot live a thousand years, therefore if we will make this separation we must find the cunning or knowledge by the which we may do it sooner; but this we cannot do by no ways except we do put unto them things divers and contrarious, for by his contraries ought ye to separate the Elements by our Knowledge and Mastery, therefore when two contrary things be mixed together one worketh in another, and so maketh him to give off his complexion and virtue, part thereof; for this cause ye must first learn to know the Complexion and Properties of all things, before you do enterprise to make commixtion together in their proper Natures, and it is needful that you know the work of Nature which you intend to do, and how much and what everything doth give, of his Nature and Complexion, and how much, and what he lacketh of another Complexion and Nature, by the means of the working which you do, and by the Nature of contrary things, which you do commix together, and if you do err in any of these, to know how much and in what; for if you know this, then you do know how to rectify anything of the world, and to reduce anything unto his first matter and complexion, or to any other thing according to your desire; then by the contrary, if you know not this you shall not enterprise to meddle, but by means of some things lo attempt to make ingression or such like until you do know this, and this is in light or in light things, and the Philosophers do say that if any man do know how to convert one nature into another, he knoweth all the whole mastery; and Avicen doth say the same, that so it is, all your desire ought to be to this, for this which I have said be the beginnings or Roots of Alchemy philosophical and medicine. And without knowledge of these Roots if you will do any work or medicine, which is called the Elixir in this Art to transmute imperfect Bodies into Sol and Lune, (of whatsoever the medicine was in his confection) you must think well of four things which I shall tell you.

The first is, that you do know how to prepare well all your things, and that you do know how to remove that which doth hurt most, and that which doth comfort your intention, and that you know the sign when you have that which you desire to have, and that you know how to remove that which you ought to remove: For all that man doth hath an end, and a certain term, for according to philosophers when nature intendeth to destroy anything, to generate another thing, worse or better, it intendeth to seek a certain degree which it doth not pass beyond and so standeth, and then another thing preparate, doth so provoke another special form which he had not before.

The second is, that your things separate you do know to commix them well together, and that is of sundry and divers things to make one Substance to be inseparable forever; for if you know not how to mix your things well and naturally, so that everything be destroyed, and so brought first unto their own primary being and proper species, and one new thing to be generated of them, it is worth nothing that you have done, and that you know the sign when your mixtion is completed.

The third is, that you know the certain proportion, that is, the certain quantity of such things as thou oughtest to mix together, and also to know by reason why it should be so, that thereby you may be sure to find the thing that you look for: By the quantities that you know to have mixed upon your melted Bodies, it will away at the last slowly or quickly how well soever the things were prepared, without they were mixed together according to Knowledge and Nature thou hast lost all thy labor as much as the final complement doth contain, and that shall be well perceived in the examination thereof, when the body trans muted is put to examination in ashes or the test, for there he will consume and waste away according as there was too much or too little of his proportion at the first; but if the proportions were rightly mixed according to Knowledge and Reason, then it shall not do so. And Rasis saith, if thou knowest how to convert Lune into Sol, thou knowest the contrary, that is to say, Sol into Lune. But to know to do this, there is a certain term and quantity hidden, which for to know thou oughtest not a little to study, that is to say, thou oughtest thereabout greatly to study, for Rasis saith, that the wise men did never hide anything but quantity and weight, and we care not whether people do know it or no, for we have made and written our books unto you that understand what we mean, and to our sons and children. And when you know that, then may you well perceive that no author or hook doth agree or accord with other in weight and quantity, and therefore for lack of the knowledge thereof riseth a great error, and it is hidden for this cause, that none but a wise man and learned may compass to accomplish the fame, which doth all his things with knowledge and reason, of the subtil knowledge of natural things; for if it might be had othenwise, men which do meddle without knowledge and reason, but only through foolish boldness, might have come to the end, they would no more have cared for the Learning and Wisdom of wise men, than for dogs, if that their own proper industry and wit could have helped them to have found or gotten it.

The fourth thing which you ought to consider, is the greatest secret of all and might wisdom, that is, that you know how to fortify your medicine and multiply his vertue, and this is a work of great prudence and wisdom, and if you understand this last, one part of your medicine will not only convert ten parts of anybody melted but a hundred, a thousand, ten thousand ten thousand thousand, and much more without end, according to the several circulations you shall make. And this which I have now said if you do understand, it sufficeth you, and I have touched all things that is needful, and they which do understand those things, they know the Art and none other, and to speak of this Art is to speak by means as we have spoken, and to work the Art of Alchemy is to work as we have said, and to reach the Art is to teach as we have taught, and he that teacheth any other teacheth nothing, and he that worketh any otherwise worketh nothing. For whom, so desireth this Art, if he does err in any of the aforesaid articles he shall never come to good end, until he knoweth the foresaid articles, and the wise man that glass purgeth metalline bodies corrupt, and cleanseth them: For glass maketh the metalline bodies of hard fusion, soft in fusion, and this is a secret. And with salt bodies are calcined and dried, for salt doth cleanse the bodies in as much as he dried up the sulfur which is in them, by which humidity they stink and be black and burnable, for the bodies calcined is clean suffering the fire without stinking, and this is a great secret; but know you that it is spoken for another secret, which I will not show here, nor yet will write of it, for it is the secret of all secrets; for by that secret, when it is well and perfectly known, a man may come to the secrets of all other kinds, and of this secret, I have showed you part, and if you know not that which resteth, I will declare no more neither by tongue nor pen. Now is ended the Glass of Alchemy which I have given for his name worthy the same, for in that you may when you will, behold, and see as in a Glass contained all the Articles pertaining to this Art, which you should desire of wise men, I believe that the Roots were never so gathered together as they be here, for which, understand you, and bear it in Memory according to knowledge, and that you do both hide and open according to reason, and as it ought to be, and not to show it to every ribald according to the lightness of the mind, for then that shall be vile which now is precious. In all the aforesaid Articles I will make you answer, if I have life and health, either by mouth, writing or words, so that you shall understand it if God will, and thus endeth the true Glass of Alchemy.

Finis.

This article is taken from a rare volume entitled "Chemical Essays" published in London by William Cooper at the Pelican in Little Britain, 1683. In the following issue, we will briefly consider the interpretation of this rather unusual alchemical tract.

## THE SYMBOLISM OF OUR NEW CROSS

BEHIND all symbolism stands two forms, the line, and the circle; the line is the positive, masculine symbol because it has no boundary, while the circle has differentiated between the within and the without and is therefore concrete and negative. There are two forms of lines, the vertical and the horizontal; the vertical is boundless life or intelligence of the Adi plane while the horizontal is boundless matter or cosmic root substance. The cross is composed entirely of angles and lines, and, like the masculine body, which is usually angular, represents the positive expression of struggle. From the union of the vertical, abstract intelligence and the horizontal abstract matter form is produced which is the concrete child of two abstract parents. Form thus becomes a cross composed of two lines which cross each other at differing angles, the intelligence of the form depending upon the angle where spirit and matter meet. On the other hand, the circle is composed entirely of curves; the curve being a feminine, concrete sign representing concrete expression, whereas the cross represents abstract expression. At the point of the crossing of the two arms of the cross a radiation begins as in the crossing of electricity and magnetism or the electric and magnetic currents of the earth. The spiritual ray pouring off from these two at that point of union forms a halo which assumes a circular shape. This energy striking matter builds a globular form, which is the concrete area of its intended manifestation. Therefore, among the ancients, three symbols were given to the abstract spirit of creation; the Father was shown as a dot, the Son as a circle (which is the feminine symbol for the Christ is cosmically feminine), while the Holy Spirit Jehovah is given the cross because His work is the building of form by the bringing into play of vertical and horizontal forces. The dot is creation; the son is manifestation, and the cross is crystallization; thus, we have the Brahma, Vishnu, and Siva of the Hindoos. The All-Seeing Eye of the gods is composed of a dot in a circle, which is usually hung at the crossing line of a crucifix to represent the Trinity in manifestation.

Among the ancient astronomers and astrologers, the cross in the circle was the symbol of the earth because the abstract power of the ever-existing cross was restrained by the concrete power of the circle which limits its manifestation. All spiritual bodies are born through the cross, all material bodies are born through the circle; the occultist and philosopher is the servant of the cross, while the mystic is the servant of the circle. The ancients built their temples of lines and curves to represent the alternately positive and negative in nature and how all creation is a blending of these two, but the great occultists built their temples without curves, as the pyramid, while the great mystics built their temples without lines as in the Grail legends where the whole building was a mass of domes and arches without a straight line. The curved and of ten circular windows in churches are all symbols of Matrapadma the Mother Lotus for they are remnants of the ancient worships which, under the sign of Geminus, instructed man especially in the laws of the positive and negative expressions of energy. The circle is symbolic of the cosmic egg while the cross is the germ of life which finally breaks through the shell of the egg but which is prevented from wasting itself prematurely by the protection of the shell. The sun, by precession of the equinoxes, has given us the cross. In Cancer, the Calvary was built or the base of the cross which, according to the Hindoos, was raised upon the back of the turtle, which turtle is the crab of astrology. Under the symbol of Geminus, the Phallic pillar was raised which is still worshipped in religion as the stamen of the lily. In ancient Atlantis, which was under the sign of Taurus, the horizontal or earthy bar was added making the cross into a letter T. or Tav. In Aries, the head, a globe was added to the top of the cross which became the croix ansata of Egypt which they knew as the symbol of immortality because immortality rests in balance and the union of the cross and circle symbolized the union of God and matter. The cross has three divisions; that part above the cross line represents spirit, the cross line is the veil between, and that below the line represents matter, consequently the proportion is one above and two below because only one phase of the three-fold spirit is yet superior to matter.

With this brief analysis of the cross in general and its origin, we will now take up the symbolism of the emblem which has been accepted as the symbol of my future work.

Behind all is the circle representing the area of manifestation differentiated for the creation of a specialized labor. The four arms of the cross extend beyond this confining line, symbolizing the removal of the wall between the circle of one man's intelligence and the circle of another's. The circle has in its center an opening, invisible from the surface, which represents the power of the Logos pouring out through forty-nine rays, these rays representing the seven root outpourings and their seven rounds.

The signs of the zodiac represent the field of endeavor and are the twelve divine avenues of expression as they are symbolized in astrology; they are the twelve gods and also the twelve creative forces and the twelve centers in the human body, seven revealed and five concealed; they also represent the twelve Apostles gathered around the table in the center of which is the calyx or flower which is the symbol of the Holy Ghost. This circular outpouring represents the birth into unreality, in which the universe dies by becoming manifest, for manifestation is the point of death in all creation while the cross is the point of liberation.

The white cross with the twelve knobs represents the human body; the temple of God built in the form of a cross. It also represents the ignorance of the world, which is the cross the Master must carry. The twelve knobs are the twelvefold constitution of the human and of the divine organism: three bodies, three minds, three souls and three spirits, only one part of the threefold spirit having descended into matter. The human spirit is doomed, as was Siva, to drink the world poison, for it is keyed to form and is now expressing itself through the ninefold constitution below. But the mystic occultist is seeking to lift his consciousness until Vishnu, the cosmic Christ and the second spirit, shall be awakened and the reins of rulership shall be turned over to Him as the preserver and refiner instead of to the builder of form.

The seven points of the star represent the Seven Elohim or the spirits before the throne, which pour out from the solar Logos. Everything in nature has seven divisions; there being seven great human races, seven great animal kingdoms, seven great plant kingdoms and seven mineral kingdoms. There are seven senses, seven colors, seven sounds or notes and human life is divided up into periods of seven years. There are also seven metals which belong to the Seven Elohim and are the vibratory poles whereby They manifest in form.

The sun and the moon appear upon the emblem but are there for want of more complete information. In other words, they are substitutes for two other spheres which are not known at the present time. The metals of the planets are as follows: Saturn, indigo, lead; Sun, yellow, gold; Moon, pale blue, silver; Mars, red, iron; Mercury, violet, quicksilver; Jupiter, sea or cobalt blue, tin; Venus, green, copper; and Saturn, once more as the point of entrance and the point of going out, covering all colors and containing all the primary shades within Himself. These represent also the seven ductless glands under the rulership of these respective

## THE SYMBOLISM OF OUR NEW CROSS 157

planets and the seven Great Ones who come to the world at the beginning of each new race.

The star also has four divisions horizontally. The lowest division is earth, the center division is water, and the next division above is fire, while Saturn's point alone is air. On the star rests the Indian lotus of ten petals, five above and five below, which ten petals represent the ten numbers of the numerical system and also the ten original zodiacal signs before Virgo and Scorpio were split by Libra.

The center medallion is threefold in significance. The diamond represents the Father and also the soul of man revealed by his unfolding consciousness, the petals of the flower; the rose represents the Son or Christ, the heart; while the lily is the Holy Ghost, Jehovah. The five leaves constitute an inverted star which is so symbolized because it represents matter or the black force which is slowly being obliterated by the unfolding lotus above. These three, the eternal Trinity, rest over the opening which can never be filled, and which is left blank in honor of the first Cause who is unknown. As a hypothetical spot in a vacuum, this unknown radiates power but cannot be measured by it.

The four arms of the cross represent the Cherubim with four heads, also the four headed beast of Ezekiel and the four gospels of the Christian bible. The four revelations represented by the arms of the cross are basically as follows: the physical history, the emotional concept, the mental revelation, and the spiritual doctrine.

The four little triangles are earth, fire, air, and water; the Matthew, Mark, Luke and John's powers, and the expressions of the Lords of Scorpio, the builders of form; they also represent oxygen, hydrogen, nitrogen, and carbon, the four basic elements from which bodies are composed. The four small diamonds and the large one in the center represent the five points of liberation, the hands, feet, head, and side of Christ from whence the blood and water poured. These are the five hidden truths and exoterically the five senses of man which are the jewels in his bodies, also the five vowels which we use at the present time in our languages. The unfolding star and jewel in the center of the cross represents the human larynx, and the creations born out of the mouth of the godman. The entire cross in its measurement is two by three which when multiplied produces the interlaced triangle and the philosopher's stone, and when added produces the five-pointed star of the Christ, one the priest and the other the king. The symbol stands for the Order of Melchisedec which is the perfect blending of all known symbols and workings. The crimson rose (robe) surrounding the diamond represents the crimson robe of the Christ who came to bear witness of the Father. Mathematically the cross contains all the geometric angles, philosophically it contains all the natural laws which again are the seven points of the star. The whole diagram also represents the brain, surrounded by the four secondary brains. It also contains both the primary and secondary colors. The seven world religions, as the outpourings of the Logos, are also shown and the entire drawing is symbolical of the World Soul which is being slowly unfolded with the consciousness of individuals who are seeking to find the philosopher's stone, the perfect expression of spirit and matter. It is worn over the heart to symbolize the effort in man, which is the crowning jewel of his life.

## QUESTION AND ANSWER DEPARTMENT

What is mediumistic materialization and trumpet seances?

Ans. In materializing a body the departed intelligence does so by taking the life forces of the medium and those attending the seance, using them to build a temporary vehicle. The same is true in trumpet seances, where the strength to express on the physical plane is gained through sapping the vitality of the medium and sitters. This is a detrimental, unproductive method of securing information, seldom accurate but always carried on at a terrible expense to those present.

Why is an ego sent to a family out of harmony with it?

Ans. Inharmony is the basis of growth, for it furnishes the opportunity to learn to love and appreciate the thing which it is not naturally attracted to. It comes to teach creations born out of the mouth of the godman. The entire cross in its measurement is two by three which when multiplied produces the interlaced triangle and the philosopher's stone, and when added produces the five-pointed star of the Christ, one the priest and the other the king. The symbol stands for the Order of Melchisedec which is the perfect blending of all known symbols and workings. The crimson rose (robe) surrounding the diamond represents the crimson robe of the Christ who came to bear witness of the Father. Mathematically the cross contains all the geometric angles, philosophically it contains all the natural laws which again are the seven points of the star. The whole diagram also represents the brain, surrounded by the four secondary brains. It also contains both the primary and secondary colors. The seven world religions, as the outpourings of the Logos, are also shown and the entire drawing is symbolical of the World Soul which is being slowly unfolded with the consciousness of individuals who are seeking to find the philosopher's stone, the perfect expression of spirit and matter. It is worn over the heart to symbolize the effort in man, which is the crowning jewel of his life, the value of harmony through showing the suffering of inharmony. The ego comes to settle old scores and to make new growth rather than to

# THE SYMBOLISM OF OUR NEW CROSS

find harmony.

Will man develop more rapidly from the spiritual standpoint in the near future than he does now?

Ans. He will never develop any faster than he does now until his whole life is better than it is now, a few million years do not make much difference unless he changes his mode of living.

How would you treat a drug addict or a cigarette fiend?

Ans. Patching up the effects will never produce a lasting cure. The higher side of the nature must be appealed to in some way and the consciousness of the individual raised to a realization of the blasphemy of his acts.

What is the life in man?

Ans. The life in man is that spark of the Divine Fire which, in search of experience, has robed itself in the garments of matter which it is slowly transmuting until its prison walls shall become a glorious dwelling place to be finally united with the Life itself.

What does man carry with him from life to life?

Ans. His consciousness. Upon the seed atoms of his various bodies, the records of every thought, action and desire which have animated his being are impressed. These form the basis of karmic payments and future growth and unfoldment and will remain with him until he has absorbed all of these experiences into the soul.

Is man perfect now?

Ans. Perfection is a matter of relativity. To be perpetually perfect requires perpetual adjustment with ever finer planes of spiritual influx. Each divine Ego is perfect but this perfection must remain unexpressed until evolution and experience molds the bodies into worthy implements for the life within.

Is there any shortcut to perfection?

Ans. The longest way around is the most successful. The fineness of adjustments is the basis of the estimate of perfection and those who have done their work the most thoroughly have in reality done it in the shortest and most satisfactory manner.

What is man's work here?

Ans. His duty is to learn through experience and to harmonize his mentality with the finer heart sentiments. It is the union of spirit and matter, heart and mind, the marriage of the sun and moon which man is striving to attain through an equal development and harmonization of his thoughts and emotions.

What is man's true position in the universe?

Ans. He is, according to the ancient poets, "'twixt heaven and hell," halfway between perfect consciousness and absolute negation. He should stand in the center of his spiritual and intellectual world, drawing towards himself from all extremities of the universe the powers that he needs but always remaining true to his own center and never identifying himself with any of the tangents.

Was Masonry known in Atlantis?

Ans. Wherever the Wisdom-Religions are found, be it, East, West, South or North, we find Masonry, from the heart of China to the jungles of South Africa. Masonry undoubtedly had its foundation in the sun worship of ancient Atlantis.

Do dreams mean anything?

Ans. Some do and some do not. They are often partial memories of things we have learned and done while the bodies were asleep; sometimes they are only thoughts of the day which have automatically repeated themselves even after sleep has deprived us of conscious power. Sometimes the brain does not all go to sleep at once and faculties will labor all through the night while the brain is otherwise asleep, causing dreams and hazy memories.

Are we taught individual immortality? Is not race immortality sufficient?

Ans. The fact that we are evolving individualized organisms, no two of them alike, proves that individualization and not merely racial progression is the ultimate end. Everything reduces itself into the singular before it is through therefore individual salvation had upon individual effort is far more inspiring than race immortality where the laziness sneaks through with the hard workers.

## DESCRIPTION OF LAST MONTH'S PLATE

The plate in the November issue of the All-Seeing-Eye is the frontispiece of a rare and unobtainable work by Robert Fludd, the great English freemason, alchemist and Rosicrucian. The original folio was printed in 1619 in Latin and is really two books in one. The first book deals with the metaphysical creation of the heavens and earth and is a work of a student of Rosicrucian lore. It is now generally admitted that Robert Fludd was connected with that sacred order. He is said to be the first English exponent of cosmological alchemy and the philosophy of the Phoenicians and Chaldeans, and is known all over the world as one of the deepest occultists of any generation known to man.

Technically, the plate is astrological, dealing especially with the planetary centers in the human body and also the centers of the twelve signs of the zodiac. You can easily trace the position of the twelve signs by following the dotted line on the human figure, starting with Aries which governs the head and ending with Pisces which governs the feet. The power which is turning the wheel of eternity and unwinding the cord of human destiny is the threefold beast which has since become a part of the Royal Arch banner of freemasonry. This creature is the most outstanding feature of the plate. He represents the three great principles of nature, manifesting through the three grand divisions or kingdoms of his own body. The feet belong to the animal world, the human body belongs to the human world, while the wings belong to the celestial or divine world. The wings represent the creative power of God the Father, the human body represents the preservative power of God the Son, while the legs and feet represent the procreative and disintegrative power of God the Holy Spirit. On his head the creature carries an hourglass which shows the passing of time and illustrates the principle that the spirit of Time is eternally unwinding the cord, which unwinding causes the universe to twist on its central axis. The whole diagram is surrounded by clouds which represent Chaos and the great sphere is Cosmos in Chaos.

The human body represents the five-pointed star of Masonry and also shows the position of the various centers of the human body in relation to the threefold world of nature. This is the microcosmic and macrocosmic man; in other words, the evolving human consciousness and also the cosmic consciousness of nature. If you will turn in our magazine to our astrological section, you will find each month the keywords of one of the zodiacal signs which if analyzed in connection with this chart will make it much more intelligible.

The twelve concentric circles of the outer sphere represent the twelve spiritual hierarchies or the worlds of the external heaven. The seven spheres in the secondary circle represent the home of the seven Elohim or planetary deities while the three inner worlds represent water, fire, and air, and the solid globe behind the figure the principle of earth. The five points where the human body touches the sphere of the seven planes represent the sense perceptions of the human consciousness, while the little figure of Saturn over the head of the figure is the key of source. Above the figure is the terrestrial sun and moon, while still higher are the celestial sun and moon, much greater and more brilliant. The heart and mind are the sun and moon of the human system and in their union lies the power of an Initiate. Time is turning the Wheel of Life round and round; sometimes man stands upright as he is shown here, later he is inverted and assumes the position which you can study by inverting the picture. And this endless going round and round, first up and then down, is the Wheel of Life, to which the threefold deity of concrete creation chains the spirit of man. Only when he releases himself from the wheel of creation is he capable of releasing himself from the wheel of destruction, for as the ancients said, "Sure is death for the living, and sure is birth for the dead." The wisdoms of the ancients lay not in combatting the principles of nature but in freeing themselves by their knowledge and understanding from the Wheel of Life and Death. This is the tenth card of the Taro, the Wheel of Fortune.

## THE DANCE OF THE VEILS

IT was in the native quarter of the city of Agra that the first act of a strange drama took place. There is no spot in all India more picturesque, more unusual with its domes and mosques, its wondrous tombs and latticed palaces, than the ancient City of Agra, the gem of India, known all over the world as the city of the Taj Mahal. In the native quarter, however, it is not different from other Eastern cities, with its bazaars and shops, its merchants, its dogs, its filth and little running children that are eternally tangling themselves up in your feet.

Here, dressed in a spick and span white suit with a pith helmet and a flowing fly screen, walked John Thurlowe, retired American race-track expert and prize-fight promoter, who, after a successful life at the plying of his trade, was now globe-trotting in order to, as he expressed it, get an "inside tip" on things. John Thurlowe was a florid faced man some fifty years of age; he was built on Taurian lines with three layers of superfluous neck draped over his collar, while a large linked gold watch chain spread across from each side of his trouser pockets, lacking vest. He was decidedly over weight and every little while he would take off his helmet and wipe the perspiration from a perfectly shiny head, sans every sign of hair. Two small eyes gleamed out like those of a contented hog from a tiny crevice between eyebrow and cheek, which threatened to close entirely if he ate much more. The Eighteenth Amendment meant absolutely nothing to John but to fairly respectable American whiskey he had added infinitely worse Oriental concoctions which, in his own words, "could kick the side out of the statue of Liberty."

John Thurlowe was one of those individuals with whom pomposity was an innate quality. Everything he had gone to front, both mentally and physically, and as he half walked, half waddled, among the bazaars mild-eyed Orientals viewed him with strange expressions, mangy dogs looked at him inquiringly while heavily veiled women went on the other side of the street. John Thurlowe was out for what he could get, his recommendation being a long pocketbook and an exceptionally short conscience.

A little wiggling brown urchin did the apparently superhuman achievement of crawling in between his feet, which were long, large and ponderous, and Thurlowe, with a choice epithet, brought a heavy snakewood cane down across the child's body with a resounding whack, with a howl the streak of brown lightning vanished somewhere among the swaying portieres of the bazaars. A few beggars held out their hands for annas, but Thurlowe was not there for the purpose of financing India, so he passed on with a disdainful look and wound his way with trunchant dignity among the bazaars and narrow streets. A whiff of a strange odor suddenly broke upon his nostrils and his olfactory nerves dilated; he stopped, took off his hat and fanned himself for the millionth time that day. "Ah," he murmured, "this is the first decent breath I've had today! They surely can raise stinks in this country." He was standing in the shade of the awning of an Oriental perfume bazaar and it seemed an oasis of loveliness in counter distinction to the city sewerage which lay on the streets in front of him.

Thurlowe saw an opening before him, a series of arches where the narrow streets seemed ready to come together and were separated only by spans of clay and plaster. He passed into one of these arches and found himself in a deserted niche where the traffic of the thoroughfare did not apparently enter. As he stood there, there dashed madly from the house beside him, a figure howling like a maniac and pouring forth streams of English profanity. Thurlowe turned and looked at the figure. It was that of a white man, but his long unkempt hair and beard and his skin, tanned by the Indian sun, seemed almost that of an Asiatic. His clothes had originally been white duck, but they were now torn, dirtied and battered until their original color was almost obliterated. In one hand, this strange figure clenched some object while with the other he seemed to try to disentangle himself from some invisible network.

"Get away, you red demons!" he screamed, "you can't have it, you can't have it! Get away, damn you!" He spun around, twisting, tearing, and clenching at the air, his eyes wild and bloodshot and his whole being that of a madman.

Suddenly, he spied Thurlowe and rushed up to him in an apparent frenzy of desperation.

"My God! you're a white man!" he screamed, falling upon his knees before the corpulent form of the American race-track magnate. And then in a wild, discordant voice he babbled forth an almost unintelligble harangue.

"They've got me!" he kept muttering, "the red fiends have got me!"

Thurlowe looked down cooly. "Opium or hashish?" he asked, wiping his face once more. "I've made a mint selling them, but I don't advocate their use.

"No, no!" screamed the wild figure. "it's not dope, it's red devils, it's red devils!"

"Sounds like Indian hemp to me," answered Thurlowe, "but what do you want?"

"You're a white man and you'll do something if I ask you to, won't you?" What is it?" asked Thurlowe, "I've found it don't pay to make rash promises."

"I'll tell you," gasped the other. "A year ago, I was just as prosperous and well-heeled as you are. I came out here to India for a special reason, I went up into the North mountains, way north, to a temple that has been sacred for many ages to Krishna, the great Brahmin god, Get away from me, you red devils! I can see you blinking at me, but get away, damn you!" and the disheveled figure broke into a grating, unearthly laugh. "I stole it, I stole it!" he laughed. "I stole the eye of Krishna and I've got it still, but they've sent red devils after me! Promise me that you'll take it back to them when I am dead or they will haunt me in hell forever, promise me you'll take the eye back here on this paper is the place to take it to. Promise me you'll do it!"

"All right," answered Thurlowe, "what is it, a glass eye?"

"No, no!" screamed the disheveled figure. "Here, you will take it. The demons are strangling me! Help! Help!" and quickly slipping the little package into Thurlowe's hand, the figure leaped to its feet. Clutching at his throat, he rushed straight into the opposite wall of a near bazaar. He battered himself against the wall screaming, "Red demons!" And then suddenly he straightened up and his body swayed in a strange unearthly way, his eyes gazing into an unknown depth.

"What on earth is he doing?" exclaimed Thurlowe.

Then the thought flashed into his mind that the crazed man was dancing. Though no sound broke the air, the figure swayed back and forth to the tune of some Oriental nautch tune. Back and forth, the crazed man danced, his movements becoming more and more eccentric. The American followed him as, dancing this strange, unearthly pantomime, he passed down the street while the passersby stepped aside fearing that he was insane. Suddenly he danced past a bazaar filled with wondrous implements of gold and silver, where steel scimitars and inlaid daggers were exhibited to the throng. The crazed and obsessed man grabbed one of the scimitars and spinning it in his hand, twisted his body back and forth in the ancient Hindoo Dance of Death, the sword gleaming and swishing through the air in strange parabolas. At the same time, the bearded figure with its crazed face and ragged form laughed and screamed. Slowly the movements became slower and at last, exhausted, the figure sank to the ground and when the crowd reached it, they found that in falling the scimitar has passed through his body. The crazed man was dead.

Thurlowe, having seen one end of the story, now turned to the package in his hand and unwrapping it he gave a gasp of amazement he was gazing down upon a great blue-white diamond as large as a pigeon's egg, gloriously cut in the manner of ancient India and appearing more like a flaming torch in his hand than a piece of stone. Thurlowe staggered back against a supporting arch.

"Good heavens!" he muttered. "That stone is worth millions! So, that is the eye of Krishna? That bird sure had some eyes. um-m-m-give it back? Give this stone back to these greasy heathens? Not much! Oh, I'll give it back! John Thurlowe, this stone alone makes you many times a millionaire. You know the more I see of this country the better I like it!" And slipping the stone into his pocket, he slowly wound among the streets until he again reached his room in a well-known European hotel.

Locking the door and standing a chair against it, Thurlowe sat down on a three-legged stool and took out the stone. As he did so, a voice whispered in his ear: "Take it back, take it back, take back."

"Like hell I'll take it back," muttered Timrlowe, "when little Johnny gets his hands on it. It will take a pickaxe to pry it loose. Why this rock is as big as the Kohinoor, and I understand they built a tower over in London to put that in? My history ain't very good, but I seem to have a strange ability to pick up diamonds."

The voice kept whispering, "take it back, take it back, take it back."

"Those little red demons ain't going to frighten me. This belongs to yours truly from now on." And flipping it in the air with his thumb, John Thurlowe spun around and caught it as it came down. "Pretty soft, I'll say." He went to his valise and opened a little leather bag and put the stone into it, and placing the stone and bag together under his pillow, prepared for the night.

John Thurlowe's method of life did not tend to actuate the nervous system, for his entire constitution was more animal than human. Consequently, no chills ran up and down his spine, no worries beset his soul, and, lying flat on his back with his eyes on the ceiling, his lids slowly fell (with them his lower jaw) and John Thurlowe, race-track plutarch and present owner of the eye of Krishna, entered peacefully into slumber land, his long rythmic snores reverberating through the hotel.

This scene of nocturnal placidity left nothing to be desired.

\* \* \*

About three hours passed in perfect stillness and Thurlowe never dreamed that his peace would be broken. There were other plans in the wind, however. Under his window stood a slender turbaned form, his arms folded. The figure was dressed in well-fitting English clothes but his face was that of an Oriental and he walked slowly up and down before the window of Thurlowe's room, looking up to the second story behind whose shaded window peacefully reposed the rotund form of our friend John.

He was not awakened by the soft turning of the doorknob, which attempt was foiled by the chair against the door. A few seconds passed and from the edge of the roof above there was lowered down a thin silken cord on the end of which hung a tiny incense burner of bronze, carefully padded. This swung back and forth in the window of Thurlowe's room and then its motion changed. The hand above was swinging it far into the interior of the room. At last, with a very long swing and it passed over the windowsill and was lowered with the slightest thud onto the floor. From it there poured forth a stream of fine blue smoke, the cultured hashesh of the Orient prepared in the temple and certain in its effect.

Many moments passed for in the East nothing is done hastily. The fine blue pencil of smoke was driven by the gentle breeze about the room, which slowly became hazy with its fumes. Thurlowe slept on in peace but slowly into his slumber crept strange dreams which were not won't to disturb his peace. He seemed to be in a strange place filled with clouds and dancing lights and he swayed among these lights like a creature in a dream, but all seemed very real to him. Then, through the thick clouds appeared faces which seemed to leer at him with strange blood-shot eyes and were of strange red flaming appearance. Somehow, he realized in his sleepy way that these were the red devils that had tormented the crazed man on the street a few hours before. Voices began to speak to him, always whispering of the diamond.

John Thurlowe stirred in his bed uneasily and rolled over on his side. He tried to wake up, but a great weight seemed to be upon him. Something was pressing down on his chest and his breath came in short gasps. He tried to sit up, but fell back in a stupor. The red leering faces came ever closer to him. He swept his hand across his face to try to drive them away, but they only laughed. Although he did not know it, they were the dzins appointed to protect the treasure of Krishna's eye.

Thurlowe was now tossing and twisting in his bed. His eyes were open, but he was still asleep. At last, he rose from the bed and his hand fell under the pillow where the diamond was.

"No, you shan't have it!" he kept muttering, "s'mine, s'mine-get away from me, you hell demons! S'my diamond! S'my diamond!" and he lurched to the other side of the bed.

As he sat there, a strange sound suddenly broke upon his ears. It was the weird tune of Eastern music such as the dancing girls have on the streets and in the semi-darkness his eyes saw a strange figure sweeping through the clouds of ether a strange, veiled form that swayed and twisted in rhythm with the music, a houri of the opium dreamer. This figure, like the very subtle mystery of the East itself, swayed back and forth in its draping's of veil, holding out long swaying arms to Thurlowe, twisting round and round him in a wild dance of the East. Soft black eyes gazed up at him and a curving form twisted and turned amid the veils, holding out round arms to the American.

Had you been able to be in that room you would have seen Thurlowe rise to his feet and stretch out his arms to the figure, his glazed eyes seeing only the beings of another world. Slowly, he joined the strange dance, twisting and turning with the figure of the dream. The weird cry of a flute and the endless chant of a drum inspired him, so round and round with the veiled creature of his dream, Thurlowe twisted and turned. This mystic figure draped its veils, through which the slender form but faintly shone, and drew ever closer to the window. Thurlowe in his dreaming followed her, weaving and swaying as though wrapped in the veils of the dancer. Through the silence came the soft jingle of anklets and clinking jewelry, while the soft odor of Oriental incense and rare perfumes seemed to fill the air. Thurlowe, hands outstretched, dancing the same weird dance that the man on the street had danced the day before, reached the sill of the window. The alluring figure floated out into the vapors beyond, still calling, still enticing. Thurlowe stepped up onto the windowsill, still swaying to the strange music, and after one moment of hesitation, leaped off into space. Like a rock, the body of the American fell from the window to the ground beside the form of the Hindoo, landing with an awful thud.

The Oriental, his hands still folded, gazed down upon the crumpled form at his feet. The American was dead, his neck broken by the fall. Leaning over, the Oriental took from the hand of the dead man the little brown leather sack that contained the eye of Krishna and in reverence he clasped it to his heart.

"The gods protect their own," he murmured, "and the dzins, the red demons from the scarlet lake, forever entwine this sacred thing with their shielding presence."

A few seconds later, another Oriental met him. He was the one who had lowered the cord into the window. In his hand was the little incense burner and the silken line. Together they vanished in the night, taking back to the temple the eye of Krishna.

## THE LAW OF NON-ATTACHMENT

MAN'S attachments bind him to the physical world like the Lilliputians hound Gulliver in the ancient story until he is hopelessly involved with material unrealities. Of all the things that hamper his usefulness in this world there are none that make him as much their slave as his senses for instead of illuminating him they tie him up in endless complications until he learns to extract from them their essence without accepting their short-comings. Man spends ages trying to untangle this knot of human destiny until, like Alexander the Great, he loses all patience and cuts the tangle with a single blow. This sharp steel is discrimination and its shining blade divides the false from the true, for from discrimination is born divine reason which proves to man the illusions of materiality.

Man must learn to divide, in the depths of his soul, the eternal quest from the passing fancy and in his ability to do this lies the degree of his mastery. The Initiate has learned to pass consciously from the mortal Maya to the immortal Nirvana, the one who rests strong in the reality of the eternal and whose consciousness is united with that of the eternal meditator. Such a one is free from all attachments, and attachment to particulars is the basis of limitation. Let us go out into the world and study the curse of attachment as it stalks like the spirit of death, of which it is the essence, over our world, gathering into itself all who accept it or who fall victims to the mirror of matter which it carries, so the ancient Aztec said, upon its belly. In their legends, the demon floated as a great flame over the universe and all who looked into this cursed mirror lost their soul. So, all who pause to gaze at themselves in the mirror of illusion become involved in Maya, which slowly destroys all who are not free from its vanity. There are two worlds floating in space, it is said, the world of temporal things and the world of eternal things. In the world of material things lies the spirit of man, hound to oblivion by the ties of matter. He lives for today alone; he serves the passing fancy; he struggles to retain the illusion and then falls broken hearted as the hand of infinite law slowly dissolves the visible things into the unknown reality.

As the material universe, its works completed is resolved into the unformed Being, those souls still tied to its spinning wheels by crystallized thoughts and animal desires pass with it into dissolution while the sage, perfect in realization, insomuch as he is free from the illusion, passes on to his already realized Nirvana.

Many in this world, in fact nearly all, are fighting to gain liberation while by thought, action and desire they are tied to the spinning wheel, and in their thoughtless effort become only more involved in the very problem they are seeking to remove. Man cannot climb to liberation and still serve the ties that bind him to the earth, so the ancients taught, as the first step to immortality, the realization of the unreality of mortality, not that the objective universe did not exist but that it only existed as a means to an end and as such should he accepted, considered and mastered but never assumed.

Attachment is the base of sorrow, the parent of crime, the inspiration of lust and the causeless cause of limitation. Man must battle it through the realization of one great truth, that attachment to matter is the renouncing of spirit and that attachment to spirit is the renouncing of matter. It is written that man may not serve God (spirit) and Mammon (matter). The sage is free in the realization of the immortal reality while the fool is chained a prisoner by his acceptance of the immortality of matter.

The ancient prophet, wandering over the earth, cried out in his agony, "There is no rest among the children of earth, there is no peace in the cities of the plains, nor in the forts among the mountains! Release me, oh God, from this molal clay which hinds me with its stony fingers and dooms me to death the day that I was born. Oh, unhappy fate! That bears to slay and slay that it may bear again!"

Here, take up your staff and walk with me among the children of the earth, long bowed like the tribes of Israel under the rod of Egypt's blackness-matter. Attachment is the rod and flail that stripes the back of a man with the red welts of mortal agony. It is the heartless slave driver that breaks the back of the spirit and the heart of each soul that falls victim to its wiles. Yet out of this land of darkness comes the new race, born of sorrow and widowed by the loss of light; out of matter rises the spirit triumphant which spreads its wings and draws upward to the freedom of reality.

There is but one consciousness and it is not in matter; there is but one truth and that is the realization of immortal purity; there is but one quest, the search for reality; there is but one reward and that the attainment of reality; there is but one devotion and that the love of reality; there is but one sin, the loss of the reality; there is but one death, that is the death of reality. When the clouded soul of man loses sight of the star of truth that gleams through the veil of maya, as the clouds of old concealed the body of Deity, so the clouds of attachment shroud truth in a winding sheet of limitation.

Let us watch the people whom we daily pass all slaves to attachments, crushed by ignorance as to the will of the planner or the wisdom of the plan. Little better than beasts they are who know not when nor why but, like little puppets in a shadow show, follow the strings they have placed upon themselves. The Master is aside from these, strong in truth and steadfast in reality, and when He comes to earth, he comes not with peace but with a sword, its blade sharpened on the grindstone of the eternal Wheel, sharpened to slash the veil of maya and to divide the false from the true. Watch now the ghosts we call men and women who, while still living, are in truth dwelling in the death of matter.

First, love comes with bowed head and tear-stained face, for all today who flutter moth like around its hallowed flame sink broken-hearted at the foot of its altar. The price of love in the world today is loneliness and sadness because we have not learned to unveil the mystery that love is of the spirit and not the body. The attachment to form is today the measure of affection, and in form there is no rest, no peace, below that line that borders immortality.

Then comes pride, a god that many worship. Man fights and dies to be superior and to gather around himself things that other men cannot attain, but when the victory seems won, the hand of eternity sweeps all away and leaves the soul crushed by its broken dreams. Then vanity, that which seeks to beautify the unreal, and leave the living truth unadorned. It decks with flowers and stones that which is already dirt and bows before the dazzling array of worthlessness.

After this, the specter of lust appears in the role of a human being but with the soul of a beast. It crushes the thing that it adores, slays the spirit it claims to worship, and with the call of fleshly sense, seeks to answer the divine call of the spirit within.

There is a cloud upon the soul of man and he knows not the way that he should go, nor does he realize the path that shall take him there. He seeks entrance where angels dare not tread but is not willing with the sharp blade of non-attachment to sever the cord that binds him to the great illusion. He aspires to heaven but is still chained to earth with every fear, with every habit, and with each desire.

This is the story of Vedanta, the philosophy of the unreal. For thousands of years, it has been taught that there is but one true thing: the spirit -and that as it gathers ever changing bodies around itself; it changes in the eyes of mortal man, but the life of it is ever the same. With the keen sense of discrimination, man finds peace by seeing the noble striving of the spirit and not the fleshy failings of the body. Until he finds this and accepts this, there is nothing in his soul to fill the emptiness of a heartless world.

As the gifts of Santa Claus come down through the fireplace so man's gift to the spirit comes out of the flame of suffering, which tempers the steel of the sword of spirit. In experience lies infinite possibility, man's free will must choose experience above comfort for by this path lies unfoldment of the human soul.

## THE WHITE ELEPHANT

THE White Elephant is the ancient Oriental symbol of transmuted matter. For ages white has been used to symbolize purification, to represent a cleansed or bleached surface exposed to the light of the sun, spiritual or physical. According to science, those substances which absorb light are black or dark in color while those which reflect light are white or pale in color. The unpurified earth absorbs the light of the sun, as do all the other planets, therefore is called negative while the sun is a vitalizer and the life-giver and is called positive. For many ages, the white robe has stood for a purified body, trimmed in red for transmuted emotion and sky blue for spirituality. As man's first labor is to purify and prepare matter to become the throne of a divine essence, the end of this process is concealed under the symbol of the white elephant which is the symbol that India has given for the redemption of matter and its transmutation into a purified garment for the manifestation of spirit.

It is said in the ancient stories that Buddha was conceived as a White Elephant and that at the moment of his conception a great spiritual ray descended into matter. Most of the great Initiates are said to have been born of Immaculate Conceptions. The reason for this is that ages of preparation are necessary before the master is either ordained or the vehicle for his manifestation properly cleansed and prepared. All the initiations that lead to immortality are taken on the physical plane while the candidate is in a concrete physical body. There are no initiations between lives and every candidate for spiritual enlightenment must pass the tests of initiation here in this world of matter. There are no records of a Great One who was born conscious of his mission. Some have received light very young, one at twelve years of age, while another did not comprehend his mission until he was nearly ninety years old. This does not mean that the Great Ones do not possess their knowledge before birth but that it takes the incoming consciousness from twelve to ninety years to bring its sacred wisdom out through the body which it is manifesting through. The consciousness of the enlightened is so highly developed that only the most finely attuned instrument is capable of registering it in this world.

The Immaculate Conception is that process in nature which prepares for the coming of a great Adept, Initiate or World Savior, for such do not come alone into the world but are properly heralded and their way prepared. He could not come in without the world knowing it, for certain qualities come with him and one of them is a great dynamo of flaming light. In the case of the Master Jesus there were chosen as his parents, two of the Order of the Nazarenes, sometimes called the Essenes. They were set apart from all mankind, both in spirit and in life, so that their bodies were purified to the degree that the shock of the coming fire-globe might not destroy them. If this preparation had not taken place, they would have died from the rates of vibration set in motion. Before the coming of a World Teacher, there is always a period of preparation, during which time his body is chosen for him, and the atoms of the vehicles purified to the utmost degree possible.

The children that are brought into the world at the present time bring as their heritage about sixteen generations of scrofula and not one child in a multitude is born free of inherited disease or physical imperfection of a serious nature for which the parents are responsible. When the Master or Initiate is coming into the world, he cannot use these physiological concoctions commonly known as bodies for they are the basis of limitation. Every impurity in them limits him more and more and his work demands freedom of consciousness, for he has come to assist in the overpowering of limitation. And so, in order to facilitate his work every care is taken to see that he is supplied with as pure a vehicle as the world can make and when such a one is found or prepared the great consciousness descends as a ray of light into it and takes control. But no matter how fine the body may be, it always retains some impurity for there is no living thing at the present time that is one hundred percent perfect as the very food we eat, the water we drink and the air we breathe assist in defiling the body. Therefore, it takes the Initiate from twelve to ninety years to impregnate this body with the full consciousness of his power.

Before the ego is capable of revivifying his bodies, he is as much in darkness as other men and often in his younger life the Initiate to-be does not live in accordance with his wisdom. All have to fight the hereditary instinct. This inheritance is not a part of the spirit but is the incessant voice of the bodies and ofttimes it takes ages before the voice of the appetites can be stilled.

We say that Buddha was conceived as a White Elephant, that is, in the most perfect body that could be prepared for him. When the spiritual consciousness entered it, all nature felt a vibratory thrill. Anyone who has studied vibration realizes that even the presence of a great power will cause nature to quake. The first time that the occult student meets his teacher he is usually prostrated. No unfoldment of consciousness can come to the candidate here without a disintegrating effect upon the physical body; when the candidate takes up his work and comes in touch with those powers that be in nature, these occult qualities often tear down his organisms, causing him sickness and suffering. A certain teacher in this country was once sitting reading at a desk when the form of Master appeared to him for the purpose of giving a certain message. At the moment of his appearance, the person sitting in the chair was electrified by a shock not unlike the feeling that comes over us when we touch a live wire; in spite of nerves of steel and an indominable will power, this person was unable to stand up or move but just sat there with the tears running down his face.

Madame Blavatsky said that electricity is the fringe of the garment of an unknown deity whose heart no man knoweth. The electric force generated within the body of the Master would put the average individual to sleep, and if it be a great Master the rates of vibration may destroy the student. This is the same thing which often embarrasses the student while studying or listening to a lecture. There will come over the man overpowering d sire to go to sleep; it is not a normal desire but the result of the presence of rates of vibration that are too high for them.

So, we must realize the necessity of preparing for discipleship and the coming of a great master, whatever day or age of the world it may be. The great spiritual entity that takes control must be properly welcomed and prepared for. There are not three bodies in the world at the present time capable of bringing an Initiate into the world and you can count on your fingers those who could bring in an Adept without disintegration. Only the lowest egos are capable of finding bodies at the present time and when there are not a certain number of older souls to guide the race, it speedily collapses. The fall of a race takes place when the bodies of its members become so crystallized that the teachers are incapable of working through them. As long as there is one body in a race that is capable of giving entrance to the powers of the unseen, then that race shall live, but no longer.

The coming of the Great Initiate is the White Elephant, the rarest thing on earth. When we are able to produce the environments, bodies, and qualities necessary to bring in great intelligence, then we shall have the influxes of knowledge needed for the development of a race. Two things are necessary for the manifestation of a World Savior; one is the spirit descending into matter and the other is matter ascending into a spiritualized state. A Great One cannot come down into crystallization, neither can inanimate substance become a god in such a length of time, and so they meet at a central point.

Buddha was not born consciously as a Great Initiate and in his early life he undoubtedly did many things that were not in harmony with the great wisdom which later expressed through him. He is not to be condemned for the limitation but is to be treated and considered generously, as all living things though they be gods incarnate, are limited in some manner by the bodies that contain them. The desertion of his wife and child has always brought condemnation to Buddha, but let us consider it for a moment from a broader standpoint. The reason for Buddha's youth is shown in the story of his boyhood; the great soul coming into the world was enmeshed in materiality, which was symbolized by the flower garden of the king; he was ever surrounded by the animal and human qualities which seek to prevent the release of the Buddha within and it was not until he had wandered for over forty years that he consciously connected himself with the message he had come to bring and through the living of which knowledge he gained liberation. The

Buddhas are men who have reached liberation from the wheel of birth and death and many of them are wonderful because of the purely human side of their being. All through his life, Buddha loved with the finest side of human sentiment; when he sat under the Bo-hi tree waiting for the last revelation and the realization of his two great truths, all the demons of nature came to tempt him. But he is said to have remained in silence, unchanged and unmoved, saying, "I have no attachment for these things, for they are the unreality." The last temptation that came to him was the vision of his beloved wife and child. Then, it was said, that great Siddhartha groaned. But he gave them up also and in this he won illumination; he gave up one for the good of many, sacrificing his own love for the service to the world; two were sad, five hundred million were gladdened. So, we cannot help but believe that he took the wise course.

And so, they have all, these Great Ones, wandered years before they found themselves, searching to discover and lift out from the shroud of the body the knowledge that they had gained in the past and the memory of the work they had come to do. Always behind the veil of mortal things, there are those who are glad and willing to serve their brothers in the world; the saviors and sages of the ages are there but are unable to act, for between them and us is a wall which can never be pierced until through the Immaculate Conception we build a body here for them to function in. The greatest thing that stands between the world today and the Golden Age of a spiritual Renaissance is sixteen generations of scrofula, thoughtless parents, and general inharmony in the home and in the world. These are the things which man himself has created and they alone prevent the advance of his gods and the spreading of his light. From the unseen worlds behind us, around us, and before us, comes everything that we are, have been or shall be. Tiny lives come to us that seem too small to fight the battle and yet mayhaps in their souls is the wisdom of the gods and through these tiny organisms, when unfolded by the conscious labor of the spirit within, will come the masters and gods. So, the story of the conception of the White Elephant is the way to perfection by the purification of bodies that the Lord may ride among his people upon the back of this stately beast.

## THE CRIME OF VACCINATION

HOW much longer people will have to pay to have smallpox is the problem confronting a large number of people. They send their children to the public school and are forced to allow a pedigreed concept to pump smallpox into them under the refined heading of vaccination. It has been proven conclusively that a great train of ills, in body and in spirit, follow after vaccination. Many vaccinated people have succumbed to smallpox while many exposed to it have not taken it, although unvaccinated. The karmic debt for vaccination is two-fold. First, to our bodies, which we deliberately defile with smallpox serum and vaccine. Secondly, to the animal who goes through untold suffering and is itself given smallpox in order that from the ulcers, the drops of vaccine may be extracted and pumped into us. The occultist is fighting tooth and nail to abolish vaccination and supplant it with good common sense. Smallpox is primarily a filth disease and if people would live right, bathe right and eat right they would not get it for the healthy body is perfectly capable of taking care of its germs. We look forward with great hopes to the day when we will remove from the fair name of our race the blemish, mental and physical, the swollen glands, the tonsil trouble, the nervousness and debility, the rashes and outbreaks, not a small percentage of which can be traced to vaccine which kills the best in us in order to save the rest.

## THE SONG OF THE SOUL
### From One of Our Prison Friends

"What is the purpose of life?" I said
    As I sat by the fire alone;
"When my heart is still and my body dead,
    "Will my soul live on and on?"
I pondered long on the unknown end
    When life should cease to be,
Would I know my soul as a foe or friend
    When death's hand sets it free?
Then the touch of an unseen hand I felt
    And a soft voice whispered low,
"There's a region of light where your soul once dwelt
    You may see if you choose to go."
Then the scene around me grew strangely dim.
    And faded at last from sight,
I could not choose but follow him
    Who spoke to my soul that night.
Then my thoughts went out to those sun-kissed realms
    And my soul kept them company
As we winged our flight with an unseen helm
    To the brink of eternity.
I saw the earth in the sky below
    Just a tiny brilliant spark,
My gentle guide sang soft and low
    In the hush of the voiceless dark.
Then a glorious orb of golden light
    Appeared in the distant sky,
And we stood revealed in the splendor bright
    My guide, my soul, and I.
I had never dreamed a thing so pure
    As I saw my soul to be
Could long on the tainted earth endure
    In a form we both called "Me."
I fathomed the depths of its astral eyes
    And read immortality,
I caught the first glimpse of the paradise

That awaited humanity.
My gentle guide then took my hand
And I gladly followed him.
Till we took our stand on celestial land
On Saturn's golden rim.
Such scenes of splendor mortal mind
Had never yet believed,
And yet the soul of all mankind
Was 'mid those scenes conceived.
Me thought that sounds seraphic rung
Throughout that broad expanse;
On every tone my senses hung,
My mind seemed in a trance;
The zephyrs wafted sweet perfume
That thrilled me through and through;
Each law of nature seemed in tune,
The sun, the air, the dew.
And long I stood and gazed upon
That ever-changing scene,
It was not day, but early dawn,
No night could intervene.
And countless forms of misty white
Rolled by in endless streams,
Their faces lit with heavenly light,
As oft we see in dreams.
I looked upon my own pure soul,
Which seemed a thing apart,
I saw it join the onward roll,
I felt the tear drops start.
My guide then spoke in gentle voice.
Each accent full of love,
"Be not alarmed, it had no choice,
"But like the cooing dove,
"It follows where love leads the way.
"It cannot choose but go,
"For love rules in these realms always,
"Such love no mortals know."
"But must I then resign my soul?"

# THE SONG OF THE SOUL

I cried in deep concern.
"Perhaps as on the ages roll
"This lesson you will learn,"
My guide replied. He took my hand
In tender sympathy,
"For years that soul on Earth's dull strand
"Has struggled to be free.
"Your ears were deaf to all its pleas,
"You scoffed and scorned, and sneered,
"You quaffed the wine, it drank the lees,
"You spurned all it revered.
"That soul was yours by grace of God.
"And yours it shall remain,
"But never more on Earth's cold sod
"Shall you that soul reclaim,
"Until thru years of suffering
"And humble contrite prayer,
"Beseeching, sorrowing love, shall bring
"Your soul to join you there.
"Come hence, and to your mortal eyes
"I will a sight unfold
"That has no equal in the skies
"Which now those eyes behold."
We rose into the midnight air,
Nor paused to say farewell
To my own better self. I dare
Not speak to break the spell.
Once more I felt my trembling form
Flit past the brilliant stars,
Until at last the fiery storm
Revealed the planet Mars.
And then we stood on mountains bare
And viewed the silent land,
The hush of death was in the air
And on the burning sand;
And as I gazed methought I saw
Stooped men go slowly past;
Their nude forms knew no mortal law,

Their hollow eyes downcast.
"And who are these?" I cried, amazed,
"Who walk with footsteps slow.
"And act like men with senses dazed?
"And whither do they go?"
"These forms, like you, are soulless men.
"And this is their abode,
"Nor can they join their souls again
"Until the weary load
"Of selfishness, lust, and greed,
"That ruled their passions then
"Has forced them to their knees to plead
"Their soul's return again."
"Why do you come to this dead globe,
"This gloomy, living Hell,
"Where men without nor shield nor robe
"Their lamentations tell?"
I asked in quaking voice, but no!
My gentle guide was gone!
My heart grew sick with fear to know
I stood there all alone.
I cried aloud, none heard my cry,
For no one could afford
To reach a hand or lift an eye
In all that soulless horde.
Each nursed a grief the same as mine,
Each mourned for pleasures past,
When life meant love and mirth and wine,
Too glorious to last.
I sought to go as I had come
From yon bright, distant star;
I sought in vain, each sense was numb,
Tho' Saturn smiled afar.
The fierce sun blazed over the sand
And quivered in the air,
No cooling breath my hot cheeks fanned,
My parched lips moved in prayer.

"Lord, give me back my loving soul
"That erstwhile walked with me,
"That I may gain my destined goal
"Of immortality!"
I listened, but no answer came;
I knew my doom was sealed;
My greed; my selfishness, my shame
Was to my mind revealed.
With drooping head and heavy heart
I joined that grewsome throng,
I felt the burning teardrops start
As we slowly passed along.
And so the days, the months, the years
Passed slowly one by one,
And all seemed dead save only fears
Of what was yet to come.
Annihilation waited me
When life's brief span was over,
No hope that I should wake to see
That promised Golden Shore.
And then I knew that life on Earth,
So filled with hope and love,
Was builded on the soul's rebirth
In blissful realms above.
I knew that in my ignorance,
My sinful pride and lust,
Offense was heaped upon offense
Against my soul. Disgust
Of all Earth's petty vanities,
Of shams, deceits, and lies,
Of mockeries, Profanities,
And other mundane ties,
Welled up and set my heart aflame
With hate for every deed
Of my earth-life; then in my shame
I heard my lost soul plead.
"Oh, Pray for light that you may know
"The hopes you knew of old;

"Oh, pray for firm strength to forego
"The power of glittering gold!"
I knelt me down, and as I prayed
Behold, a vision fair
Of spirit forms above me played,
Upon the sand dunes there.
And from that throng my own fair soul,
With arms outstretched, advanced;
I felt the heavy burdens roll
From off my heart. Entranced,
I felt the soft warm glow
Of hope and faith and love.
Throughout my yielding body flow
I soared to realms above.
I knew my soul and I were one,
Re-born on Earth to dwell
I saw where Mars still, brightly shone,
A fiery living hell.
And when my feet touched earth at last,
We knelt, my soul and I,
Full grateful that the test was passed
We two should never die.
I knew the love, the faith, the hope,
I'd never known before,
No more would I in shadows grope
As I had done of yore.
The weary years of dark despair,
On Mars when hope was dead,
Had taught me that the earth was fair
Whereon to lay my head.
And then my gentle guide appeared,
"Farewell, my Spirit friend,
"We may not meet again," he feared,
"Until earth-life shall end.
"But thou hast seen what few have seen,
"And lived to tell the tale.
"Go forth and spread the message free,
"That faith shall never fail

"To keep love's shining light aflame
"Betwixt their soul and them
"You saw, you know, you felt the blame,
"No man your pow'r can stem.
"For life is Love-God's only law
"Thru all eternity.
"Twill lead them on without a flaw
"To Immortality."
Thus spake my guide, then passing on
To that oblivion vast,
Where people of our dreams have gone
Through countless ages past.
Then consciousness in full returned,
I was myself once more
The bright fire in the grate still burned
As it had burned before.
Methought myself an aged man
When I awoke again,
Long passed the ordinary span
Of three-score years and ten.
But lo! an hour had scarcely passed
Since first my guide appeared
The vision grand, from first to last,
Was not as I had feared!
A weary stretch of wasted years,
But just one hour had flown.
Farewell to grief, farewell to fears,
My soul and I atone.

## THE KOJIKI

THE Kojiki is a very ancient book of the Japanese having to do with the creation of the universe and the building of the first land. Among the Japanese we find many interesting mythologies not the least of which is the ancient Japanese story of creation which we will very briefly consider in this article.

The Kojiki opens with the story of the coming of the three gods. Every nation has its trinity, and this trinity is the expression of all things which come into creation. The moment abstraction is concreted it divides itself into three forces which are the Trimuti of India or the three phases of human life. God, the Unmanifest, manifests Himself through three creatures for there are but three expressions of force in the universe, the creative force, the projective and perpetuating force, and, thirdly, the disintegrative or reductive force. The moment that any life essence assumes matter, it becomes subject to these three gods who are in reality, the rulers of Maya or of the created universe. The only reality is the Uncreated, which is the beginning and end of all creation.

In the ancient doctrines of Japan, there are two kinds of deities: heavenly gods and earthly gods. The heavenly gods refer undoubtedly to those beings who dwell in the spiritual planes or else those beings who, while manifesting in the world, descended from the spiritual planes. In other words, they are those forces extraneous to ourselves which assist in the molding of our consciousness, while the earthly gods are those who, though born of men, achieve immortality and become deified as the fruitage of their labors here. The Kojiki shows two divisions to the universe, the heavens and the earth. The heavens came before the earth which was born out of water by the actions of two gods who are called Izanagi, the Male-Who-Invites, and his sister Izanami, the Female-Who-Invites (literal translation). These two were the creators of the earth and represent the principles of polarity, which bring solid matter into existence. It is said in the ancient hook that in the plane of the superior world called the Most High Heaven there were three deities born out of nothing, that were differentiated from That Which Is Not. They were parentless creations, self-born androgenous creature creations, self-born, androgenous creatures known and, according to the ancient story, withdrew themselves from creation after the appearance of two secondary deities. The first of these self-born ones was called the Master-of-Heaven's-Center; the second was called the Most-Distinguished-Producer-of-Wonders; and the third the Divine-Producer-of-Wonders. They appeared in clouds floating over the heavens and the source of their being was unknown, but they are seldom symbolized because even their shape is but a hypothesis. From them came two others that were born of a strange hollow stick or reed like growth which came out of the earth at that time when it was a floating bubble in the center of a great ocean. The names of these two deities were The Elder-Reed-Shoot deity and the Heaven-Born-Eternally-Standing-Diety. They likewise were unseen to mortal men and were born without parents.

These five constitute the eldest of the ancient cosmogony and in modern occultism represent the Elder Brothers or the five Great Initiates who never leave the temple but, like the ancient deities, hide their person. The Wisdom-Religion is divided into two divisions, the five god-born or god-reclaimed ones and the seven man-born or man-unfolded ones. It is these two divisions which constitutes the mystery schools of the ancients. The higher group contains five which is the number of the astral plane or the high priest, while the second contains seven which is the number of the Mosaic law and the earthy things. In the ancient wisdom, the five-pointed star stands for the elder five whose thrones are in the human brain. It is through these five superior deities that man secures liberation cosmically and they represent the wounds of the crucifixion and are the most secret of the ancient wisdom. According to the sacred books and early literature of the East, edited by Professor Charles F. Horne, PhD., the literal names translated into English of the next seven gods and goddesses are as follows:

First, the Earthly-Eternally-Standing-Deity and the Luxuriant-integrating-Master-Deity. These two were heaven-born without procreation and were unseen in the mortal world. Then came the Mud-Earth-Lord and Mud-Earth-Lady, the Germ-integrating-Deity and his younger sister the Life-integrating-Deity; the Elder-of-the-Great-Place and his sister the Elder-Lady-of-the-Great-Place; the Perfect-Exterior and his sister the Oh-Awful-Lady; the Male-Who-Invites and the Female-Who-Invites. From the Earthly-Eternally-Standing deity down to the Female-Who-Invites we have what are termed the Seven Divine Generations. These represent the seven Logos or the gods of the planetary chain who are the outpouring of the five unseen First Causes which are the outpouring of the Three most sacred centers which Three are the Witnesses of the Unknowable.

In Masonry the numbers Three, Five and Seven are of great significance and Masonically it means exactly the same as in the ancient Japanese mythology, the three great tools, the five senses, and the seven liberal arts and sciences. The seven liberal arts and sciences are the lowest and belong to the earth, corresponding to the Entered Apprentice degree of Freemasonry which is keyed to the number seven.

The five, which is the number of the priest and is called the Hierophant in the ancient Taro, is the mind which thinks through the heart system and is best expressed by that old saying, "As a man thinketh in his heart, so is he." As has been said before, five is the number of the astral plane, is the key to the Fellowcraft degree of Freemasonry, and is the number of sense perception which is the fruitage of the astral plane. The Master Jesus, expressing the principle of the astral plane, wore over his white garment a crimson robe as the symbol of the blood system. Three is attuned to the mind, is the Master Mason's degree and the key to the third degree of Masonry. It belongs to the mental world and the mind-born gods are without father or mother, being born in the subtle mind stuff of the Saturn period. Thus, we see the ancient cosmogony played out in both spirit and matter.

The gods placed the last two named deities upon the Bridge of Heaven or the Antakhrana which is the bridge connecting the divine with the human, sometimes known as the Heavenly Stairs. Handing them a jeweled spear, they told them to stir the brine floating in the ocean until it should curdle. The spear was then drawn up and the brine that dripped from it piled up upon the surface of creation, forming a mighty island which was called Onogoro or the First Land. Upon this they built their first temple and a hall eight fathoms square, from which point all creation was carried on.

This legend undoubtedly refers to the ancient mystery of the descent of the spiritual hierarchies on to the North polar cap of the earth which was the first point to become crystallized. The spear was the ray sent down by the sun upon which ray the spiritual hierarchies descended and the sun drew up the water, leaving the earth. The ancient myth tells that the spiritual hierarchies built their temple upon the sacred island of the Gobi Desert, where it has remained even to this day. From this point, all the work of civilizing and unfolding human thought, race, and culture has been carried on. It is at this point which the occultist believes to be the place where the spiritual bridge or cord connecting the planet with the sun passes into the earth. This is the beanstalk of Jack, which we read off in the fairy story, which grew all the way up to heaven.

In the temple of Shamballa, we find the sacred cosmogony played out again. Of the twelve Masters or Elder Brothers who inhabit it seven are demi-gods attuned to the concrete world, while five remain in the shrine all the time as the invisible life and power of the great work in the world. In this way the ancient Japanese creation exactly agrees with that of the Hindoo, the Jewish, and the Chinese, for, while the deities differ in name, in each case they represent the laws and properties necessary for the creation of concrete manifestation out of abstract possibility. They all have taught us that the gods became mortal themselves when they entered mortal substance and that all things are subject to birth, growth and decay, the trimuti of human expression, until they are superior to Brahma, Vishnu and Siva, the concretions of the Absolute.

This is all played out again in the body of man, in the zodiac, and in many other stories and allegories of the various religions of the world. All these doctrines have twelve gods or demi-gods of which one is the leader, three are His messengers and all the remaining are demi-gods. All of these gods carry out the dictates and orders of their Leader who in turn is born out of the parentless abyss and carries sacred or magic implements of power which are the basis of His superiority over mortal men. The implements which make the gods greater than men are all to be found when we analyze the Masonic implements and instruments, which are symbolical of mental, emotional or physical body qualities which in turn symbolize the spiritual expression of man seeking manifestation in partially crystallized bodies.

The great Japanese colleges of learning, especially the Buddhistic colleges, are beginning to take great interest in unraveling the mystery of mythology for they realize, as the Christian world must eventually realize, that mythology is the most accurate historical data on spiritual subjects which we have preserved to us and that the keys of wisdom, both scientific and theological, are concealed in the mythologies of ancient people. Neither history nor literature as an entire has preserved truth but mythology has been honest and it makes little difference whether you are searching for the effects of a chemical combination, the birth of a planet, or the effect of contradictory emotions on the human soul, you will be perfectly safe in accepting the mythological characters and their word in solving a problem. A country that knows its mythology is fortunate indeed, and in this respect, Japan is especially blessed for it has one of the most fascinating and inspiring mythologies known to the world today of which this little word we have spoken is but the beginning of a study that could involve life-times and has astounded all who ever attempted it.

# ASTROLOGICAL KEYWORDS

The sign of Libra was put into the Zodiac to divide the signs of Virgo and Scorpio, which were once one in the time when the Zodiac was divided into ten instead of twelve signs. It is called the Balance and symbolizes the division between the signs. It naturally rules the seventh house, but its great keyword is Balance, and it is to that end that egos take bodies under Libra that they may learn to harmonize and co-operate their faculties. All growth is the result of discrimination, and discrimination is the mental process of weighing values against each other.

Briefly considered the keywords of Libra are as follows:

Moist, Hot, Airy, Sanguine, Western, Diurnal, Cardinal, Equinoctial, Movable, Masculine, Human, Speaking, Whole, Changeable, Sweet, Fortunate, Autumnal, Southern, Obeying, Sign of Long, Ascension, Day house of Venus, Exaltation of Saturn, Detriment of Mars, Fall of the Sun.

General Characteristics:

Libra is usually just, honest and fair in its weights and measures mentally, physically and spiritually. In this following out the symbol of its sign; but if a bad square exists in the horoscope of Libra, the native will become dishonest, untrue, and far from virtuous for in Libra the scales tilt very easily from one extreme to the other.

Just, Sweet, Upright, Square, True to principle, Rather religious, Lovable, Romantic, Changeable, Fond of travel, Usually material.

Physical Appearances:

Tall, Well made, Elegant in person, Round beautiful face, Ruddy in youth but inclined to be plain in old age, Subject to disfigurements of the face through skin diseases, eruptions, etc. when old, Blue, or gray eyes, Flaxen, auburn, or yellow hair, Slender, Straight, Usually long in body.

If Venus is well posited in Libra, it adds greatly to the physical beauty, but if the Libra body is not properly taken care of, it soon shows it in becoming run down and disfigured.

The diseases Libra is most subject to are:

Ruptures Weaknesses of various, General debilities kinds, Locomotor ataxia, Mild forms of venereal, Wasting of spinal complaints, marrow Corruptions of blood, Ulcers Weakness in small of back, Corruptions of Blood.

Domestic Problems:

Libra being ruled by Venus and being a fruitful sign is often fortunate in matrimonial problems but seems to be more subject to disappointments through the insincerity of the marriage partner than many of the other signs. Also, being airy is rather subject to wandering. It is not quite as satisfying in the home as some of the other signs.

Countries Under Influence of Libra:
Austria, Lavonia, Alsace, India, Savoy, Ethiopia, Portugal, Part of Greece.
Cities Under the Control of Libra:
Lisbon, Fribourg, Vienna, Placentia, Frankfort, Antwerp.

## Author and Managing Editor

Darrell Jordan is an acolyte of the August Fraternity, former Noble Grand-IOOF and Freemason. He is also a member of the Theosophical and Philalethes Societies.

Darrell Jordan

## BOOKS BY THE AUTHOR

- Illustrations of Masonry
- Surviving Document of the Widow's Son
- The Undiscovered Teachings of Jesus
- The Initiates
- Jefferson's Bible
- Master Masons Handbook
- Forgotten Essays - W.L. Wilmshurst
- Forgotten Essays - Waite
- Forgotten Essays - H. Stanley Redgrove
- The Writings of Sigismond Bacstrom M.D.
- Forgotten Essays – Reincarnation
- Masonic Writings of George Oliver
- Masonic Lectures by Wellins Calcott
- The Fellowcraft Handbook
- Secret Societies
- Vibration and Life
- Key to the Rosicrucian Characters
- The Revelation of John
- Life and the Ideal
- The Philosophical History of Freemasonry
- The Magic of the Middle Ages
- Musings of a Chinese Mystic
- The Life of the Soul
- Christian Mysticism
- Krishna and Orpheus
- The Eleusinian Mysteries & Rites
- The Crucifixion Letter
- The Mystic Key
- You Paid What?
- The Illustrated Pioneer History of the America
- Montana Freemasons 19th Century
- Washington Freemasons 19th Century
- Idaho Freemasons 19th Century
- Rock Metaphysics
- Emblems: Jean Jacque Boissard and Otto van Veen
- Emblems: Nicholas M. Meerfeldt
- Alchemy Art: Manly P. Hall
- Emblems: Manly P. Hall
- Alchemy Art & Symbols
- Splendor Solis

For the latest information, please visit author's book site: Parallel47North.com/collections/esoteric-books

If you have any question, suggestion, or feedback, please contact: info@Parallel47North.com

www.ingramcontent.com/pod-product-compliance
Lightning Source LLC
Chambersburg PA
CBHW020247010526
44107CB00002B/141